Gender and Culture

Studies in Austrian Literature, Culture and Thought

Translation Series

General Editors:

Jorun B. Johns
Richard H. Lawson

Rosa Mayreder

Gender and Culture

Translated by Pamela S. Saur

Afterword by
Susanne Hochreiter

Ariadne Press
Riverside, California

Ariadne Press would like to express its appreciation to the Bundesministerium für Unterricht, Kunst und Kultur for assistance in publishing this book.

.KUNST

Translated from the German *Geschlecht und Kultur*
© 1923, Eugen Diederichs Verlag, Jena

Library of Congress Cataloging-in-Publication Data

Mayreder, Rosa Obermayer, 1858-1938.
 [Geschlecht und Kultur. English]
 Gender and culture / Rosa Mayreder ; translated by Pamela S. Saur; Afterword by Susanne Hochreiter.
   p. cm. -- (Studies in Austrian literature, culture, and thought. Translation series)
 Includes bibliographical references.
 ISBN 978-1-57241-162-3 (alk. paper)
 1. Sex. 2. Women—Germany. 3. Marriage—Germany. I. Title

HQ21.M4617513 2009
306.7082'0943--dc22

2008053964

Cover
Art Director: George McGinnis
Designer: Beth A. Steffel
Photo: Bildarchiv der Österreichischen Nationalbibliothek
Vienna, Austria

Copyright 2009
by Ariadne Press
270 Goins Court
Riverside, CA 92507

All rights reserved.
No part of this publication may be reproduced or transmitted
in any form or by any means without formal permission.
Printed in the United States of America.
ISBN 978-1-57241-162-3

Contents

Foreword 1

On Culture in General 4

Civilization and Gender 19

The Crisis of Fatherhood 29

An Essay on the Double Standard of Morality 58

Gender and Social Politics 64

Sexual Ideologies 87

The Evolution of Female Eroticism 140

Transformations of Marriage 162

On the Essence of Love 191

Excursus on the Imaginary Self 219

Afterword by
Susanne Hochreiter 248

Bibliography 262

Foreword

When *A Survey of the Woman Problem* appeared in the year 1905, I said to my friend Carl Kunn, the first promoter of the book, "Now I must set to work and write the sequel." He said laughingly, "I hope you don't need fifteen years this time." However, it turned out worse than that. Not only have more than fifteen years passed – in the meantime, cataclysmic events have upset my life, inwardly and outwardly, and created a chasm between these two volumes. Death and illness have taken a cruel toll on the small circle of people nearest to me, and just as cruelly war and disaster have taken control over the German-speaking world to which I belong. In the midst of such devastation, for a long time it seemed impossible to maintain the world of the intellect; faith in its significance has been shaken, and years had to pass for the realization to return that the intellectual gifts which one is given cannot be destroyed by external circumstances.

At the beginning of the war, the essays that comprise this second volume had for the most part already been written and the title that encompassed them had been chosen. I do not know if today I would have the courage to choose it. For in the meantime, the world has had its fill of the word "culture" because of its misuse; it has been overused, emptied of meaning, and rendered ineffective as much as any term in the rust bucket of intellectual values; it has acquired a considerable aura of empty verbosity. Many people today think that the end of Western culture is inevitably approaching; they regard all theoretical musings about culture as impotent chatter about a way of life that we no longer possess and can never retrieve. Others believe that culture must dissolve before the foundation of a new order can emerge.

Is culture only a series of episodes in human history that again and again must alternate with periods of barbarism? Must humanity inevitably lose that which it imagines has been acquired as a permanent possession every time a particular epoch has played itself out?

But however the present defines its culture within world history, whether as a time of inevitable decline or as a time of transition to a new stage of life, we must by all means recognize that we have the task of seeking the lines that lead from the past through the present to the future, the lines that trace the path of humanity through the centuries of our historical development, the paths of those mental creations that we refer to collectively by the name of culture. The course we take can be traced only from a historical viewpoint, and if those ignorant of history wish to intoxicate themselves with the illusion that they are creating something new in the world, something independent of our entire past, the historical viewpoint fortunately will offer the possibility of fleeing from a desolate present, lacking soul and ideas, back into the past, in order to create the guarantee of a better future. What once was a cultural possession cannot be lost; it will be reborn in a new form. If the ancient evils that cling to humankind cannot be eliminated, neither can the wonders of human creation from past times. This book seeks to appeal to the *evolutionary conscience* of both the conservatives who regard the past as a noble and proven heritage to be preserved and the radicals who want to destroy the past with violence because of its flaws. This conscience aims at preserving and expressing the organizational connections of all cultural processes.

In *A Survey of the Woman Problem*, I addressed gender psychology primarily as a problem of individual predispositions: a project that regarded freedom of the individual as limited by the constraints of gender. In this volume, however, I consider the values of societies and cultures as, in a fundamental way, determining the patterns of life of the genders and influencing the development of the individual, insofar as he or she is a social being and is malleable by cultural influences.

A Survey of the Woman Problem begins with the question of what woman *is,* defined according to her 'nature' and it shows that this question, posed in this general way, cannot be answered at all. This book, in contrast, begins with the question of what woman, according to her nature *should be*, a question that, to all appearances, likewise cannot be answered at all.

In this day, who would dare to try to create new social norms? The flowing river of our times rushes forth, carrying new and old along; nothing permanent can maintain itself. Here I have limited myself to considering cultural influences connected with the gendered nature of human beings. In doing so, I can not completely avoid overgeneralizing. Freedom of self-determination according to individuality is one pole of development; the determination of one's life through the agency of a higher culture is the other. That these poles cannot be brought together without contradiction lies in the nature of a polarity, which is a fundamental opposition in all life. The historical development of the female gender in the future will not shape the lives of those individuals who are able to create their own laws of life by the power of their personalities, but it will affect the passive majority of people.

Moreover, it is less a matter of the creation of real conditions and circumstances of life than of the particular ideological directions in Western culture that have determined the development of the relationship of the genders to each other, as well as the relationship of the individual to his or her gender. Actual conditions are affected only to the degree that they are symptomatic of this problem of historical development. That elucidation may thereby cross the border into poetry is a possibility of any such attempt. I confess willingly that I give only a subjective view of the world. My own experiences, what I have learned from other people and from books and, not least of all, I myself, bear the responsibility for the viewpoint I have developed.

Rosa Mayreder

On Culture in General

It was once the task of religion to answer the great question of the meaning of life; as faith has dissolved, however, so have the answers it provided. Whoever can no longer conceive of a hereafter must find meaning in the here and now. Another power has taken over the role of religion, lending order and regulation to the here and now as religion does to the hereafter – that power is culture. The great significance of culture corresponds to the high status that it enjoys in serious thought at present, as zealous theoretical efforts are underway to cultivate, promote and maintain culture in all areas of life.

However, reality presents a sharp contrast to this situation. The power from which modern life expects its rebirth seems to be in an irreversible decline, threatening to disappear just as it approaches its point of greatest significance.

Let us admit to ourselves that we no longer possess culture as an objective attainment, as a common heritage of higher human life. But is this loss permanent? If at present, theorizing about culture is taken as a symptom, it indicates that the powers are still effective that enable a people to make cultural achievements. Cultural collapse can be understood as the condition and prerequisite of the transformation of renewal. The present can make no judgment about this, for only in retrospect is it possible to recognize a period of decline as the sign of a final collapse. Within a culture, flourishing and decline are not necessarily unique or final events; only in retrospect does any judgment interpreting them find confirmation. The conditions of every epoch – which are defined but little by its limitations – hardly correspond to the generally held cultural viewpoint whereby people only rarely recognize themselves as members of a flourishing time, so overly loud are laments about downfall based on comparison with perfect conditions existing only in the imagination. As Goethe said as early as the beginning of the nineteenth century: "It is maddening for those of us growing old to see the world around us rot and dissolve back into its elements." Twenty years later, he expressed his judgment of his times with these words: "Confused doctrines added to confused behaviors rule the world." To us, the world out of which these words came is viewed as an epoch distinguished by the flourishing of high culture, unaffected by the social forces of mechanization hostile to culture, still determined by unbroken traditions. And yet we hear from the mouth of the era's greatest son, Goethe, the same lament that crosses our lips when we think about our present situation!

That every culture will run its course according to certain laws may be in general indisputable, but this course cannot be predicted by drawing conclusions based on analogies. In the great plethora of possibilities, there is no guarantee that past developments will be repeated. Even when historical analogies seem obvious, as in comparing the conditions of the present with those of the declining Western Roman Empire, they may fail to take the most important facts into account. The fate of the present is determined by an unheard of and never before existing technological mastery over nature, by the entrance of the machine into the history of humankind – an event that has had no equal since the invention of agriculture and the domestication of animals in prehistoric times.

It is no coincidence that a conflict between culture and civilization began to be visible at the time when the consequences of machine use became evident in the social conditions of life. From this point on, our ways of living changed decidedly. To be sure, this change was regarded as progress at first and the designation as a highly civilized epoch assumed to be advantageous. Nevertheless, it is increasingly assumed that civilization has negative consequences with regard to culture. The growing but gradually increasing awareness of an unfavorably altered condition seems to be expressed more and more in our times.

Even Buckle in his *History of Civilization in England* saw no difference between these two concepts. He considers both our increasing technological capabilities and the process of moral perfection to be factors contributing to the development of civilization without regard to what degree technological progress has been destructive, even hostile, to moral perfection. In this connection, of course, linguistic usage must be considered, for the word "civilization" is used differently in English than it is in German; Lester Ward points this out in his *Pure Sociology*; however, when he asserts that the German word for culture refers only to material relationships, while the English equivalent also encompasses psychological, moral and spiritual phenomena, it becomes apparent how variable these expressions actually are.

A detailed comparison of culture and civilization is given by Karl Joël (*New World Culture*); according to Joël the word "civilization" stems from *civis*, referring to the city, while "culture" is rooted in agri*culture*. "Civilization is based on customs determining the relationships of people and refined personal behaviors; culture creates values as concrete things." A similar conception is represented by Lujo Brentano, who understands by culture the mastery of human beings over nature, whereby he also locates the origin of the word as referring to tilling the land. The word "civilization," on the other hand, according to Brentano points to the behavior of human beings in interaction. It refers to the foundation of justice to replace caprice and violence. Starting with the same etymological tracing of the word "civilization," Müller-Lyer places the beginning of civilization in the early epoch of human development in which established states, with their legal institutions, took shape and made possible corresponding orderly patterns of life. Finally, Spengler, in *The Downfall of Western Civilization,* identifies civilization simply as the final stage of every culture, without, however, giving an explanation of how one should distinguish between culture and civilization. He borrows from Nietzsche the view that culture is a certain unifying force shaping the way of life of the people in a certain geographical area at a certain epoch. A culture is born in the moment "when a great soul awakens out of the original souls' condition of eternal child-like humanity, and it dies when it has exhausted all its possibilities; its blood flows out, its powers fail – it becomes civilization. Culture is to civilization as the living body is to the mummy."

From such a view of the relationship of culture and civilization we learn not much more than the fact that death is the end of life. Civilization, conceptualized as the final stage of a process whose content is nothing other than the sum of all the activities of a people – no one will be satisfied with this explanation that the living process of culture is a temporally and spatially unlimited phenomenon, whose changing phases never end and which outlives individual peoples because it is generally human.

Culture as an achievement of a single, temporally and spatially identifiable community and culture as the natural condition of the human species, the product of its long journey, from times earlier than our countable centuries, do not amount to the same thing; if the former, like an individual, is subject to death, then the latter is something timeless and indestructible like the human race itself. This means that the end of a single culture cannot be an absolute end. Moreover, how deeply an individual culture is entwined with the collective culture can be seen in the achievements that reach far beyond the borders of a race, a geographical area or an epoch and spread widely from one culture to another. Does not the Babylonian culture, which is temporally and spatially far removed from modern Europe, still have clearly demonstrable influence in our day? (see Winckler, *Babylonian Intellectual Culture.*) Is there not a hidden thread that connects Egyptian intellectual tradition to the Greek and Roman by means of Judaism and is still alive in the ideas and practices of Christianity?

Perhaps Chamberlain was one of the first to invest the concept of civilization with a negative quality. He states that civilization is "a constantly growing and developing, ever increasingly industrious, comfortable, and unfree existence like that of an ant colony." He conceptualized civilization as a basically superficial condition that in and of itself can be defined only in relative terms. He stated that "a higher civilization may only be regarded as advantageous if it brings about an increasingly intense intellectual and artistic formation of life as well as inner moral illumination." At that point, civilization would become culture, if perhaps not conforming to Chamberlain's view, for he defined culture solely as the daughter of the creative freedom, that enables great individual artists or philosophers to create and shape the human world.

The essence of culture as a condition of human society is not captured by that vague definition. For example, how would it help us assess the cultural significance of Spitteler fashioning anew the Greek Pantheon of Gods according to his individual Swiss viewpoint?

In a general sense, one can define *civilization as that condition of society in which a highly developed mastery of nature is applied to the purpose of making people's lives easier, both practically and in terms of ideals.* But, it is obvious as well that modern conditions of life have another relationship to civilization. From its origins in the drive toward an easier life, civilization has developed according to its own laws, laws that are not parallel with cultural interests and actually push them into the background in the end. The goal of a highly developed civilization is not merely the easier satisfaction of natural needs, but rather the satisfaction of new, refined needs that are constantly being created by the complicated apparatus of civilized life, as well as by ever-evolving technology (Goldstein, *Technology*). If civilization actually were to be understood, as Ziegler says, as "practical behavior determined by the conscious goal of achieving well-being," then the behavior of the human being participating in culture would have to be labeled as quite impractical.

At its inception, the first results of modern civilization are all kinds of sickness, misery, and decline, the destruction of the conditions needed for human well-being. The same unfortunate fate of peoples exposed to higher culture and unable to adjust to its conditions is experienced to a certain degree by populations affected adversely by new technological achievements.

The limitation of civilization as a *technological* force of life perfection lies in its lack of governing ideas of a *higher* type of life perfection, for it develops according to laws that do not correspond to the goals of culture. All technological inventions are driven forward on a course of development set by intellectual and economic conditions; the nature of their effects on the condition of the human soul has thereby no influence whatsoever. For that reason, Einstein presented to us the idea that the word "technology" in the consciousness of a refined person brings forth notions of "greed for profit, exploitation, social division of people, class hatred, soulless mechanization, racial degeneration, and hasty, senseless drives" – all companions of modern civilization. Through them, we experience the terrible drama of ever unfolding technological means of power with which comes the destruction of culture, aesthetic and educational values, even the decline in the health and capability for happiness of the generations so affected. If civilization results in mechanization of life which puts human beings themselves on the level of machines, it hardly can be said to create conditions favorable to the cultural development of society or individuals.

If one delineates the difference between culture and civilization in such a way that civilization refers to the technological and economic directions of life, and culture to the artistic and intellectual directions – a delineation which allows one to see in civilization only a cancerous growth or an ever increasing decline – then one may well say that civilization has never been as highly developed as in the present. This conclusion is not altered by the fact that it has suffered terrible losses due to war. The dominance of the technological and material has played a considerable role in the catastrophe of war, and especially in the atrocious way in which it is waged. This confirms Dreisman's assertion that culture and civilization in a certain sense should be viewed as antinomies of reason and a moral world order; they need not exclude each other, but for the most part do (*Ways to Culture*).

According to Dreisman, culture is "the ability of the soul to resist outside corrupting influences, seductions of appearances and illusions of the senses . . . a feeling of unity with the basic foundation of life and a sense of life that gives rise to an undefeatable power to persevere and create." With this view of culture as limited to a purely internal condition, as a kind of religious-philosophical attitude, Dreisman's definition corresponds to that of Fr. W. Förster, who says, "Culture is the subordination of all individual needs to the intellectual forces of life, a mastery of human beings over their own natures," or to that of Simmel, who sees culture in the deepest sense as "the perfection of the soul through the blossoming of all the seeds and realization of all possibilities present within the self to create the noblest works of humankind."

These definitions of content relate to only one aspect of culture, namely personal ethics, just as other definitions view other single aspects as central. For example, Kemmerich defines "the most important criteria of culture as respect for life, honor, freedom, and other people's convictions," and Weininger opines, "One must view the essence of all culture as a sense that has two sides. One condition for all culture, and, in a purely intellectual sense identical with culture, is a sense for problems. For this reason all culture is based on individuality, for problems exist only for individuals." (This is, by the way, one of the most one-sided and inadequate utterances about culture as a social problem).

In its objective meaning, culture is a community manifestation that can come into being only within a society. *Culture in this sense is a condition of the social order, through which external patterns of living are set by a certain rule-governed relationship to inner psychological processes;* it is the increasing mastery over nature through the *incorporation of intellectual values* into community life. Without the pre-dominance of ideas directing the way life is led, culture cannot exist. "Culture is the active reshaping and use of natural materials with clear intention and in service of the idea of human perfection, the will to perfection." (Eisler, *Cultural History*) However, the idea of perfection alone is not the essence of culture. Inseparable from it is an aesthetic-formal element: *Culture as a social phenomenon is a general shaping of life through which an ideal content is expressed*, or in other words, culture refers to the life patterns of a society whose higher tendencies correspond to its external conditions. Neither the acquisition of material goods nor the acquisition of intellectual goods, the mere collection of increased knowledge, has anything to do with culture, nor does extensive artistic or even religious activity if it is not decisively influenced by the kind of thinking and behaving that belongs to the identity of a social group, if it does not create a shared *form of life*.

In addition to the form of life and the ideas that direct it, the *content of life* that is brought forth also belong to culture: culture means, in addition to creation of life content, the enriching of life permitted by nature by means of the mind. Even the lives of so-called primitive peoples living close to nature are determined to a significant extent by cultural concepts.

Culture requires a correspondence of thinking and being; otherwise it would not create shared life forms as expression of an ideal content. This is the source of the debates on whether a truly Christian culture has ever existed because the Christian viewpoint largely rejects life here on earth; and so it would not be able to bring its ideas into material form. Nevertheless the monastic way of life of the early Middle Ages did take form, and it fulfilled the concept of a genuine culture completely insofar as it incorporated Christian ideas into a fully developed organization of life that was not lacking in aesthetic-artistic activity.

Not as thoroughly, but nevertheless still substantially determined by Christian convictions, was the worldly way of life during the era of chivalric courtiers. While the Renaissance openly borrowed from the classical age in order to merge it with the Christian world and create an artistic synthesis, incidentally thereby losing a great deal of ethical seriousness, it was not until the eighteenth century that the influence of the Christian religious element in literature receded.

These epochs, which to us seem to be the high point of European culture, were interrupted by periods of deep decline. Around the year 1000 the circumstances in Europe were so dismal that the pious assumed that Judgment Day must be imminent because they saw no way out. The fourteenth century was (according to Taine) "a sad, bleak era, that entertained itself with merriments, but was oppressed by a widespread misery of suffering and fear, lacking any comfort or hope." These words describe precisely the situation of the present, just as they apply, in many respects, to the time after the Thirty Years War.

The uniqueness and emptiness of the present day, however, stem from the misunderstanding of culture and civilization. In no earlier epoch was the technological perfection of life so far removed from the cultural. As soon as the tempo of the progress of civilization substantially surpasses the ability for culture to develop, then culture and civilization must necessarily move into opposition as enemies. The lack of stability that results from the rapid pace of technological innovation, along with accompanying economic upsets, prevents culture from thriving and growing.

II

When life in Western culture was knocked off balance by technological innovation, another development occurred at the same time, revealing that influences from within culture can have effects just as disadvantageous as innovations from outside. The downfall of culture is not caused entirely by its degeneration into civilization. This is shown by every period of decline not accompanied by a relative growth of technological means of power. The strongest influence, from the inside, on the condition of human culture for the last hundred years or so, has been, next to economic upsets brought about by the machine, an intellectual process that one can identify as the loss of beliefs from the past. Reason has taken the intellectual lead; it provides insight into the laws of events and understanding of the self in individuals. This process of recognition is irreconcilable with the controlling power of established traditions and customs. Their power declines to the same degree as individuals face themselves in a critical way. In doing so, they free themselves from the prejudices of tradition: this is the advantage of such a rational emancipation, but at the same time it destroys the means without which culture has no ability to exert influence over people.

Culture in a general sense, as a societal condition, rests on religious, social, and aesthetic values that maintain their validity in the life of a community through *tradition*. Tradition is that complex of ideas and judgments resulting from the communal experience of many generations transmitted to individuals to serve as guides. For culture to be an organic union of individuals within groups, it must be maintained through the endurance of values, giving direction through continuity. Tradition is the prerequisite for unity in all expressions of life, the style of a culture; it comprises such a substantive element of culture that many see it as the main content of the concept. Schurtz understands culture as "the legacy of the work of previous generations, insofar as it incorporates the established structures, the consciousness, the work and the products of work of those living at every time," and according to Vierkandt, culture consists precisely in a "quintessence of established forms" that are impervious to the whim of the individual. As soon as tradition loses its binding power, culture as a social force simultaneously disappears, for nothing that requires community can remain alive without individuals yielding to the general, to an overarching order.

Culture in this sense is therefore not to be equated with a rapid increase of civilized achievements of civilizations leading to a transformation of a society's economic foundations nor with rebellion against traditions that have become unworkable, that inhibit individuals in their development instead of appropriately giving order to their relationship to the general community. Such rebellion is, however, a necessary, concomitant condition of development. Traditions as tools of the cultural process have only a limited life span; their coming and going is inseparable from the rhythm of culture itself that moves upward and downward. Obedient submission that unconditionally honors the expression of the general will and its superiority gives way to critical rebellion, with which individuals reject norms that no longer mesh with their personal makeup. Only when submission to prevailing norms at the cost of individuality is not enforced by violence, can individuals appreciate, with a free mind, the meaning that tradition brings – a stage that paves the way for the development of new traditions.

At present, tradition in all areas has lost its influential power, its ability to evoke a sense of duty, its power over the stubborn will; its claims no longer awaken respect and submission, but rather disdain and rebellion.

An example follows. Traditional concepts of femininity and masculinity, as recently as two or three generations ago accepted as norms governing personal development and assumed to be beyond any criticism, have become, in the course of the nineteenth century, a matter of debate that no thinking person has been able to avoid. Ever fewer are those who insist on remaining in the condition of obedient submission; ever greater the number of those moved by the polemics of rebellion from which emerges free, personal evaluation, founded on the basis of deeper understanding.

The social condition that mirrors itself in the rule of authoritarian tradition is of course never stationary; every generation brings forth changes in it that, however, in epochs of upward movement do not amount to preponderant negation. And the relationship of the creative individual to tradition is always different from that of the average person. For the latter, control by inherited norms has a similar meaning as control by instinct for primitive creatures; it gives an intellect of a level too low to make appropriate independent judgments direction or guidance. For the self-sufficient individual who is capable of independence based on good judgment and power of the will, the loss of tradition is a far less significant matter than for the great majority, who thereby fall prey, with no protection, to all the inadequacies of human nature.

If tradition loses its enforcing power over the majority, then the crudeness of the base level of existence emerges once again uncurbed. Culture ceases to be a community phenomenon; the relationship of the individual to the majority, the few to the many, that in every culture is ordered in a particular way suffers a disturbance.

According to Nietzsche, the goal of all development is the sovereign individual, the human being who freely shapes his or her own life as directed by inner impulses, independent of the influence of external circumstances. However, the significance of the sovereign individual is not exhausted by the fact that he or she develops apart from the human community to realize the highest possibilities of the species; it consists just as much in his or her creative activity that lends content and form to the lives of others. Thereby is his or her inner relationship to the human family created – a relationship of which Nietzsche was fully aware.

Deep insight into this relationship of the exceptional individual to the many is given by Ernst Lissauer (*Celebratory Workday*). He considers in turn three types, the normative, the normal and the abnormal, and comes to the conclusion that "the strongest power is the normal at the border at which he becomes normative; one can say that the normal person, not developed to the level of genius, is the born friend and student of the normative." In this connection, he points to Goethe, whom he respects as a normative type of the highest level: "Goethe is the new norm, developed over the centuries. . . . It is fundamentally possible for the middle-level person to learn from him, just as it is fundamentally impossible for the abnormal person."

The criterion that distinguishes the normal from the abnormal in respect to cultural development would be, according to this conception, found in an individual's relationship to the normative, in his or her capability to learn from it, while the abnormal person wants to stand alone, to be separate, and such a person defines the significance of the self in possessing something solely his or her own, apart from all community – in the art of free will, in the products of the free will of the person totally lacking connections.

The relationship the individual to the community to which he or she belongs, and the way individual achievement has effects through its reception, one sees perhaps most clearly in the development of language. All linguistic inventions, neologisms, and expansions are created by individuals, but they are meaningless play, nothing but acts of inconsequential whimsy if they do not expand and endure by being taken up by the majority and incorporated into the lexicon through tradition.

Culture as a life form of the general community, determined by shared principles, creates an interaction between the creative individual, the great personality, and the community, whereby the latter forms the receptive, the former the productive power. The way that this interaction takes place is, however, not linear, as, for example, between a teacher and a pupil. In the delineation of prominent social classes with their sharp rejection of outsiders, in the keeping secret of religious doctrines and customs that exists also in artistic and craft activity, one sees the tendency of culture to create select groups of people. At the same time, however, such exclusion awakes in others the striving to acquire the advantages and privileges of the elite for themselves and to change elite cultural property into common property, reachable and accessible to all.

That which endures over thousands of years in the high realms of culture repeats itself in small ways in daily life over small spans of time. In the effects of fashion, one sees an example of how the elite selects a new fashion for itself and regards it as a distinctive possession until it is imitated by the mob. Then the charm of newness loses its distinctive quality and the fashion must be replaced by something else. For this reason one can see fashion as in a certain sense a microcosmic reflection of cultural processes.

It is impossible to calculate or measure the degree to which the content of an individual life is determined by the person, how much it has in common with the community, or the level and role played by cultural change. Certain, however, is that those who willingly follow civilization's irrational course and let their life content be determined by the technological and commercial exploitation of nature do not belong to a new elite. If the situation of the present resounds with the tumult of technological and mercantile interests and the battle cries of power groups in mortal combat, both intellectual and artistic work seem without substance, unimportant, and superficial, this is a byproduct of cultureless civilization, whose emptiness and lack of ideas becomes obvious the moment that one thinks about the sense and purpose of such a life. It is amazing that this viewpoint appears even in works in which civilization is portrayed as the death of everything worthwhile in life, namely in Spengler. In his writing, the individual life sinks to the level of complete insignificance; he says expressly: "If, under the influence of this book, people of the new generation turn toward technology instead of lyrical poetry, navies instead of painting, politics instead of epistemology, then they will be doing what I wish." This claim is all the more disquieting in that Spengler completely rejects the uniqueness and value of the individual. In every genuine talent, the will of nature speaks; its direction toward artistic and intellectual activity is a sign that the soul of a culture that speaks out of this activity has not yet been exhausted. Whoever is driven by inner inclination away from the horrors of profit-hungry mechanization and toward nobler forms of life may recognize therein the power whereby external powers can be resisted, even if one thereby runs the danger of being set by Spengler on the level of "fools, charlatans, and pedants." In this spirit, Ruskin had already started a battle to protect culture against civilization, to be sure without stopping the changes in living conditions that go along with the growth of the capabilities of civilization, but nevertheless offering an admirable model of the will to achieve culture that may allow a great individual to go against the currents of the times.

This resistance is the condition of all personal culture in the present times – a conscious setting apart of the self and a desire to be different, accompanied by insight into the conditions that connect the individual with the whole. If *social* culture means a generally valid organization of life in which an ideal content guides the community by traditions, then one can regard *personal* culture as the ideal pattern of life to which an individual subordinates the self through the exercise of free judgment. In a time without tradition, personal culture is the only possible form culture can take. Spengler himself thought that the greater the urban growth of emptiness and triviality in the practical, applied arts and sciences, the stronger would be the retreat of the posthumous spirit of culture into very narrow circles, where it would give rise to ideas and structures that could be meaningful to only an extremely small number of superior people.

It is, however, quite possible that in such a narrow circle the posthumous spirit of culture will not have its last blossoming, but the future will have its first. Tönnes makes such a suggestion (*Community and Society*): "Because the entire culture has been transformed into societal and state civilization, culture in this altered form will cease to exist, unless it happens that its disseminated kernel stays alive so that the essence and ideas of community once again are nurtured and a new culture secretly unfolds within the declining one."

It will require the work of generations to reshape civilization's attainments of the last decades into appropriate cultural conditions, to bring them into correspondence with the higher tendencies of human nature, and to make them able to serve those tendencies. It remains to be seen, however, if this work can be achieved on the basis of a new social foundation and whether the creative power that can bring about such a rebirth has not already been extinguished in the peoples of Western culture.

Such a fateful question cannot be answered by historical analogies that are open to varying interpretations. It is just as possible that the condition of cultureless civilization will lead into barbaric primitivism as that a new cultural life form, shaped by noble ideas, is in the making. The decision depends entirely upon the individuals of a future time, on those few in whom the necessary creative power will need to become dominant, and on the many in whom respect for that power will need to take effect.

The extent to which future individuals possess the power of resistance co-existent with the power to create new forms will be the factor that determines the future existence or non-existence of culture. The belief in culture, in its permanence despite ups and downs, in its ability to be transformed by new influences, is one part of this power. And in this formulation may the words of Goethe strengthen us. Goethe discussed the aforementioned complaint about the downfall of culture in conversation with Sulpiz Boisserée. Boisserée asserted that he had hope for the future because young people had tried to save treasured books, their legacy of education, as the best thing that remained after the plague, in order over time to become teachers and thereby also leaders of future generations. Goethe commented, "What you say is right. But to see things thus, character is necessary, for character is a part of resignation."

Civilization and Gender

It is the tragic fate of human beings that we always become slaves to our own creations because we are incapable of realizing in advance the results they will have. And so it happens that, even when we successfully employ our acumen and gifts of invention to tame the fundamental forces that challenge us, we fall victim once again to powers we cannot control.

The technological advances of the last hundred years are so great that they outweigh those of all past centuries. Viewed with this fact in mind, civilization offers an overpowering stimulus to intoxicating feelings of triumph and fulfillment. Such feelings, however, lead to the senseless overvaluing of technological achievements that shape modern life everywhere, along with a general view that is virtually blind to the accompanying destruction that this epoch of highly developed civilization wreaks not only on our noblest cultural achievements but also on our health and our competence at living.

Civilization shapes our ways of living through practical advances, not higher directives; a fateful lack of direction and perspective is seen in the excesses of both work and leisure. The existence of the civilized person has lost not only the balance of leisure and work but also all aesthetic dimension in the area of leisure and pleasure. As high as our control over nature has risen, so deeply has sunk the mastery of the individual over his or her own life. In Western civilization, human beings are masters of nature, but not of our own lives; instead of living our own lives we are letting them be governed by outside forces.

At the same time, the consciousness of a higher purpose is progressively diminishing in our existence; the person entrapped in the values of modern civilization can identify no purpose to life outside of civilization. If one asks what the whole bustling business of civilization has contributed to deeper happiness, no answer is forthcoming. A vivid portrait of this emptiness is given in Kellermann's novel, *The Tunnel*; there the Moloch of civilization inflates himself – independent it seems, of the intention of the author – and in his horrifying inner lack of center or purpose, devours the inventor, the employer, and the worker without revealing what purpose the loss of these victims serves. That in the future a twenty-eight-hour railroad trip between Europe and America will replace a ship journey of many days – what does that signify, beyond a mere business advantage? But, so beholden is the world of the present to the values of civilization that no one can see past the showy display of such innovations to perceive their ridiculous lack of significance.

Likewise, the noisy spectacle of civilization together with its material advantages deceives modern individuals by hiding the bankruptcy of inner values it causes. In a highly civilized society, the individual no longer perceives the unknowable and unreachable in the form of uncontrollable powers of nature but in the form of unrealizable human accomplishments. The trappings of civilization have given human beings mastery over nature – but now things have gone so far that we must defend our mastery over our own lives against the forces of civilization. If this generation still had time to come to its senses, it could perceive its own senseless, life-destroying hubris simply by considering the number of nervous breakdowns affecting the competent as well as the incompetent, the former because they are too vulnerable to excessive demands, the latter because they cannot cope with the life of the average person. Hubris, seen in excesses beyond all rationality, is the fundamental characteristic of modern civilization.

If one tries to trace the causes of these developments, one finds, among other reasons a disturbance in the balance of participation of the two genders in civilization.

At the end of the last century a respected physician, an opponent of the women's movement promoting social equality, pointed to the immeasurable riches of civilization's achievements and coined the slogan, "All the work of men!" To be sure! The whole of modern civilization is the work of men; the participation of women is so minimal and of such recent date that it can be dismissed. One can without reservation identify the man as the creator of civilization. Men are superior to women in technological abilities in all fields.

On the other hand, however, it is noteworthy that civilization, in its technological aspect, would seem to be in its origins a feminine achievement because women everywhere were the first farmers, potters, weavers, tentmakers, in short, the first technicians. And because inventions are usually made by those who are involved in a field, one may conclude that the original inventions, now shrouded in anonymity, which began cultural life, were made by women. After all, without a certain degree of technical expertise, culture as the aesthetic formation of life cannot emerge; culture cannot co-exist with the complete lack of control over the elemental powers of nature which characterized the lives of primitive human beings.

The same ability which prepares the soil for culture is the worst threat to culture as soon as it becomes dominant, and the fate of culture is analogous to the fate of the female gender. The technological skills that distinguish women on the lowest levels of culture are transformed into a hostile power as soon as the consequences of female nature in culture become apparent. If individuals, not only female, but also male, exist in cultural conditions that make their gender-based life fulfillment difficult, our highly developed civilization is to blame for difficulties and complications. Our natural sexual predisposition toward procreation, in particular, is offered no protection in the world of civilization. All influences are directed toward hindering it and the drives that serve it. It is well known that the more highly developed a civilization is, the less favorable are the conditions for raising children. The child, as the human being closest to nature, is the most harmed by life that has been made artificial. And along with the child, the woman is harmed, for nature has bestowed upon her the whole weight of the task of reproduction, for which the man bears no responsibility.

The root cause of all inequality between the sexes is the unequal division of the task of procreation. This task burdens the female gender disproportionately, whereas men have no certainty of their biological relationship to their progeny. These facts of nature strengthen culture as a male-dominated form of life and promote inequality. The life of the genders in the animal realm is in no way similar to human life which is determined through the responsibility of motherhood or the uncertainty of fatherhood. Only with the origin of culture does the historical process begin, in which the inequality of the positions of the genders increases over time, an inequality based on the woman as mother versus the man as father. *Motherhood and fatherhood are the basis of the culturally determined relationships of the genders.*

As soon as the man lays claim to his progeny as a possession, he is required to make provisions that give him the certainty that they are his offspring that nature does not, and, in doing so, he comes to realize his freedom from the burdens of reproduction, in contrast to the woman's duties of pregnancy, birth, and nursing children, which make her unable to accompany him to the realm of more important work. The fundamental reason for his superiority lies in his freedom from bonds to the succeeding generation whereby he wins room for the unlimited unfolding of his intellectual potential, and in the unique conditions of fatherhood, which require him to maintain his mastery and possessor's rights over his children by providing for them through vocational achievements of various kinds.

On the most primitive level, motherhood does not operate as a barrier to a woman's participation in the tasks of social life, any more than men are limited if their consciousness of fatherhood is completely undeveloped when contrasted to women's consciousness of motherhood. However, the ever greater degree of vocational specialization and its life-altering effects worsen the situation of the female gender, just as men gain more power, to the disadvantage of women, by developing a consciousness of fatherhood based on the concept of possession of offspring. As long as men feel a strong duty to procreate freely, based on strict family morality and strengthened by religious impulses, reproduction is also a solemn duty to them. However, their whole intellectual power is liberated only when this morality slackens; significantly, the great growth of civilization's achievements coincides with the decline of religious and familial tradition.

Heretofore, gender-based freedom has always been regarded

as a natural advantage to the male gender, precisely because it frees men to unfold their higher abilities in all fields of life, whereas the female sex, bound by the service required of wives, has had to remain behind. However, the unrestrained power of modern civilization, which devours and destroys the individual, brings out the great disadvantage of male freedom – excessiveness. This quality is already a danger stemming from the male nature in itself, with its physical lack of restraint, its necessity of striving ceaselessly for ever shifting goals, its seeking for objects that are out of reach; hubris is an expression and result of the natural male character, and it is intensified by the plethora of creations made possible by the freedom men have enjoyed.

Let us consider out of this plethora the highest achievement of mental life, which puts to shame all the great epochs of human thought of the past, namely science. It is by no means a failure to acknowledge the superior position of science to say that the modern scientific drive – which has been almost entirely exercised by men – has reached a point at which greatness threatens to devolve into monstrosity and a destructive aspect of science threatens to become dominant. Overburdening of the memory that can no longer grasp information amassed, one-sided specialization that destroys any connection to the totality of life, overgrown abstraction unconnected to the facts of reality, experimental procedures that overvalue the provable and lose themselves in endless masses of details – all together, these developments contribute to a hubris of the intellect, an explosion of intellectual productivity that greatly overwhelms intellectual receptivity.

These developments all reflect the one-sided male nature of modern civilization. The overwhelming emphasis on productivity leads to an underestimation of the value of receptivity; the prevailing modern viewpoint assesses intellectual achievement solely on the former and does not recognize that the neglect and stunting of the latter make all productivity useless in the end. Indeed, one could ask of modern civilization whether its current conditions allow any room for art and the true appreciation of art. The one-sided specialization of male education, which limits the individual to one field - and even one field can no longer be mastered – seriously threatens receptivity to artistic experience. In his autobiography, Darwin confessed that he hadn't read a poem for many years. But he didn't consider this aspect of his intellectual development since childhood an advantage. He wrote, "I have lost the taste and the understanding of such things; a loss of joy that has probably damaged my intellect and very likely the moral side of my character, insofar as my emotional life has been weakened and truncated. . . . My intellect seems to have become a kind of machine, designed to distill general laws out of great collections of facts." To become such a machine, from the point of view of the intellectual values of civilization, is a sign of a "truly masculine" mental condition. If, nevertheless, artistic gifts are still demonstrated by men at an undiminished level, this is a sign that these gifts are a product of nature that cannot be destroyed by outside forces as easily as receptivity has been. Education, based on receptivity, is not as essential a component of human nature as is the productive drive. As Goethe wrote, "to express oneself is nature; to receive expressions as they are given is education."

Every productive power, in the physical world as well as the mental, is dependent upon a receptive power to take effect, but the life conditions of modern civilization are such that created products have their greatest effects in the centers, in large cities, where the peace, quiet, and leisure necessary for receptive work cannot thrive. This fact is the most sensitive issue regarding the development of culture, for receptive abilities are the means for implementing the achievements of civilization in an orderly pattern of life. The only way that the flawed relationship between culture and civilization underlying the great majority of technological advances will not signify the end of culture, but rather a phase of its development, is if balance is restored by liberating the repressed powers of the human soul to be of use to external means of improvement. For this to happen, a reduction, not a growth in productivity will be needed.

Those who lament feminine influences operating in modern life do not realize that precisely the feminine side of intellectual culture, the receptive, is lacking in the present day. The very ability without which no cultural form of personal interaction or noble social interactions can exist, namely, the ability to listen, is steadily declining among men. The character of modern civilization is also masculine in the sense that it promotes mass media of all kinds without waiting to assess their cultural effects, for it is the nature of the masculine organism to waste core resources, unconcerned over their potential to unfold, while culture resembles a female organism which brings forth new forms of life through slow growth. At least in respect to receptive ability, then, the most serious flaw of modern intellectual life lies not in its excessive femininity but, on the contrary, in its excessive masculinity.

According to the traditional viewpoint, the females' mission in culture consisted of receptive-conservative activity which enabled them to be educators and maintainers of beauty in life. Moderation in all things was viewed as the first and most superior quality. Examples of this viewpoint are so numerous and well known that one can regard them as convincing evidence of the actual stake that women have in culture. It would seem that the ability to give form to practical life and to lend expression to inner conditions through external procedures and arrangements by excelling at personal transactions is much more often found in women than in men. The house, conceived of as the homestead of the family as well as the stage of noble social and cultural interactions, forms the sphere of female cultural achievement. It follows that contributions to the maintenance and development of life forms, manners, and customs can be viewed as a substantial achievement of women. It could be that the basic impetus to creation, analogous to the male physical nature, does come chiefly from men although there is plenty of evidence that certain individual women possess it as well. Nevertheless, for the majority of women, social achievement seems in accord with a physical nature that encompasses the organic processes of becoming and growing.

But the cultural conception of the lady, like that of the housewife, belongs more or less to a bygone era; the effects of the living conditions of modern civilization have reached the female gender. One of the most severe objections, heard loudly in the beginning of the women's movement, stemmed from the fear that change in the woman's social position would abolish her ancient cultural mission. She would become estranged from her natural inclination as mainstay of the family, robbed of the aesthetic-contemplative leisure that is the foundation of a noble, deeply meaningful ordering of life, enmeshed in the nerve-wracking competitive struggles that accompany modern civilization, and even seized by the blinding ambition of intellectual productivity! Why direct women's efforts toward areas that are already overpopulated with men? Why should woman enter professions through which man, with his resilient nature, has been mechanized into a soulless machine?

How superfluous, from this viewpoint, it is for women to take part in the male work of civilization! The division of labor many people imagine, of men taking responsibility for the work of civilization and women for cultural tasks, would actually not only be impossible to implement, but also undesirable, for what form would life take if only women promoted harmony and aesthetics, and men were mechanized barbarians? In a narrow slice of society something similar actually does prevail: the man is the hard-bitten provider, the woman the consumer of luxuries who gives meaning and purpose to his empty pursuit of money. But this is only a compromise existing at the margins of modern civilization through the survival of antiquated views. If only out of self-interest, a man should oppose such a solution to the gender question in civilization and perceive the threat uncontrolled competitive striving poses to his humanity. Moreover, are there not voices enough that warn men that marriage will impede their productivity? However great man's natural freedom may be, civilization without some limitations of gender duties will tear him away from the roots of his own humanity. And how could the cultural aspects of a society last for any length of time if they are assigned only to the female segment? The types of female roles that were still considered ideal two generations ago are now completely out of date and cannot be maintained, despite family pressures, because they lack not only an economic foundation but also masculine support of these cultural phenomena.

Women are accused of exerting an inhibiting influence on progress because they move more slowly than men. It is claimed that their physiological nature, designed entirely for procreation, denies them the ability to keep pace. It cannot be denied that women, even if they forego motherhood for other pursuits, are nevertheless much more limited by their physical constitution than are men. However, those who view the nature of civilization as fundamentally destructive of life recognize that the churning flow of technical innovations not only increases the discord between civilization and culture but also does not constitute progress, or at least not a far-thinking vision of progress. If this criticism were justified, it would actually signify an advantage in the interest of creating harmony between culture and civilization.

Precisely in the alleged inadequacy of the female constitution, in its role's greater determination by nature, lies one of the hopes of restoring balance in our culturally determined living conditions. The tendencies to excesses of the senses as well as the intellect which are typical of the male nature in general and find their latest expression in modern civilization are counterbalanced by the female nature with its tendencies toward balance, self-contained peace, and form-giving order, all of which encompass many valuable cultural advantages. In the past, these two natures operated in two different realms: the male in the public and intellectual and the female in the social and the domestic. However, now that the feminine can operate in the same sphere as the masculine, the possibility exists for it to gain a controlling power to dam the powerful forces of civilization. This is only a possibility – for it may also be that what is generally understood to be female nature may not be a fundamental, irremovable aspect of the female constitution but only an adjustment to external influences, historically formed and therefore capable of being changed as external forces change.

If, however, the assumption proves foolhardy that the entire historical past of the female gender will have no further effects within a few generations, it is even less likely that any external changes will wipe away the natural differences between the genders, based on their unequal burdens of procreation. An eventual abolishment of that difference through a radical transformation of society would be based on the unconditional social equality of the genders. Women would enter all the masculine professions and face the danger of being caught up in the turmoil of masculine life drives at the expense of feminine cultural qualities.

Up until now, the man has been the measure of all things; it could come about in the future that the woman becomes the measure of all things. Arrangements that are hostile to women's reproductive mission will not last indefinitely because every society is dependent upon satisfying the desire for motherhood of its female members. Every society must provide protection and measures that let motherhood flourish. The economist Rudolf Goldschied has shown how closely women's lives are connected to social conditions. Our current cultural problem is not that women's physical nature prevents her from full participation in the building of society but rather how to best accommodate woman's natural reproductive mission within her circumstances of life.

To be sure, women must learn to understand the cultural significance of the limitations placed on them by their gender, in contrast to the freedom men enjoy. Since the beginning of the epoch of modern civilization, many women have understood the changes it has wrought in women's lives and the roles women must assume in the new social order. It is incumbent on women to give meaning to the new position in society that they must assume if they, like men, are to profit from change. Civilization has made man a slave of his gender's freedom, and it is to his advantage if culture offers him a way to curb the excessiveness to which he has been heir.

And was there not long ago, on a now barely recognized turning point of human development, when man made use of his gender-based freedom in order to take over a function of the female? The conditions under which the rights of fatherhood took over were to all appearances more difficult than modern males would bear and yet they are the source of his historical power and domination.

The Crisis of Fatherhood

I

No one has any doubt about the meaning of motherhood in the lives of females. The correlate in the male psyche, the feelings and images that connect fathers with their children, is, in contrast, kept far in the background. It could be, however, that all female relationships have moved to the foreground of public attention because great changes in the position of women have made female lives in general a current issue. Nevertheless, one does wonder why the meaning of fatherhood in the lives of men has received so little attention. Perhaps this situation stems from the fact that it is such an ancient achievement of the male gender, such an everyday matter, that the puzzling aspects of its nature have long gone unnoticed.

In addition, it seems that, in regard to this unequal attention to motherhood and fatherhood, a role is played by universal numerical differences. If one disregards every person of either gender whose soul has absolutely no relationship to offspring, one can say that in the majority of women motherhood is a predisposition of the soul that determines the entire nature of her female identity whereas a minority of women adjust to the reality of motherhood through a strongly instinctive, physiologically based inclination toward a newborn child.

The situation is almost exactly reversed in the male gender. The great majority of men know fatherhood solely as an accompaniment of the social position of the father based on *possession* and *a position of mastery*, and it does not express itself until the later stages in the lives of growing children. Only for a small number of men does fatherhood have the mark of an instinctive inclination based on physiological connection, a *consciousness of identity* and a combination of feelings that, however, does not come anywhere near its maternal counterpart in its instinctive strength.

This analysis is based on the frequency with which, in real life as well as in literature, expressions of fatherly and motherly feelings appear. No approach to fatherhood as a problem of the modern psyche other than the subjective-empirical method is, for the time being, possible. To be sure, attempts have been made to research the gender-based aspects of male life through the method of interview but, significantly, a question about the moment of becoming a father is never asked. In vain does one search in the literature on the topic, in sociology, gender studies, or pedagogical studies, for pertinent discussions. Also, literary portrayals of fatherhood as an instinctive life power springing from a man's sense of personal identity are very rare, with the exception of some that imply that the relationship between father and child is a natural reality, as, for example, Balzac's *Père Goriot* or Augier's *Pelikan*. Fatherly devotion in those cases entails complete self-sacrifice, without, however, being accompanied by any explanation of its nature or essence.

The gradual emergence of fatherly feelings in an individual life and the way they eventually gain control over their strongest counter influence, namely uncertainty, was portrayed by Goethe in *Wilhelm Meister*. Wilhelm, who has so many reasons to doubt that his child is really his, feels a stronger and stronger wish to possess him, not through adoption but through genuine fatherhood. When he receives his letter of indenture in the scene in which he learns the truth about his own experiences, the first question he poses to the Abbé is whether Felix is his own son. "You are blessed through this question," answers the Abbé. "Felix is your son." Then Wilhelm takes the boy in his arms and cries, "Yes, I feel it. You are mine." And once again the wiser man says, "You are blessed, young man! Your apprenticeship years are concluded; nature has brought you forward."

Wilhelm's fatherliness is not awakened until he interacts with the already somewhat developed child, but it appears at the exact moment when his life as an individual acquires a deeper significance through his consciousness that he is carrying out the will of nature. Wilhelm no longer sees the world as if he were a migratory bird; the wish for permanence and continuity in his undertakings is born in him, and "along with the feelings of a father he acquired as well all the virtues of a citizen." As a result, he is able to view the strictness of morality as unnecessary "because nature itself educates us lovingly to become all that we are destined to be."

That here the power of fatherhood is shown to an illegitimate and therefore unwelcome child illuminates the essential problem of fatherhood, whose weak point is after all the uncertainty of fatherhood itself. In Wilhelm's case the voice of blood conquers all doubt, and this is Wilhelm's distinctiveness – a wonderful intuition into what fatherhood means in its deepest sense.

Quite differently oriented is the conception of fatherhood found in the model created by the Christian view of the world. Saint Joseph is not a real father; he knows that his child does not belong to him through the connection of blood, and so his fatherhood cannot be based on a sense of identity. In him is embodied only the fatherly functions of the protector and provider, to which he is expressly called by a message of God in a dream. It is, in fact, astonishing that in the "Holy Family" of the Christian world there is glorified that which social morality strives to prevent in the natural family – the intrusion of a child not descended from the head of the family, but it belongs to the Christian world view that, in order to justify the spiritual, supernatural destiny of humankind, all human feelings are divested of their natural character, and the divine is brought in as something beyond the worldly. Just as Mary becomes a mother through "immaculate conception," so too does Joseph acquire, of all the attributes of fatherhood, only the ascetic, which resemble pious feelings of a more general nature rather than feelings specifically evoked by fatherhood.

The roles of protector and provider are certainly connected to fatherhood as a natural phenomenon, but they are not its essence. That fatherhood can develop into a feeling of physical connection similar to that of motherhood is a fact that is inescapable to any observer of life. Particularly in the lower classes, where the habits of life are simpler and more honest, one from time to time encounters very tender and devoted fathers. It goes without saying too that this side of fatherhood also exists among intellectual men, only it is more hidden and reluctantly admitted.

If one thinks about the incomprehensible miracle that a tiny cell, far smaller than the size at which an object can be seen, possesses the capability of reproducing its bearer, to the point of complete likeness, in a new existence, then a heightened feeling of fatherhood would seem to be nothing more than the natural expression of identity. If one, on the contrary, considers the fact that nothing about this capability bestows a physiologically immediate certainty of a man's paternal relationship to his offspring, then fatherhood seems actually to have no basic foundation and to be traceable only to an intellectual assumption. These two opposing facts of nature, the uncertainty of fatherhood on the one hand and its thrilling reproduction of the self on the other, correspond to the two completely differing types of representation of fatherhood in the male psyche.

No less dissimilar are the intellectual ways that men themselves experience fatherhood. Most often one encounters denial of the instinctive nature of fatherhood. Because the connection between father and child is not as certain as that between mother and child, the concept of connection does not stem from an immediate feeling but rather emerges only after reflection. The mother, who has carried the child for nine long months in her body and endured labor pains to give it birth, is from the beginning in a completely different relationship to the child than is the father. In most cases, he has become a father out of motives quite other than the wish to reproduce, and after the moment of conception, he has had nothing at all to do with the development of the child. This situation leads to the conclusion that motherhood and fatherhood must bring with them completely different feelings. While motherliness emerges first of all from physical connection, fatherliness can only be an accompaniment of the masculine desire for *possession* and *a position of mastery.* The conception of blood relationship has no significance in the complex consciousness of fatherhood, aside from its uncertainty, because the relationship between father and children becomes an inner, emotionally charged bond only through the personal achievement of education and nurturing – a relationship that can be created through adoption equally as well as through conception.

According to another widespread notion, fatherhood is primarily the product of love for a certain woman. Only through the connection to a beloved female person is the wish for reproduction awakened because a child's inheritance is determined through the mother as well as the father, and progeny in general is valuable only insofar as it signifies a reproduction of one's own person in unity with a beloved partner.

Others take quite a contrary view – and perhaps they are representative of those males whose sexual feelings are conflicted and who as a result harbor enmity toward women. To them, the necessity of female participation in conception is a lessening of ideal fatherhood, which indeed is present as an aspect of the masculine soul, but it is inhibited through disinclination to achieve it through the agency of a woman. This view is expressed by the father in the drama, *Dies Irae* by Wildgans, in which all problems of parents and children have tragic conclusions: "Yes, from the father's blood and brain alone, from paternal conception, the father's children should grow . . . ! But is it so? Mixed with foreign darkness, conceived, educated, suckled by others, by strangers . . ." Strindberg also acknowledges this type of misogynistic fatherhood in his novel, *To the Open Sea*, among other places.

One unique view is developed in the book, *The Borders of Sexual Morality* by Robert Michels. He calls a newborn baby one of the most perfect masterpieces of nature. According to Michels, those men who are not able to see their children immediately after birth think they are ugly. Proof for this is that such men show by their behavior that they do not understand the wonderful feeling of delight engendered by fatherhood. They lack the most fundamental element of fatherly love: the instinctive physiological feeling of connection. According to his viewpoint the first hours after the birth of a child when the mother, exhausted from birth, has sunk into lethargy, offer the father the high point of fatherly feeling: "He who has tasted this fatherly delight of sole possession will never forget it." Michels further maintains that, next to the visual image of the tender newborn, "the most penetrating, almost delicious earthy smell" that the child emits before its first taste of milk, helps to keep the awakened fatherly instinct alive and to fan it into enthusiastic fatherly love. Michels thus documents a sensation in men, evoked by the physiological connection with the child that most people regard as solely a quality of motherhood.

In order to discover the fullest development that instinctual fatherhood can reach, one cannot limit one's observation to human fathers in whom cognitive processes can cover up instincts. Among animals, unaided by intellectual contemplation of the bonds between generations, the instinct of fatherhood is equally as strong as that of motherhood. A general conclusion is difficult to draw, however, because nature, in this area as in so many others, displays great diversity. There are species that are completely devoid of parental instincts, others in which it is limited to one gender or the other, and still others in which it is equally divided among both.

Nature, seeming quite indifferent in this area, allows countless lower forms of life to have absolutely no concern for their progeny, and the future of these species is not jeopardized by their lack of care for their young. Even the instinct that in higher forms of life compels individuals with such great power to serve the interests of the species by uniting sexually distinguished cells does not exist in some species that nevertheless reproduce through sexual difference. For example, male and famous starfish live side by side without sexual attraction although their species produces endless numbers of sexually distinguished cells. Starfish simply let them float continuously away, indifferent as to whether the reproductive cells in the water are fertilized or not.

But as soon as concern for progeny began to appear in the animal kingdom, males developed this concern, not necessarily in smaller numbers than females and sometimes in greater – especially in those forms of life in which the physical task of reproduction is divided among both sexes approximately equally because the reproductive cells unite outside the female organism, as in fish and amphibians. In some species, the male guards the eggs against the females and cares for the emerging young with self-sacrificing effort; indeed, in the case of sea horses, the males even become pregnant in a sense, for they carry the eggs deposited by the females in pockets in their own bellies. Another example of extreme fatherly self-sacrifice is the American ox frog, who hatches eggs in a recess of his throat, and during this time becomes severely emaciated because the growing young make his throat so narrow that he cannot nourish himself. Also in many species of birds, the male and female play equal roles by taking turns caring for the young. Some male birds – namely the ostriches and Japanese air hens – monitor the hatching of the eggs and take care of the young alone, with no help from the females, who are totally lacking in maternal instincts.

From such information, striking facts emerge in opposition to common beliefs: namely, that femininity and motherliness do not correspond to each other in nature, and therefore cellular material itself, even in the sexually differentiated constitutions of highly organized creatures, is not the source of the quality that calls female creatures to care for their offspring.

The greatest disparity in the relationships of the two parents to their progeny exists in mammals, for a female mammal, directly after the birth of her young, puts her own body to their service for nourishment. In these species the female organism must not only carry the undeveloped embryo until it has matured sufficiently and bring it into the world with great labor pain, but also must provide its sustenance for a considerable time after the birth.

With the growing biological participation of the female gender in the duties of reproduction, the male's participation recedes; in mammals, the father is incomparably poorer in parental instinct than his counterparts among numerous other vertebrates. However, he does not completely lack this instinct. Monogamous mammals lead during their fertile years a kind of family life in which the father divides the duty of defending and nourishing with the mother, and one can even describe the gorilla, who prepares a nest at the top of a tree for his female partner and their children every night, as a pater familias.

This near relative of the earliest humans leads us to the conclusion that the human male from the beginning must not have been without a fatherly instinct, that he has always known fatherhood as *an instinctive reality*. As an instinctive reality, fatherhood presents a problem that leads into the deepest secrets of life. Unlike any other type of instinct, it touches the conscious realms of the human soul, and difficult questions present themselves to us that we cannot avoid if we wish to penetrate to the essence of fatherhood. What relationship does it have with what is called the "voice of the blood"? Is it the expression of an instinct that is rooted in the unknowable workings of consciousness beyond the intellect? And what may one understand by the designation "instinct," a word always used whenever behaviors cannot be explained as caused by rational motivation?

II. Excursus: On the Essence of Instinct

A wide detour and some rather bold premises are needed to define the instinctive as a phenomenon of fatherhood. We must assume that in nature a type of consciousness prevails that is different from that of human beings. Our species' unique consciousness separates human beings from the rest of nature. Human consciousness is superior in many ways, but it can also lead to estrangement and even enmity between human beings and nature. The human kind of consciousness, namely apperception by thinking, diminishes the understanding of the type of natural consciousness that we call the subconscious; it becomes incomprehensible to us even though rational apperception makes up only a small fraction of human consciousness. So it is that what one explains with the word "instinct" is basically only the designation of a characteristic of the animal soul that is not reachable by the human intellect. We observe its effects without being able to understand its origins.

Explanations of the reproductive instinct that are based on inherited habits through natural selection of mating partners or that see it as a product of repeated tendencies of association over generations suffer from the limitation that purposeful behavior without knowledge of its final purpose, as instinctive life may be characterized, cannot be explained as habit, for in order to have received its first impulse, it must be directed by awareness of purpose. Also inadequate is the explanation that brings in the mechanisms of desire and lack of desire; according to that view, animals may fulfill purposes unknown to them by wanting to satisfy a drive that appears in their consciousness in order to obtain the satisfaction associated with a particular desire. In this way the reality of instinctive behavior is described but not how it originally came into being, for it is not revealed how actions can create desire in an individual that can often lead to self-sacrifice of that individual for the good of his or her progeny, based upon subordination of the self-preservation instinct in the interest of the species. What happens in these cases must stem from a much deeper cause.

Natural science regards consciousness as a physical characteristic of the human organism and memory as one of its general functions, as Semons explicates in his work, *Memory*, as Ewald Hering did earlier in his writings that are equally distinguished by their depth of intuition as by their clarity of presentation. He explains the phenomenon of inheritance through the function of memory as a physical property. He says, "Hunger and the drive for procreation stirred the oldest and simplest forms of the organic world; therefore, living creatures have the strongest memories of these drives and the means of satisfying them, and the resulting drives and instincts even in our day may take hold of human beings with the power of an elemental force."

Hunger and the drive to procreate, or more generally expressed, self-preservation and maintenance of the species as instinctual reality, comprise two fundamental tendencies that govern organic life. They make their appearance only in the individual. What distinguishes organic substance from inorganic is the ability to renew itself through reproduction. If an element of consciousness is connected to this process, and it has impressed itself into the original physical memory of creatures, it must be that of the unity or *identity* of life in its renewal. The renewal of organic material by reproduction, however, is conditioned upon the *individuation* of a single living being and the simultaneous formation of centers of consciousness. Indeed, it rests upon individuation. That identity, the form of inorganic life, and individuation, the form of organic life, are different aspects of the same thing, serving different interests, makes itself clear only when the individual consciousness reaches its highest development.

It belongs to the nature of individuation that it strives to move from the general more and more to the particular, from the undifferentiated general form of the species to be divided again and again into numerous subtypes, into smaller and smaller groups, the smallest being a family of two, down to the single individual. The single being is distinguished from all other forms of individuation by its consciousness, which the human being knows as the awareness of the ego. On the hierarchical ladder of organic life forms, however, an individual consciousness appears to have very different gradations. The lower the stage of life, the less developed is its individual consciousness. In the beginnings of animal life, it could distinguish only the border between an individual and the essence of other species, for individualization as an element of the consciousness of a single creature did not yet distinguish a creature from its species. The individual and the species are at this level hardly distinguishable; identity at this stage forms only an immediate reality of consciousness. Through the sex drive that separates an individual creature from all other species is each living being connected to a unity with other members of the same species, and the awareness of this unity, conveyed by odor or other sensual perceptions of gender difference, has the additional effect of keeping predatory animals from seeking prey among their own species. In fact, the sex drive is not always necessary to the development of a consciousness of species unity, as the example of the worker bees shows, for they unmistakably display a high degree of consciousness of unity, even though it is limited by their formation of groups.

In the human species, there is considerable divergence between ancient primitive communities and cultured peoples in this respect: in primitive Indian tribes, for example, the individual does not distinguish himself or herself from the tribe. However, in the course of development, more and more areas of the life of the soul are understood by rational apperception so that the individual becomes more and more distinguished from all other living creatures.

The disadvantage of this process of development lies above all in the inadequacy and uncertainty of rational apperception in comprehending events of nature; only after numerous errors and false conclusions can it achieve results that the instinct arrives at immediately. After all, its organ, the rational mind, is egocentrically constructed, biologically constituted to serve the interests of the individual. Therefore, the growing rationality of the life of the soul affects most strongly the relationship of the individual to the species. That which the primitive human being knows as immediate instinctual reality, thinking awareness can achieve only after a long process, taking ever more from the individual the consciousness of his or her identity with the species, which it opposes as an individual being. As a result, renewal of life in procreation versus knowledge of one's own individual death, a condition of that renewal, as a factor of one's individual consciousness is greatly lessened in power.

And yet, on the level of the rationally constructed individual consciousness, the original elements are maintained, stamped in memory from the beginning, and they create in human life phenomena whose power cannot be completely explained as long as they are traced back to intellectual motivations alone. Among these effects on the species produced by the formation of the consciousness of identity is to be reckoned the nesting drive that binds so many animal species into groups and even in human life forms the basis of all communities. In the human species, strongly developed awareness of the ego usually influences consciousness of identity by its promotion of individual interests; in the highest human types, the social and religious geniuses, individual interests are completely transcended by the sense of identity. This is the motivation of charity, or love of one's fellow human beings, and it has its most sublime expression in the idea of salvation connecting godly creatures, willing to offer themselves as martyrs of redemption, with the whole human family. Carried to extremes, one finds this religious consciousness of identity in a legend of India that invokes the chant "Tat twam asi," or "That is you," in an attempt to completely eliminate the individuation of the chanter's ego. When Buddha, experiencing a deep feeling of the unity of all living beings, offers himself to a hungry mother tiger unable to nourish her young, this signifies the absolute victory of the consciousness of identity over all the limits set by individuation. Thereby, however, life as such is denied, for individuation is the condition of the renewal of life through procreation, and its delineation according to species is essential for the continuation of the human species.

The most complete expression of the equality of these two basic drives in nature is found in the parental instinct. What on a fundamental level connects parents and offspring in the animal kingdom, where the relationship is not based on rational insights and conscious motivations, namely the instinct to care for one's young, stems from the original memory of organic matter that recognizes itself as unity in separation. If hunger and the sex drive are imprinted physically in memory as the most important factors of maintaining life, how could it be that the very cause of the sex drive, the even deeper drive to renew life through procreation, would through its modality have left no trace in physical memory?

Identity in individuation, uniqueness in oneness connected to the succession of generations, coming to being through life renewal cause nothing other than the awakening of the parental instinct; it is a mnemonic manifestation of nature in which physical memory proclaims most strongly the unity of life and its renewal through procreation.

In fatherhood, however, is revealed a special quality in the tendency toward individuation. For, next to sacrifice caused by the sense of identity, the strongest motivation of the fatherly instinct is the recognition of the unique nature of one's progeny. The content of the fatherly instinct is not simply having a child so that life can be maintained and carried forth, but rather that the new creature stems from a certain lineage of which he, the father, is a member. The identity of life within the frame of individuation is, reduced to a general formula, the essence of fatherhood as instinctual reality. That thereby the egocentric tendency of individuation is completed through the division of reproduction into two, which by means of the maternal part unites a second generational line in a new creature, can prevent the grown egoism of a morbid masculinity that rejects the desire for fatherhood; in the realm of nature, the dividing in half of reproduction is one of the most miraculous natural arrangements, for it serves not only the manifold diversity of the formations of life, but because also its protection from the burden of inherited influences from only one side.

III

It is true that, like his ancestors in the animal kingdom, the human father has always been obsessed with fatherhood as an instinctual reality. This is surely so, but is it a conscious reality? Has the human species always been aware of the connection between the sex act and the birth of a child? Have human beings always had sufficient rational understanding to correctly understand the paternal connection with offspring?

Numerous reports, myths, sagas, and customs of ancient cultures and tribes at a low level of development suggest that the causal relationship between the sex act and conception was unknown to human beings of past epochs, and the position of the father in relation to the younger generation was based on other motives than the recognition of physiological commonality. In his book *Primitive Paternity* Hartland provided numerous examples for the belief that pregnancy was caused in some way other than through sexual intercourse. He presents some of the strangest ideas, namely that conception may be caused by eating and drinking, bathing, magic substances, a touch with the foot, a glance, a smell, even a mere wish. Also the sun, rain and wind have been thought to possess fertile powers that may penetrate through the eye or the ear; the moon, stars and fire are additional purported causes. For centuries too, even in our own times, a vestige of these ancient beliefs can be identified in the form of the Catholic dogma of the Immaculate Conception.

For primitive minds, the connection between events as distant in time as conception and birth is not immediately recognizable, especially in view of the fact that our conscious sex drive exists quite independent of the idea of reproduction. "For many eons," says Hartland, "the fact that a child comes into existence solely as a consequence of a sex act was not recognized by human beings, and up into the present, this fact is still only partly recognized by some peoples and is even fully unknown to others."

For this reason, he reaches the conclusion that, quite opposite to the rights of the mother, which are rooted in the consciousness of blood kinship, the rights of the father stem from social and economic causes, which in their origins had nothing at all to do with the consciousness of blood kinship. It is rather the *sense of ownership* that, besides being the root of jealousy, is the source not only of fatherly power but also of fatherly affection. Among the many pieces of evidence that can be gathered from the customs and viewpoints of the past and the present for the assertion that blood kinship is not the basis of fatherhood, the most widespread is the custom of the adoption of children. How far in some situations the concept of property determines the paternal relationship is demonstrated, for example, in those African tribes in which a man may let his wife seek a new relationship but will not relinquish the children of their marriage, whom he claims as his property because in the lives of these tribes children do not represent a burden, but rather an increase in workers.

However, the evidence that Harland offers as proof of the lack of recognition of the physiological connection, which he views as a weakness of paternal consciousness, namely the many fictions that have emerged regarding the concept of fatherhood, is taken by others as evidence of the need for progeny in the masculine psyche. In his insightful critique of Harland's work, Emil Goldmann asserts that "the longing to be called a father, to continue a family line, to be guaranteed perpetual existence, is the motivating power that initiates in the legal realm of many societies the institutions of adoption, arranged conceptions, daughters as heiresses to wealth." Moreover, many myths attribute conception to other than a sexual cause in extraordinary people; they explain their extraordinary natures through extraordinary births. One could also see in these myths evidence for the fact that primitive human beings consider it possible that conception can occur in other ways than through sexual union but not evidence that the natural connection between the sex act and reproduction is completely unknown to them, it being highly probable as well that primitive people learned of these connections through the lives of animals, which were always available to be observed.

Also in regard to this question, a great difficulty arises that often blocks ethnographic research into the lives of primitive people – namely the difficulty with which modern people, with their developed mental capacity, are able to penetrate the psyche of primitive people, determined as it is by a conception of the world that we can no longer comprehend. However one may interpret existing vestiges of this conceptual world with respect to fatherhood, there must have existed an epoch in human mental development in which the instinctual reality of fatherhood was transformed into a reality perceived on the basis of observed cause and effect for "that human beings since the beginnings possessed insight into the elementary facts of reproduction," as Emil Golmann says, is, however, as little evident as is an original human insight into other events in nature whose connections are much more obvious and yet were certainly recognized at a much later stage of evolution. We can only be certain that primitive human beings must have had insight into the process of birth and the immediately consequent and obvious connection between mother and child.

If we attempt to follow the course of the human recognition of natural connections, we must begin with the original condition in which human beings, as well as their closest animal relatives, lived together with their offspring in monogamous or polygamous relationships, whether of short or long duration, depending upon the available food supply. To apply the concept of marriage to this original form of cohabitation, as some do, merely results in confusion, for marriage is a form of sexual union based on legal definitions that did not exist when human relationships began.

The first traces of such legal definitions that we have been able to identify in this regard are matriarchal. This means that the original form of families based on couples, in which parents and children are connected by the instinct of belonging together, but without any basis in law, *were changed by the original rational perception that the blood relationship between mother and child was the immediate, primary basis of rightful family bonds.* Thereafter, the recognition of the man as father was virtually absent for an indeterminately long time. Compared to the recognition of the maternal right as primary, fatherhood, which as yet had no rationally established foundation, earned a man only the functions of defender, worker, and provider for all the children of a certain group. So it happened at a certain level of human intellectual development that the man for the sake of his sexual freedom was disadvantaged, and he had rights and influence over offspring not as a spouse with paternal rights, but only through his female relatives as brother of the mother of certain children.

When, in addition, the position of the female gender in matriarchal organizations was elevated in other ways, such as through economic factors, nothing changed the fact that the man with his fatherly instincts, including, as in many other animals, sexual jealousy, was under the influence of these instincts.

Compared to instinct, the intellect has the disadvantages that it is able to attain knowledge only through errors, false conclusions, and hard-won experiences and that it obscures and weakens the certainty of instinct. In no area of human endeavor do these disadvantages display such far-reaching effects as they do in fatherhood. In his odyssey from the harbor of instinct toward the landing of true insight, man as father is not always the victor; the struggle with other powers in his own breast may lead him far away from that which benefits his fatherly role and create habits that, to a puzzlingly high degree, run counter to the interests of exclusive sexual relations, the cornerstone of fatherhood.

In matriarchal legal hierarchies children are not counted as belonging to the paternal family line but rather the maternal, and the mother's brothers are considered their next of kin and guardians. The same arrangement prevails in group marriage systems in which a certain number of women live together with a certain number of men. These systems are incompatible with a concept of fatherhood based on a feeling of personal identity. That this degree of fatherhood even today is not attained everywhere is shown in polyandry, in which, according to Wilson, nearly thirty million people live in an honorable, socially sanctioned form of married life (Westermark). The only fatherly feelings that the children of a woman who is married to several men can evoke in one of those men would be as a provider and protector along with his fellow husbands; the rationally recognized personal feeling of fatherly identity based on an exclusive sexual relationships cannot develop sufficiently to have social effects. To be sure, polyandry in our day is not accompanied by an especially powerful position of the mother and is usually merely an economic arrangement for making life easier on infertile land; one must nevertheless point out that when fatherhood has found its full personal development, economic influences are not the primary determiners of social arrangements – in fact, individual men may take the greatest burdens on themselves in order to secure sole possession of wife and child.

The exclusivity of sexual relations that is said to have had such an enormous effect on the position of the female gender in the recent development of fatherhood is a requirement of only the fully developed sense of fatherhood; in the customs of primitive peoples which in many respects provide the only remaining documentation for the original thoughts and feelings of human beings, there are a few that are quite incomprehensible if one does not turn to the unperfected state of the intellectual sense of fatherhood as explanation. To these customs belong the so-called hospitable prostitution, according to which the head of a household gave his wife to a guest for the night as a sign of friendship or the custom which required a bride at the wedding party to give herself in turn to each of the male wedding guests. These customs are interpreted as vestiges of an earlier matriarchal form of community in which the individual had no right to sole possession, as well as the more recent system in which a man who possessed one woman for himself had to pay the community in such ways for that right.

If these types of customs may be traced back to an undeveloped sense of fatherhood, another, in contrast, illuminates the condition of the soul of that prehistoric epoch during which the recognition of fatherhood was acquired. It is the custom, fully incomprehensible and even repulsive to the modern sensibility, of the male childbirth bed. According to this custom, the man, immediately after the birth of his child, lies in bed with it and, after a longer or shorter interval of time, acting according to strict rules, acts as if he had borne the child, while the mother, as soon as the delivery is over, goes about her usual business. As absurd as this custom seems, it was practiced across the earth and still goes on in Europe today among the Basques in France and Spain, who refer to the male childbirth bed as *couvade*. The presentation of this custom by Ploß in his book *The Female in Nature and Anthropology* leads to the conclusion that it is a demonstration of fatherhood, although the people who practice the custom do not actually know what it signifies. Some of them give superstitious explanations, such as the intention of fooling the demon of illness about the birth; more widespread, however, is the belief that the father after the birth of the child must be strictly protected from all harmful influences and dangers because otherwise the child will be vicariously vulnerable to them; this idea very much reflects the father's feeling of identity as a father. In order to explain the actual meaning of the male childbirth bed custom, Bastian (according to Ploß) goes back to the reason for its origin, which he seeks in the disintegration of matriarchal systems. According to matriarchal custom, the man did not acquire along with the woman the immediate right to the children; they belonged not to him but to the mother's family line until he purchased that right through transfer of his possessions. Through taking on the suffering and burdens of childbirth, the man sought to acquire a direct right to his offspring.

This explanation, however, fails to clarify why a man, if he could purchase the rights to his children from his wife, would submit himself to the hard and unpleasant custom of the childbirth bed, for, only in some places is a recent, obviously evolved form of the custom practiced, whereby the man in the childbirth bed is pampered and fed with dainties. In most cases, the suffering of the male childhood bed is worse than what the female endures, for in peoples close to nature childbirth usually takes its course quite easily. The man, in contrast, must endure many painful torments, castigations, and fasts that last up to six months; often in the end he must undergo a purification as if he really had gone through the birthing process.

Thus, one may interpret the male childbirth bed custom as an act of verifying the reality of fatherhood. To primitive perceptions, the essence of motherhood is the pain of childbirth; if a man wishes to verify his relationship of fatherhood to a certain child, then it follows that he should imitate the external circumstances of childbirth. By voluntarily taking on suffering and hardship for the child, he acquires it in quite a different way than by mere purchase. If a sense of fatherhood issued only from a sense of ownership, only from the male's need to dominate, then a custom like the male childbirth bed could not have arisen. As a form of expression of an instinct that has evolved into an understanding of reality, an expression of the need to verify a recognized connection publicly, the male childbirth bed is a proof, worthy of respect, of the serious purpose of the primitive man and his willingness to undertake suffering to acquire his rights.

A sense of ownership and the need to dominate are thus to be regarded only as components of fatherhood that in an individual manifest themselves all the stronger the less developed is the feeling of identity created by a sense of fatherhood as instinctual reality. The sense of ownership is in this connection particularly significant because in earlier times it had a broader meaning in legal systems that recognized slavery and therefore entailed a sense of ownership that included ownership of human beings.

There are also indications that in ancient times the conception of motherhood was likewise not always solely based on physiological ties, but it could be, like primitive fatherhood, shaped somewhat by the concept of ownership as well. Evidence for this concept, which to modern minds is no less strange than the male childbirth bed custom, is found in *The Book of Genesis*, where Rachel, in despair over her infertility, couples her maid Bilhah with Jacob to acquire children through her, and when she does bear a son, Rachel regards him as fully equivalent to her own offspring: "God has heard my voice and given me a son." And, indeed, she acquires physical possession of the child by holding the maid Bilhah on her lap while the child is being born.

This is, however, not to be understood as meaning that there has ever been a time when the immediate connection between mother and child was not recognized; only that, to avoid overestimation of the physiological foundation of matters related to motherhood, one must remember that other forces have operated as well; even in female creatures, the most fundamental and deepest element of a relationship to an offspring is not always to be sought in the physiological connection whereby the child becomes a part of the maternal organism. As the actual agency of motherhood there appears, transcending the close physical connection, the same parental instinct that can also affect the father, who throughout nature is connected to his offspring only through a quite transitory physical role but nevertheless may in some circumstances show the same self-sacrificing devotion and experience the same feeling of unity with them. Neither the sense of ownership nor the desire to dominate alone could have produced the powerful sense of fatherhood that, operating in several ways, became the powerful impetus leading to an entire epoch in human development.

IV

It is a general principle in human cultural life that intellectual achievements reach the high point of their creative effects soon after their first appearance and then gradually lose influence because that they have no new concepts to offer succeeding generations. Thus, one may locate the highest social-creative power of fatherhood in that epoch in which the first clear understanding emerged out of the confusion of superstition and ignorance over the natural course of conception and the role of the man in the origin and supplying of characteristics of the offspring. This intellectual achievement appears to coincide in time with the development of the sense of property; through that connection property becomes the basis of the nuclear family within a patriarchal order that suppressed the matriarchal legal system and placed all rights in the hands of men.

The father in ancient times had power over life and death. The Roman pater familias in early times could carry out a death penalty as he thought fitting, even on his adult children; among the ancient

Germanic tribes the newborn child had to be laid on the floor at the feet of the father and received the right to life only when he had it lifted up. If he refused, the child was put to death. The same right over life and death as a measure of sole ownership was enjoyed by the man over the woman; he punished adultery with death and invented many customs and beliefs in order to combat uncertainty, the bane of the authoritarian father.

With the rights of possession, the father also took on a great range of duties to feed and protect his children. No longer only through the temporary burden of the male childbirth bed custom did he demonstrate his fatherly feeling of identity with his progeny but also through the much longer lasting and more arduous task of providing their financial security, and one can certainly say that a man who carries out this achievement for a large family under demands of serving his family line bears no less of a heavy burden that the woman who brings the children into the world. Care for his children becomes the meaning and purpose of his entire life's labor, the goal of his most strenuous expenditures of energy. In addition, the compulsion to bequeath the fruits of his labor to his progeny after his own life to assure them of an easier and better life seems to have been a significant factor in originating one of our most significant social institutions – inheritance rights. The sense of ownership and the sense of identity are connected in a mutually strengthening bond: ownership fuels the wish for heirs and the existence of heirs increases the value and usefulness of ownership. Thus, in the course of human history, the pater familias ascended to a role that commanded respect and obedience; to be a pater familias meant for an individual man, however powerless he might be in other social positions, that he reigned all-powerful in his small kingdom consisting of his wife and children; in this area, his individual will prevailed absolutely.

In fact, this unlimited authority and power of the will extended beyond the duration of a father's own life; he secured the advantages of his achievements for his progeny in the future through the rights of inheritance, as well as their gratitude and subservience after his death in the establishment of the ancestor cult. He remained the god of the house who determined the fate of the household even when he had departed, the god who was to be feared, honored, and served. Even among the Romans, ancestors in the form of the lares and penates enjoyed these rights. To be sure, European fatherhood with its claims to gratitude and recompense never has been as extreme as in Asia; in Chinese and Japanese society, a son's honors and achievements are not considered his; in fact, whatever a man acquires does not belong to the man himself but to his father.

For thousands of years, beginning in a past so distant that it has left only faint traces on later patterns of human life, the man as father has maintained his superior position. Until recent decades, the family, with only slight variations, has been the uncontested domain of fatherly power. Now, however, signs have begun to appear that fatherhood as a social power is diminishing. Even a few generations ago unassailable, the pater familias, who regarded a large number of children as the pride and content of his life and who ruled with an iron fist over his self-created world, omnipotent and not infrequently despotic, has gradually begun to become an anachronistic figure. He is at present most likely to be found in rural conditions, among simple and unchanging societies, but even there he has already become an exception because both external and internal influences are changing life more and more to his disadvantage. Many conditions of modern urban life that have had unfavorable effects on the rearing of children, as well as economic and technical changes that are taking men in new directions, are the external forces that are threatening his position. Pressured by increasingly competitive struggles, by the enormous demands that urban life makes on his nerves, the modern man has neither the time nor the desire to take on the governing of a large family; doing so would no longer be a source of pride, but rather a burden.

It is obvious that the relationship of an individual to his progeny if they signify utility and power to him is quite different than if they represent a burden greater than he is able to bear. Even in a purely numerical sense, the pater familias in the modern family has lost power and importance as families have become smaller; certainly it is more difficult to instruct and provide for a dozen children than to fulfill fatherly duties for two or three offspring.

Much more significant are the shifts in values that contribute to diminishing paternal power, which was originally based on a principle of authority without regard to person. A father could demand unquestioning obedience; he did not have to demonstrate benevolence or superior wisdom in life but could exercise his authority as a right of his role, however harsh, lacking in understanding, or cruel he might be as a father. In the family, as in other areas, a force of opposition to the principle of authority has recently arisen, a force that does not tolerate yokes of oppression – consciousness of personhood.

Changes in the social position and opinion of the female gender, to the extent that they have been caused by an awakened sense of the personhood of women, have not occurred without affecting the family; in particular, they have contributed to a lessening of the power of fatherhood. Women's ability to earn money independently has already challenged the economic superiority of the man by demonstrating that it is no longer he alone who is able to provide sustenance for women and children. In addition women's independent earning power has strengthened the sense of personhood of the woman who no longer obeys male authority without question.

Also the assumptions accompanying fatherhood that determine the position of the woman in many areas can no longer be maintained due to the concept of personhood. The more the woman develops this sense within herself, the more the certainty of paternity becomes her responsibility, for the avoidance of adultery is not enforced through constraints on her freedom.

The awakening of a sense of personhood even among young people is challenging the bonds created by the father's sense of ownership of his children and his need to dominate them, which have often created in children a condition of slavish dependence long after the years of actual minority. Just as women have freed themselves from male power, young people growing up have begun to strive for emancipation as well, thereby contributing substantially to the weakening of the position of power parents have over their children. That offspring of adolescent age are still unable to achieve economic independence and release themselves from dependence on parental support only sharpens the conflict without resolving it. How strong the sense of personhood has grown among those in the last years of childhood is shown in the "youth movement," in which individuals of the same age band together in order to find a source of support outside the family. This youth movement, which fights for the rights of adolescents to their own development independent of the compulsion of parental authority, is one of the signs that the old form of the family, based on absolute paternal authority, is in a process of breaking down. To be sure, emancipation of the young curbs maternal as well as paternal powers, but increasingly the man as a father is viewed as having no authority over the mother, to whom as recently as one generation ago children used to turn to for protection against the pater familias.

It should be added that the modern youth movement is not to be confused with rebellion of the son against the father, which has occurred, at least in isolated instances, throughout the whole history of fatherhood. The father as the master over the life and death of the child, as he appears in ancient cultures, is easily perceived as the enemy from whose caprices the independent individual strives to break free. That rebellion against the father has mainly been found among sons is explained by the stronger sense of self-reliance and force of will found in males, who also play different roles in society than do females. The motive of social jealousy between father and son explains the enmity of this relationship more convincingly than the sexual jealousy motivating the so-called Oedipus complex of the Freudian school – one might add that Oedipus killed his father unknowingly and not out of conscious rebellion, and so he is hardly a typical representative of that phenomenon.

According to old beliefs, the relationship between parent and children was structured on the basis of the sense of duty and the principle of authority; a tender, intimate relationship, now regarded as desirable, would have in earlier times been thought of as inappropriate and damaging to the ideal of respect. Even the formal address forms, "Herr Vater" and "Frau Mutter," which have been replaced by various, not always tasteful nicknames, communicated the prescribed distance and, especially among dissimilar parents and offspring, created a real barrier to parents and children who ordinarily might become very close.

The relationship of children to their parents, subordinate to the authoritarian principle, rests on the absolute certainty that life in itself is, beyond any doubt, a noble and sublime good, the work and expression of divine will, which is fulfilled by the act of conception. As soon as these two pillars, faith in life and belief in divine will, begin to wobble, the relationship of children to parents also becomes insecure, ambivalent, and subject to question. If conception is no longer the work of a higher will, it becomes merely an act of thoughtless lust, and if life is no longer unquestionably a sublime good but perhaps pain and torment for the creature burdened by it, the question emerges as to whether two people have the right to grant existence to a being who will then be burdened with the duty of enduring existence as long as it pleases blind nature. Indeed, this question can be expressed more bluntly: "Who is so heartless as to wake a human being out of the slumber of non-existence?" (Wildgans, *Dies Irae*) If it is a crime to take a person's life, is it less of a crime to force life audaciously upon a person regardless of his or her will? In this view, the father is more to blame than the mother, for along with the task of bringing a child into the world comes so much effort and pain that she cannot be accused of acting to conceive as an act of pure lust; moreover, she is seen as the more passive partner, succumbing to the will of the male. The actual guilty party is the father, and for the moment of pleasure through which he calls a being into existence, he later atones by providing for its existence; then this creature owes him no gratitude if he or she does not automatically consider life as entirely good.

To counter a damaged life drive, there is no argument in favor of life, just as there is no argument to counter the undamaged drive. The gratitude that, according to the ancient view, was the basis of all children's love of their parents becomes insubstantial when life is devalued; who should give thanks for something that he or she regards as more of an evil than a good? Why, such offspring ask, have you forced me into a life in which I do not feel at home? Why be grateful for a legacy of insufficiencies and burdens that is passed meaninglessly from generation to generation?

Along with the principle of authority the *relationship of dominance* collapses, traditionally one of the essential components of fatherhood. Nor can the *idea of ownership* continue to prevail during the transformations of modern life. The wife who no longer wants to consider herself in any sense the property of her husband lays her claim to her children all the more strongly and strives to release them from the unlimited power of the father. That masculine viewpoint that sees in woman only a necessary evil for giving birth to offspring is countered not infrequently by the extreme female view that men are an evil necessary to have children and that, for the sake of personal independence, unmarried motherhood is preferable to married because it is free and unencumbered by fatherly claims.

Similarly, the child developing a sense of personal independence struggles against the idea of being property. The emancipation of the child that logically follows that of the woman is basically the last consequence of the weakening of the concept of ownership that began with the abolition of owning people through slavery and has since spread across the world. To all appearances, the global historical process that is steadily diminishing remaining forms of possession of other human beings is beginning to extend so far as to threaten the rights of inheritance, a significant creation of fatherhood.

The rise and fall of fatherhood is a fascinating chapter in the history of humanity. From the ancient times, when the father was of no significance because he did not understand the organic connections of conception, he has so grown in the spheres of power and respect as to be considered a representative of God, who is himself thought of as a father. For much of our history, the father maintained, ruled over, and provided for his family, which was his absolute kingdom. Indeed, so strongly was his ruling power based on the paternal authority he incorporated that the terms "father of the nation" and "children of the nation" became expressions used to identify political relationships between rulers and subjects.

Then, at some point, his star began to fall, just as has happened to all absolute monarchs until, from the perspective of a modern epoch that has begun to question religious explanations of the meaning and purpose of the world, he was regarded as culpable because he was unable to provide answers about the ultimate questions of life.

The same motive, however, that led from the emancipation of children to the dethroning of parenthood also bestowed on it a new justification and glorification. This motive is located, once again, in the concept of personhood. Childhood's demand for rights associated with conception collapses as soon as the individual personality asserts itself. This individual personality resists the idea that it owes its existence to another person. To reject the responsibility for one's own being and essence and transfer it somehow to another, to think of one's own self as only the product of another, means to deny one's own personhood. If the human being, which has developed into a conscious personality, can regard itself as a mere product, it is a product of nature itself, not of a couple belonging to the unending chain of generations acting in its creation as the tool of nature. Parents are a part of this unending chain; it does not begin with them. Conception is purely a natural occurrence. Through it, the individual becomes part of the original ground of being that lies beyond the conscious mind. The responsibility that results extends only as far as a person's ability to damage his or her inherited legacy; for mere life acquired through conception, a person owes nothing. Life in itself is a value-free force of nature, a mystery over which the understanding need make no judgment. The human being does not become the master of nature by rejecting what he or she cannot comprehend but rather by taking as personal destiny what is unknowable. The Asiatic illusion that the drive for life which maintains the universe can be destroyed by people if they reject it misunderstands and falsifies the position of the human being in relation to nature. According to this idea, extended to the relationship between parent and child, human beings can poison the spring from which they drink. A new concept of nature, corresponding to those deep lines of poetry with which Goethe described it, can also unite parents and children in a new bond whose basis is a new connection between human beings and nature: "She has placed me inside, she will also lead me out. I trust her. She may take control of me, she will not hate her work. I spoke not about her; no, what is true and what is false, everything she has spoken, everything is her responsibility; everything is her achievement."

With good reason, in all life-affirming religious perspectives, the father has been regarded as superior to the single man; with good reason, the pater familias has enjoyed the highest honors during the whole history of culture insofar as that culture has remained untouched by ascetic renunciation of the world. For fatherhood is the highest glory of male existence; it leads the primitive man, long before his sensations become refined in the erotic realm, beyond the egotistical superficiality of sexuality, and it moves him to take upon himself duties and burdens to which his generative power does not bind him. As a merely sexual being, insofar as he merely obeys drives that demand satisfaction, a man, from the point of view of higher humanity, demonstrates nothing requiring respect or even sympathy. The elemental nature of his sexual drive, the fleeting and unreliable nature of his impulses, and their relationship to the emotions of rage and cruelty must be ennobled either through their transformation into eroticism or through the effects of fatherhood. As soon as he achieves such a higher spiritual level, the man himself may easily develop contempt, even enmity toward his own sexuality! The truly great men, the real lords of the world, the lawmakers and founders of human society have not been simply men as men but rather men as fathers. In the role of father the ordinary man's nature reaches a moral height through the acceptance of responsibility and through sacrifice. In the old order of things, his position of power was thus thought to be fully justified by his inner qualities.

And now, on the threshold of a new era, the father, after untold thousands of years, once again stands at a turning point. If there was a past time when the instinctual reality of fatherhood changed into an understanding of cause and effect and was joined through an incomparably powerful bond with the male sense of ownership, now a time has come in which fatherhood must separate itself from the sense of ownership in order to create a social form of personal relationship based on the free inclination of a rationalized instinct. Rationalizing of the instinct, however, does not mean its weakening through superficial understanding, but rather its strengthening through insight.

If the man is no longer to be master and owner of woman and children but instead their helper and companion on the basis of a relationship that creates a loving bond between those who are weaker and in need of protection and those who are stronger and able to protect them., then fatherhood in the consciousness of the individual will mirror what it is at its deepest level. If it were in actuality only the fruit of the idea of possession, only a byproduct of the male need to dominate, then prospects would be dim for its future significance.

Not the idea of ownership but rather the feeling of identity is the strongest force of fatherhood. And it can only be comprehended in its full depth if it separates itself from its connection with the idea of ownership. The feeling of identity with which the individual, through his relationship to his offspring, connects his own fleeting existence to the immeasurable continuity of the family line is a bond that cannot be lost through any social change, for the individual has every reason to anchor himself, looking both forward and backward, with all the power of his feelings to past and future within the chain of generations whose legacy he carries. He looks forward through dedicating his love to the children who descend from him and backward through dedicating his love to the parents from whom he is descended. The mystically deep basis of parental love as well as filial love is the same; it is rooted in the essence of the succession of the generations, which is the eternal basis of natural life.

An Essay on the Double Standard of Morality

The differing moral standards by which the sexual lives of man and woman are judged could at first glance seem to reflect the privilege always exercised by the stronger over the weaker. It is, however, a notable fact that the man, going against his own sexual interests, judges as completely moral only that female creature for whose submission he pays the highest price he can offer – his bond to her in marriage. That the man fundamentally despises the woman who gives herself to him without this social premium cannot be explained simply by their sexual relationship; for according to simpler and more natural logic, he should be thankful that he owes her no compensation, or as little as possible.

Also marriage in its monogamous form as a male creation does not correspond to the sexual interest of the man. As a sexual creature he has no inclination to limit himself to a single woman. If marriage in its patriarchal and polygamous forms seems to be more advantageous to the man and his paternal interests, monogamous marriage in essential aspects also provides advantageous protection for the female, protection she needs due to the task of procreation and the associated loss of physical attractiveness, as well as provision for herself and her children, for which she has full claim to one man's care. Because, however, at the time when monogamous marriage originated among human cultures, the female gender did not have the social influence to advance her interests in competition with the male, a force other than the female or the sexual man must have promoted it.

In his feelings toward the woman, the man as father differs quite significantly from the man as sexual creature. The stronger the feeling of fatherhood is in a man, the stronger is his instinct toward his daughter determined by the feeling of identity. His son, who will have the same rights as a man and the same conditions of life as the father and thus represents the direct continuation of his existence, creates no conflict between being a man and being a father in the soul of the male individual, except that which exists in general between one man and another. But in the daughter, in her who is also flesh of his flesh and to whom he feels strongly connected through the mystical voice of the blood, he himself experiences to a certain degree that fate which had seemed to him as long as he stood opposite the female as a man, to be the naturally ordained submission, the necessary hierarchical order between means and goal of creation. His fatherly feelings cause him not to identify with the man who now wants to make his daughter serve these purposes. If the solidarity with his gender that ordinarily prevails in social life can be easily repressed in the psyche of a man through jealousy and rivalry as soon as his sexual interest comes into play, how much less is its power when the sense of possession, along with the imagination of physical togetherness, has developed into a feeling of identity!

That, in this relationship, erotic feelings play a more or less conscious role, one can acknowledge without generalizing about pathological impulses; to be sure, the relationship of father and daughter cannot be completely free of erotic undercurrents. Yet, one does not need to include the motive of incest to draw a complete picture of the fatherly position in matters of morality concerning the daughter. On the contrary, the very fact that the man as a sexual being is excluded where his daughter is concerned makes him capable of identifying with her as a father. And the father is stronger than the man; he fashioned in a monogamous marriage a creation that transcends the male sexual interest and grants the daughter as a spouse a level of importance and protection that she as a woman in such early times could not have achieved. So it happens that in this arrangement the father requires of the son-in-law behavior toward a woman that he as a man would not have required of himself.

The father is also the one who, in the interests of his daughter, defends her from men's advances outside of marriage; to the full extent of his fatherly power, he protects his daughter by means of the double standard of morality from male sexual demands. Women from a different class or women lacking familial protection are therefore the ones a man seeks as objects for his sexual life removed from the realm of fatherly interests. Even though in matters involving physical drives logic never has an influential place, the illogic of the double standard, through which individual male actions forbidden to women are given community license, could not be explained except through the opposition of maleness with fatherhood. As long as a man remains a bachelor, the attitude of the libertine governs his actions toward women; the transformation of his moral judgments emerges quite distinctly when the libertine becomes a husband and father, for the interests of fatherhood demand unwavering exclusivity in sexual relations with the wife and must place the greatest honor upon her commitment to this exclusivity as the highest virtue of woman; in fact, it is often equated to "virtue" itself.

Also the overvaluing of virginity is founded to some extent on the interests of fatherhood. The man in relationship to the children he will sire sees in the social premium of marriage, which the woman demands as a condition of sexual submission, the strongest guarantee that her motivation for intercourse arises from the desire for motherhood along with the desire for exclusivity. Exclusive union with a chosen individual under social and familial approval forms the essence of female honor; especially for the man as father this union encompasses qualities of the highest value. A woman, in contrast, who gives herself to a man without the social premium of marriage communicates thereby that the desire for motherhood is not her motivation; she arouses the suspicion that in her inner life the sexual drive itself has the foremost position – from the standpoint of paternal interests a despicable situation because it is accompanied by a lack of ability to resist seduction.

Only at one point does bourgeois morality place the man under the same requirement as the woman – in fatherhood itself. To be sure, it is not as devastating for his honor, but a man's admission that he has an illegitimate child in some circumstances has negative consequences for his social standing. According to the assumptions of the double standard, the premarital sexual life of a man, whatever it involves, is accepted without reproach as long as no illegitimate child is born as a result. This double standard tolerates the most mean and destructive form of sexual relations, prostitution, while it condemns its potential natural consequence, conception, as illegitimate.

This is symptomatic for the nature of the man in whom social motivations play an important role. While the female psyche in general is ennobled through its closer connection of the sexual sphere with higher activities of the soul, the male psyche is disciplined through motives of a social nature. To the average male intelligence the power of social motivation is so strong that it completely determines the valuing of woman. Without doubt, the frequently found difference in fatherly attitude toward legitimate and illegitimate children can be traced back to the fact that the former appear as sanctioned, the latter as without value to the male psyche. It is a social superstition in the male psyche that perceives legitimate birth as sanctioned; the illegitimate child lacks the social guarantee of genuineness. It is the fatherless one, possessing only maternal rights, who, in a social order ruled by paternal morality is a disreputable child whose existence throws a shadow not only on his mother but also on the one who sired him. For the man who recognizes an illegitimate child threatens this moral system at its core by violating the apparatus of social stability that it values as holy.

Threatening to an even higher degree is unmarried motherhood. Although the progress that is beginning to reduce the social stigma of unmarried motherhood should be welcomed, this progress is accompanied by the ever weakening influence of fatherhood as a social force. The accompanying development in this case is a benefit in the sense of greater humaneness. At the same time a symptom of the ongoing reduction in fatherly power is a change taking place in the double standard of morality, leading to more freedom in sexual relations.

The women's movement, which has taken up battle against the double standard, has sought to bring about a situation of equality by subjecting the man to the same strictures as the woman. The movement has adopted the paternal system of sexual morality for the female and placed it at an even higher level than the male does. What is now happening in reality, however, looks more like an equalization of female sexual morality with that of the male.

The son released from the power of the father is not in a

different position in the world than before; no new demands are being made of him. The situation is different for the daughter so released. In case she does not want to adopt the old views of womanhood, that is the masculine and paternal, as she was compelled to do as long as she was subordinate to these authorities through economic dependence, she can discard them only through effecting a cultural change, replacing traditional views by adopting new ideals and values for herself. Men have the disadvantages that correspond to their psychosexual constitutions; they are governed by qualities that are not present in the average women. The creation of a single morality conforming to the male system would merely mean adding the typically male deficits to the typically female deficits.

The final cultural goal of the differentiation of the genders, in the sense of transcending the male viewpoint to achieve a higher cultivation of the soul, appears to be reached through an exchange. The two genders in their cultural development follow two curves that diverge from each other at a certain point, then gradually draw near to each other and eventually converge. Such points of convergence, at which an exchange of advances made by each gender has occurred, can be identified in cultural history. Christendom proclaimed to men that feminine values of the soul should be their model, just as the Renaissance bestowed the gifts of male intellectual culture on privileged females. Now, as women are acquiring civic equality and gaining the rights of personhood, another chance at such an exchange has arisen.

To bestow meaning on life and direction to its development is the free creation of the human being, for the future position of woman depends on her being able to contribute to culture the typically female superior characteristics that she has acquired during the historical course taken by her gender. To these belong the inner unity acquired in response to the pressure of long submission to the demands of fatherhood as well as the male concept of possession.

To the extent that it has contributed to this unified life of the soul, the high valuing of virginity has been a developmental factor for the female gender that is in the female's own interest to maintain. To a unified human being, it is not possible without danger of psychic degradation to sacrifice one's physical chastity by yielding to a fleeting sexual adventure. This type of first sexual relationship is the rule in most young men but also in their cases not without deep damage if the relationship between soul and senses is not unified. Nothing, in fact, contributes as much to the establishment of conflict, the single enduring condition of the male being, as the unworthiness of his first sexual experiences.

Achieving a unified morality in the interest of the unity of the soul is the mission of the woman. In this point she must step in as the teacher of the male gender. If the woman is unable to cause the man to alter the sexual culture that he has developed, that is, to cause him to cease to view the woman as solely the object of his wishes and ideas, and even to see himself as the object of female wishes and ideas, then the fruit of a thousand-year-long development will be lost for the future.

The sexual integrity of the bourgeois daughter was guaranteed through the power of the father and his values combating the elemental power of male sexuality. If this protection – or the maternal, which is only another form of the paternal – ceases to exist, the young woman must find in herself protection from the strong power of that elemental force. The female personality is capable of this. At the young age, however, when sexual attraction first begins to operate, the personality is not sufficiently developed. In addition, how far removed is our social life as yet from conditions permitting the fulfillment of interests of the female personality, in spite of the equality we have achieved in principle! Until this fulfillment occurs, the father/daughter bond will remain, as ever, the most influential relationship to a young woman. Moreover, the double standard as a creation of fatherhood cannot disappear until the interests of the female personality as a value-creating power gain in influence to the point that they are equal to the governing power of fatherhood in female life.

Gender and Social Politics

I

Like other social achievements, the movement toward women's social equality promotes free self-determination of the individual. This freedom, which is, pure and simple, the highest benefit for the man as for the woman insofar as they are genuine personalities, has in common with the concept of freedom in and of itself the characteristic that it has no positive content. It simply means absence of coercion; it is the preparation, condition, or possibility for a content that must still be brought into its framework. Freedom – to what end? That is the fundamental question that defines and determines the value of the concept of freedom.

Carrying out individual inclinations and drives without direction does not possess the same level, in terms of the soul, as the fulfillment of the requirements of traditional normative concepts – not so much from the standpoint of a heteronomous morality that is irreconcilable with the concept of the free personality but rather in respect to the effects that occur in the individual as well as in social life. If women can no longer fully uphold the role of the fair sex that defined for them the ideal of female beauty as the highest and most important pursuit of their lives or the role of social representative or administrator of the household – their three cultural duties according to the old style, then they must set equivalent new roles in their place. The qualities that were advantageous for their old cultural duties are no longer useful to them in their new position in life; on the contrary, they are in many ways disadvantageous. They will be as thoroughly transformed through changed conditions of life as female nature will permit, a limitation that has yet to be defined. But whoever considers the entrance of women into social life especially significant must begin with the assumption that this change will bring forth new norms, corresponding to women's natural condition, which will suit the changed living circumstances of the female as well as the male better than the historical positions of the genders.

A wide new horizon is being opened for women – to be sure also a possible source of dangerous deceptions and disappointments. Accusing voices are already being raised, claiming that women's participation in public life is setting no new direction, indeed, not even making a meaningful attempt to chart their own course away from the one men have been following. Barely having achieved political equality, some claim, they have already joined the men's parties and submitted themselves to the yoke of party discipline as completely as they were previously accustomed to submitting in private to male domination.

This reproach is not without some basis in fact but nevertheless completely unjust if one considers the brief time that participation in political life has been open to women and if one gives thought to what can reasonably be expected of women. Even though women's past position in Western culture can scarcely be endorsed any longer, it also cannot be transformed in one stroke by recently changed circumstances. The normative values underlying the past situation were the expression of the essential characteristics of an overwhelming majority of women, and it appears that the individuals who wish to free themselves from them through their unique individuality are still in the minority. Still today, without a doubt, the majority of women – that is, those of the middle class – would greatly prefer to maintain their traditional positions in the home and family rather than to burden themselves with a male profession in order to exercise their new social rights.

And still, as ever, the problem of the genders revolves around the question of whether the woman in her essential natural is fundamentally different from the man, for the existence of such a difference is the only way to justify the assumption that her new position should be developed in a different way, according to her different nature, than that of the man.

The overgeneralization that has brought such confusion into the problem of the genders is also in this case wrongly brought to bear, because one must, at this precise point, distinguish, *which type of woman* is suited to enter public life. How great the differences are among women in their fundamental natures has been addressed in *A Survey of the Woman Problem* (on women and types of women); briefly summarized, I say there that the quality that makes a woman suitable for public life is a preponderance of social interests over familial, that is, a divergence from the female majority's subordination and acceptance of the man as lord and master. Thus, just as the battle for civil rights for women was waged by women conscious of their distinctively independent personality types, it is likewise only from such women that independent participation in public life can be expected. For the others, as ever, the home and family, with the man as head, is their preferred domain. Because economic need also can push some women unwillingly into competition with men, and civil rights are granted to all women at the same time with no distinctions, one should not have too high of an expectation for the participation of women in public life. Only through the course of a gradual development can societal changes eventually increase the number of women whose personalities are mature enough for them to learn to comprehend and take advantage of their newly available opportunities to such an extent that they will be able to alter the form of the state that has been constructed by men so that it will serve women's own interests.

If woman on the basis of her absolute difference from man is to maintain her significance and effectiveness in community life, she must recognize the conflict caused by gender differentiation as the most determining factor of the female personality. However, any normative process that is based on a fundamental polar difference of the genders goes against the reality of *individual* differentiation; through overgeneralization, it ignores the most important aspect of the gender problem.

At this point an insoluble dilemma threatens. If woman, solely on the basis of her absolute difference from man, is able to forge new directions for women's lives but precisely because of this difference is barred from attaining these new goals, how can she attain sufficient influence in the male-dominated political world?

It is therefore advisable to reconsider the gender problem and all the implications of the dissolution of the old norms again and again, for as long as one keeps seeking to determine the position of women according to "the nature of the woman," hoping from this standpoint to attain new norms, the female gender will, in spite of the recognition of civil equality, possess no genuine freedom of self-determination.

Excursus over the Gender Problem

Again and again, this question arises: to what extent does the differentiation between the genders determine the essence and existence of the individual? In general there are three methods through which an answer to this question is sought: the philosophical, which addresses the problem speculatively through the metaphysics of gender; the historical, which looks at the institutions of the past in order to draw conclusions about distinct achievements of men and women, and the physiological, which explains human behaviors and traits that are rooted in physiological processes.

Since the publication of his *Critique of Femininity*, Georg Simmel has been regarded as one of the most intelligent representatives of the first method. His book is based on the fundamental polarity of the genders; in his discussions of "the relative and the absolute in the gender problem," he succeeds, through the keenest psychological analysis, in subordinating the empirical approach to the genders, in their multifaceted complexity, to his metaphysics of gender.

That Simmel tries to set the typically feminine against the typically masculine as *equal in value* distinguishes him in a positive way from many of his predecessors; even many women have often sought to establish their validation through coming closer to thinking and acting like men! According to Simmel, this approach will always present women as weaker, less significant creatures as long as they try to fulfill the same tasks and reach the same positions as men. Woman can attain the same level as man only if she becomes a *radically* different creature than he is. In the description of how she reflects this radical difference, however, one recognizes, despite the new terminology, the basic characteristics of the old norms: that of the woman as an inwardly directed, closed, harmonious *being*, that of the man as a creature divided by his will, with his drives pulling him in different directions, acting on reality outside himself in a *process of becoming*. What is said therein about the female gender, like most generalizations, does not correspond to reality; instead, subjective notions are substituted for real phenomena. That the woman is able to comprehend the truth directly through instinct without logical proof, that she wants to be what she should be, that her drives are in accord with the moral imperative of nature: in how many variations have women heard these assertions – especially German women, so often used as objects of philosophical speculation! If women really wanted to believe that they carry the truth in themselves as a matter of instinct needing no proof, to what an incredibly arrogant belief in their own infallibility they would have to subscribe! Of course, according to Simmel, everything that woman is and does is always connected to her sexual nature, from which she is in a purely physical sense more independent than man but that nevertheless governs all expressions of her being. From this, it follows that the female nature in spite of its inner absolute quality, must leave entirely to men, to the male principle, the creation of the "objective world, transcending sexuality, the theoretical and normative that operates in opposition to the ego," the world that is moved by ideas. Women, then, cannot participate in the highest and most distinctive feature of the human species – the ability to create ideas, the basic force underlying culture.

There is a certain irony in the fact that these arguments were repudiated by an essay authored by a woman and based on logic and keen psychological insights – *The Woman and Objective Culture* by Marianne Weber. She comes to the conclusion that "from the well developed metaphysical idea of a radical polarity of the genders" there is no path leading to an objective understanding of what an individual woman can signify as a representation of a thing or an idea, whether created by her or not.

The polarity of gender that shows itself in all phenomena of life is often too crudely, too superficially, and too schematically comprehended. In the personality itself the polarity works in manifold ways; the more highly the personality is developed, the more the general polarity of the genders recedes behind other characteristics (see *A Survey of the Woman Problem,* "Perspectives on Individuality"). From the philosophical standpoint, conclusive words on the metaphysics of gender were contributed by Hermann Keyserling in his *Travel Diary of a Philosopher,* in which he says that one should not dwell on the opposition of man and woman; otherwise, its truth will evaporate like an image in a cloud. He asserts, "It does seem as if the polarity of the genders were an absolute reality. If one takes a more precise and a deeper look, not even the preliminary appearance, much less the factual basis, holds true. One cannot find absolutes in the polar opposition, as has been attempted from Empedocles to Schelling and after them, again and again. What, in reality, determines the basic unique nature of the feminine compared to the masculine? That the former can create life only after a previous act of conception? If that is so, then are not all artists women, all thinkers and philosophers, even the most manly of men, the geniuses of action . . . Every human being is a synthesis of masculinity and femininity and can, depending on circumstances, appear as man or as woman."

Let us dispense, once and for all, with trying to discover behind the empirical reality of the genders something like a platonic idea as an a priori law of the essence of gender difference; all such metaphysical attempts fail due to the empirical fact of individual differentiation. What always thwarts metaphysical speculation about the absolute polarity of the genders is the diversion of the individual from the gender type, but this problem can be solved incontestably by means of physiological theories. Modern physiology sees in the psychological uniqueness of the individual the effects of the operation of the glands, to be understood as the working together of all the glands and all their internal secretions in an organism. Their products, hormones, determine the chemical composition of the organism and influence to a significant degree its psychological and intellectual achievements. For example, the pathological malfunctioning of the thyroid gland causes cretinism. Through smaller or greater effects of certain hormones, one can explain individuality and its divergence from general types.

In regard to sexual differentiation, one may draw the conclusion that an individual's degree of sexuality is determined by the relationship of the entirety of inner secretions to those of the sexual glands. The most feminine woman and the most masculine man would be so due to the result of a ratio of secretions in which the sex hormones predominate, or in other words, the outer poles of masculinity and femininity are reached when the hormones from the sex glands are in the strongest proportion in the entire body chemistry.

It has long been observed that castration, the removal of the male sex glands, causes increased similarity to the opposite gender; additional research known as the Steinach experiments produced the same finding. They showed that qualities of body and personality reflecting gender difference are the product of a gland, and if this gland is implanted in an organism of the other gender, all specific accompanying characteristics and functions of the other gender will appear. The masculine creature will become feminine, the feminine masculine through this procedure. This gland, which Steinach named the puberty gland because it does not begin to function until puberty is the source of the two primary substances that cause differences between the genders.

Yet the riddle of gender differentiation in itself has not thereby been completely solved. The primary chemical substance of the sex glands appears, strangely enough, not solely in the designated gender. According to Professor de Poehl, one of the major pioneers in gland therapy, the specific product that he has collected from the sex gland of male animals, namely sperm, can also be traced in the chemistry of the blood of females. Also, according to the theory of Wilhelm Fließ, the two opposite substances are found in male and in female organisms, and, in fact, in some cases, the male substance can predominate in a female creature and vice versa.

These physiological findings illuminating the power of individual differences in sexuality are set forth in *New Foundations of the Psychology of Man and Woman*, which also includes a *historical* factor previously not considered: the effects of the acquisition of power on the psyche. Dr. Mathias Vaerting and his wife Dr. Mathilde Vaerting, in a psychological analysis of "the feminine nature in the male state and the masculine nature in the female state," come to the surprising conclusion that the nature of the genders, assumed to be deeply rooted in physiology, is merely a phenomenon accompanying *domination*. From this standpoint, the result emerges that there exists a basic law "that the current feminine nature in its major aspects is determined by the masculine state and its exact and perfect parallel is found in the male nature in the female state. . . . The domination of one gender always bestows on the ruling gender the same position, whether male or female." Through historical and ethnological examples the authors show that the characteristics that we are accustomed to regard as basic factors differentiating the genders, or as directly connected to the differing natures of the genders, such as the inclination of women to domesticity and childcare, to subordination to a stronger will, and in men, the disposition toward an active, outwardly directed or even warlike life, are in fact simply the products of power. "The ruling gender, whether man or woman, has the tendency to relegate to the subordinate gender the home and family as their domain of work." The division of labor is not a product of gender difference but rather solely the result of domination by a single gender. According to these authors, domination in its effects on the psyche of the individual is much stronger than the developmental power of inborn characteristics associated with gender difference.

The Vaertings' examples from quite different times and peoples, showing striking similarities, are sufficient to make such far-reaching assertions if not indisputable at least credible. Not only do they show that men in female-dominated states have been responsible for domestic "women's" tasks – such as cooking, washing, caring for children – but even phenomena such as the sexual double standard, which is ordinarily attributed to the needs of a specific male nature, appear under female domination precisely in reverse form. Sexual faithfulness and exclusivity are regarded as the law of male life while women exercise the same sexual freedom that under male domination is considered the natural right of the man.

Also the causes for alternating shifts in power relations between the genders throughout the course of human history are explained, according to these authors, by the effects of the possession of power. Superior intelligence is not the *cause* of the domination of one gender, it is the *effect*.

It belongs to the essence of power that it strives for ever greater expansion; this "expansion law" leads to the misuse of power and this misuse eventually to rebellion against unbearable oppression. So it happens that domination, initially resulting in submission, later meets rebellion and eventually a gradual process of change leads to an equalization of the genders until, over a long period, the domination of the previously oppressed gender is brought about.

The effects of power on the individual – in all areas of life still too little considered – is here, through an application of gender psychology, seen from a new standpoint. But whereas there is no doubt that possession of power in the female psyche can produce the same results as it does in the male, even including misuse up to the most egregious cruelties, the accompanying evidence for the Vaertings' contention that history has seen a pendulum-swinging process of shifts between male- and female-dominated rule is neither weighty nor definite enough to be convincing. The weakness of their whole theory lies mainly in their historical-ethnological evidence, for our knowledge of human community life before the epoch of male domination is extremely limited. Most of the material that Bachofen, Engels, and Morgan presented about a matriarchal age as a general phase in the history of human development has been called into question, re-interpreted, or dismissed by later researchers. And even if we assume that the span of time contained by human memory does not reach back far enough, that the memory of this distant age has disappeared, and that ancient humanity went through many phases of development that we know nothing about, the historical facts at hand hardly support the hypothesis of a pendulum swinging between alternating periods of male and female domination.

In light of the present situation regarding gender differentiation, the theory seems improbable for various reasons. However far back in history we may seek the limits of individual characteristics and their dependence on gender differences, the fact remains that man and woman throughout all of human history have been seen as dissimilar creatures, and however little the typical characteristics may apply in an individual case, they are derived from the characteristics of the majority and are typical for most people.

If we expressly assert that there is a nearly complete independence of individual differentiation from gender it would appear not inconsequential to point to an inequality of the sexes that is not based on any social or personal arrangements. This inequality, based on nature, consists specifically in the unequal burden of reproduction. This basic fact suffices to explain the differences in the historical course of development of the genders without having to bring in any other factors based on absolute biological differences; it would also seem to be a consideration that would prevent us from accepting the allegation that there ever was an absolute domination by the female gender.

Let us once again consider the significant fact that nature placed the heavy burden of the reproductive task entirely upon the female gender and allowed the man to be free of it. For this burden, nature gave woman the compensation of connecting her progeny in the most intimate and doubt-free relationship with the maternal organism while granting the man no certainty about his biological relationship to his progeny and at the same time binding them to him by bestowing on him a more or less strongly developed paternal instinct. In addition, it should be noted that culture as one of the human species' distinctive attributes has strengthened this naturally bestowed inequality. The lives of male and female creatures in the animal world are not governed to anywhere near the same degree by either the tasks of motherhood or the uncertainty of fatherhood as they are in the human species. With the beginning of culture, as far back as one can trace it in the first unfolding of the human intellect in communities, there also began the historical process of creating unequal positions of the genders in the world.

In the drama of maintaining each species, nature assigns to

animals of the male sex the active role, to which they seem fit through impulses toward an aggressive drive for empowerment, while nature makes female animals suited, through passive characteristics, to their gender roles as the objects of domination. The human species presents no exception to this pattern among animals; it diverges from it only with the growth of culture, which is accompanied by a growing individual differentiation. The inclination to the task of maintaining the species is designated in *A Survey of the Woman Problem* as a *teleological* differentiation of the genders in terms of their primitive natures because it represents conformity to the purpose of procreation, "the purposeful nature of the physical constitution directed toward the function of the individual as a member of a species."

This teleological conformity is accompanied by another inequality. The man perceives himself as a *sexual subject*; the woman perceives herself as a *sexual object* – the significance of this difference has consequences that extend far beyond the sexual realm, for in taking on the role of object that the male sexual perception bestows on her, the woman gives up all rights that stem from the self-sufficiency of being a subject and that belong to the foundation of the personality. Through his identity as a subject the man places himself in the primary position, regarding himself as the purpose of all events. The woman, in contrast, is pushed down to a secondary position as a means to serve masculine purposes, and there she remains, unable to develop, because of her own perception of herself as an object and because of the male's egocentric self-awareness, the most important characteristic accompanying male sexuality and supporting the superior position of the male.

To be sure the characteristics of the primitive sexual nature can be changed through altered circumstances; in countless cases, individuality does resist typical gender roles, and culture itself exerts manifold influences that contribute to such variation. On the other hand, one unchangeable law, valid in all cases without exception, is that a woman, in order to fulfill her generative role, must endure the burdens of pregnancy and birth with all of its restrictive consequences, just as it is an unchangeable law that between the father and his offspring no immediate connection can be formed that proves his paternity in a natural way.

It is difficult to accept the idea that the effects of this natural inequality of the genders must prevail in every instance. However great the differences among the customs and institutions of different peoples may be, in general the relationship between the genders will nevertheless be ordered according to the primitive nature of the sexes. Of course, the insecurity of fatherhood has its effects only at a higher level of development of the intellect, only when the relationship to his offspring becomes a *conscious* reality for the man. As long as progeny were viewed as belonging only to the maternal family line because paternity was always somewhat uncertain, women could enjoy an advantageous position although motherhood at this stage did not establish a matriarchy in the sense of female domination over the males, for in that system it was always a male relative on the mother's side to whom her progeny belonged. The advantage that women possessed through motherhood due to the undeveloped consciousness of fatherhood was lost as soon as the father laid full claim to his progeny.

But even if one assumes that matriarchy referred to an actual domination by women in the past, such domination would not have come about because the female gender extended her power in order to rule; her power of maternal claims would merely have supported *paternal rights,* which the man fully exercised by placing his stronger capacity for work in the service of nurturing. And by the same token, these many thousands of years later, women are not driven by resistance to the extension of male power as much as by their inclination toward their own *development of personhood.*

Resistance as a conscious and systematic battle on the part of women did not begin until the rule of the male state had long been declining from its apex of power, and its gradual weakening was not caused by female rebellion. Rather, the same condition of consciousness of personality that may grow in either the male or the female psyche weakens submission to the law that sets women in a subordinate position, the position of a means to an end.

II

The concept of personality or personhood stands at the summit of the value system of Western culture. It has guided the development of Western culture, its direction, and its results; it is the basis of the West's leading position in the world, in an even deeper sense than the forces of technology and civilization.

Individuals in the Middle Ages defined themselves entirely in terms of race, folk, party, trade or guild, family or other forms of community; in the Renaissance era, subjectivity became very powerful, and man became an intellectual individual and recognized himself as such. (Burckhardt) This process spread to the world of women three hundred years later and brought about the struggle for the rights of personhood which form the conceptual content of the women's movement. This is not to say that women did not previously take part in culture as persons, only that such a feminine cultural unfolding was separated from the general historical process. There is no doubt that the aesthetic form of social life that took form in the salons of the seventeenth and eighteenth centuries was a creation of its female participants. This form of social interaction which facilitated an exchange of intellectual values from person to person was based on the art of bringing out one's own personal style of interaction – an art that one finds much more frequently in women than in men and that is defined by many as the specifically feminine type of genius. The Age of the Salon, which was universally centered on educated women, was a fully developed specifically feminine cultural achievement. Lucka's beautiful words about the relationship of culture to personality and its significance applies to these women. He calls personality (in *The Three Phases of Eroticism*) "the individual soul that is conscious of itself, that produces values out of general conceptual (cultural) values, fills itself with them, and assimilates itself to their higher forms."

Our current situation requires women to seek their claim on culture in various areas. It cannot be disputed that it is impossible for them to maintain themselves in their old cultural circles. They must, therefore, seek the essence of their personhood just as man must seek the responsibility to take actions that are shaped by his own authentic ideas.

For the man, the development into a free personality lay along the lines of his natural teleological type of being. His gendered subjectivism is related to the consciousness of personality and his battle for paternal authority; his position in the patriarchal age showed even in ancient times the direction that he was to take toward the full development of his personality. For the woman, however, development into a self-empowered personality does not stem from the teleological nature of her gender; she has developed in opposition to this. Thus, this development is the greatest event in cultural history for the female gender. To put it in the fewest words: female development consists of the woman transforming herself from an object into a subject, from a thing into a person. The process of this development is by no means complete. There are still significant barriers in many persistent viewpoints and customs, not to mention female and male emotions, that stand in the way of the self-empowered personality of the woman.

From the viewpoint of the teleology of gender in combination with the interests of the personality, this development can perhaps succeed in finding its own directional course without restricting the free self-determination of the individual, a course that will be taken by women seeking a new position if they are willing to take into account the unalterable, nature-given inequality of the sexes, which lies in the difference of the burden of procreation.

The difference in the subject position of the man and the object position of the woman is identified in the most marked instance by the concept of honor. That which up to now has made up the content of female honor is basically physical – sexual intactness, in the unmarried woman, virginity; in the married, exclusivity. Her lack of independence expresses itself in particular here, for a male person is partly responsible for or must stand up for her honor. For example, often throughout history, a spouse was obligated to avenge his wife's violated honor by punishing her seducer, just as a father or brother was to do for an unmarried woman.

The male concept of honor also contains some specific gendered characteristics. That a man lacking physical bravery is regarded as without honor, and that cowardice is a slur has a gendered basis – this can be seen even in the fact that the same disposition of the soul in a woman is interpreted as need for protection and enjoys the aura of an attractive quality. In a man, however, physical bravery is a component of the primitive male sexual nature, based on the drive for power; lack of physical bravery limits the drive for power, and bravery as an aggressive characteristic is both a precondition as well as an accompaniment of it.

Another part, however, of the male concept of honor is its significance as a highly regarded value for the free personality. In the word of honor, it has created an instrument through which the full power and glory of the self can be demonstrated through the offering of a pledge. If the word of honor were divested of its romantic-chivalric meaning, which would leave it capable of being broken, then it would still retain something incomparable and permanent – the voluntary connection, the entrance of the personality into an act of will of unbreakable power. The word of honor is, beyond all the conventional prejudices, the expression of a human being's possession of the inner power to make free decisions, without conditions, and to do so in defiance of all hindrances. Thus, an individual's word – significantly called "a man's word" – is the complete expression of the free personality. There is, in fact, nothing higher for the individual than the ability, under all conditions, without external compulsion, to stand up for oneself; this is the noblest and most valuable possession that the self-directed person can have: the awareness of oneself as a human being in the highest sense.

That no such word is attributed to women shows clearly that they have not yet completely acquired the rights of personhood. Nothing would be more advantageous for the woman than to acquire such a conceptual instrument through which she as a person, like the man, could in every case remove any doubt of her reliability. If the validity of the word of honor for the man in his social relationships has an incomparable worth, it would be of special and decisive significance for the woman at that point where the natural inequality of the genders up to now has affected her position to her greatest disadvantage, where her independence in connection to the male sex interests has been the most in jeopardy. We know that the uncertainty of paternity has led to severe restrictions of the freedom of females in order to prevent falsification. To be sure, the barbaric precautions of fatherhood are no longer customary in Western culture, but their final effects will not be completely eliminated until the female's word of honor has won the same respect has the male's. The only means for women to counteract natural inequality in the matter of procreation is to connect the rights of personhood with a deep consciousness that the content of her specific honor in relation to the man must be to vouch for the certainty of fatherhood. After all, there is nothing worse for the position of female personhood than the falsification of lineage. Little as the preservation of virginity has anything fundamental to do with the female concept of honor, it is, however, inseparable from the preservation of exclusivity. If women are to succeed in creating new, recognized norms that are just to the interests of female personhood, then women must be persuaded to accept procreative responsibility. The prevailing lack of instinctive certainty in women and men is shown, among other examples, by Rudolf Hans Bartisch, who, in the form of the "light woman of Karminell" glorified a falsifier of lineage without provoking any protest.

    The de-objectification of the woman as a cultural process did not become a consciously planned event until the women's movement. Its representatives have frequently been accused of abandoning the good instincts of femininity; if one regards their agenda from this standpoint, however, one cannot help but be astonished at the exactitude with which it takes up the social mission of women by reaching down to the hidden depths of the female personality. All relationships, arrangements, or conditions in which the perception of the woman as an object or mere means to an end that are still in effect in some way inhibit equality as well as the possibility of empowering specifically feminine influences in human culture. For every woman for whom personhood is the formative power in her life, it must be a never-ending task to use this viewpoint to put the problems of private as well as social life to the test.

Much discussed is the question whether a woman may govern her own body according to her own wishes without setting aside her personal honor, even whether she can make a free decision to sell her body. Dispensing completely with moral prejudices would seem to demand a positive answer to this question, and with this positive answer, one can even justify the social rehabilitation of prostitutes and thereby eliminate one of the worst inequalities of the prevailing social order. Havelock Ellis says in this regard, "To say that a prostitute sells herself is not just an understandable rhetorical exaggeration, but as inaccurate as it is unjust." Rather, he asserts that prostitutes should be regarded as belonging to the class of professional workers who receive wages for services performed.

We have not yet considered the essential and decisive question of why the reality of prostitution, even if one sets aside all moral considerations, cannot become valued through a change in society As long as prostitution is understood as a fleeting sexual relationship for which the woman is paid to serve as a mere means of satisfaction of a physiological need, it will not be reconcilable with the recognition of female personhood. One should not believe that the usual difference men perceive between honorable women deserving respect and immoral women deserving no consideration stems merely from a conventional prejudice! The woman who makes herself into an object stimulates in the male psyche all primitive and elemental impulses that are antagonistic to female personhood; she sets the sexual relationship on the level at which the woman is merely a passive instrument of male domination. However, if one maintains that a woman as a free personality should take charge of her own body as she chooses, then this view rests on a misconception: if the position of the woman is to operate in society according to the rights of free personhood, then the woman herself should do nothing that negates her personhood or justifies, in rational or emotional terms, men's old perception of woman as an object.

From the consciousness of personhood, the first condition of social equalization of the female gender, stems the single great task of women in their new position, that is the struggle against the sexual sickness that infects our society today – a struggle that also must fall to women because of their procreative burden. For the prostitute not only negates female personhood and causes women in general to seem reprehensible, in addition, she is the carrier of infectious diseases that can be passed on to offspring and so represents a scourge and a danger to all women whose life is dedicated to the task of procreation. To be sure, in the bourgeois world the idea prevails that the sexual integrity of honorable women is protected from the unrestrained force of male sexuality by prostitutes. Honorable women of the old school went along with this argument and received their husbands back from the arms of prostitutes without reproach – however, in numerous documents, the archives of the women's movement offer substantial evidence that, even in the days when such an association was viewed as a disgraceful affront to morality, honorable women did not shy from taking the consequences of this standpoint on themselves.

The relationship of the individual to sexuality can be influenced from two directions: the intellectual way through enlightenment and the emotional way through changing relations in sexual matters. The intellectual way is the easier; it has in the course of recent decades led to a substantial literature; a new science, sexology, has come into being. Investigations and inquiries have made a substantial contribution, not to be undervalued, to the struggle against ignorance and hypocrisy fostered primarily by men. However it should not be forgotten that the main cause of bringing these questions into the open was the women's movement. It was also women who first found the courage to resist the injustice, one-sidedness, and secrecy with which the authorities have handled the victims of prostitution. One need only mention the name of Josephine Butler, who for many years led an unyielding campaign in England and endured the most severe persecution for her activities.

Since the war, this task of women has been pushed into the background; their other great task requires all their powers in its service. It is the struggle against war. It is hardly necessary to repeat the arguments that have been made by women against social ills in the sexual realm in light of the enormous literature on the subject. Pacifism as a specifically female issue or movement is different. An attempt to illuminate the psychology of war will reveal the reasons why women need to oppose war more than men do.

We must recognize war as one of the inevitable consequences of the competition for power among peoples. But war is not caused solely by economic and political forces; it also has hidden roots reaching deep into natural masculinity. For war is not merely a matter of political machinations; it is also a matter of instinct. Could such a monstrous thing as war have prevailed through all phases of cultural development, instigated by small groups of power holders, if it were not spurred on by their instincts? This is not to say that every man who has participated in war is dominated by warring instincts; the mere fact that men must be legally compelled to serve would make such an assumption completely untenable. Without doubt, however, war rekindles ancient male instincts that are suppressed during peacetime. Theoretically, war represents the most extreme manifestation of male being, the last and most terrible consequence of absolutely male activity. Next to this highest escalation of natural masculinity, natural femininity cannot maintain itself as equally powerful; it must of necessity sink to the second tier beneath the dominant gender.

From the standpoint of higher human values, this lessening in status is of course not justified; for the achievements of the soul that war requires of woman – the steadfastness with which she must wait to learn the fate of men dear to her heart – demands as well a type of heroism. However, the values that prevail in war provide no recognition of this heroism. And how different are the effects of such passive heroism on the psyche from those of the actively masculine!

The man who lays his life on the line is able to experience, in certain circumstances, a kind of intoxication, and a unique tension and heightened feeling which one can call a physiological feeling of personhood. And even if the noble motives of defense of a common cause, sacrifice for the fatherland, are in the forefront of consciousness, the lust for battle does not originate in this idealistic sphere but rather in that re-awakening of the suppressed barbaric instinct that makes the warlike way of life somewhat satisfying in spite of all the associated dangers and hardships.

Nothing similar accompanies the passive heroism of women, for it is purely ethical and lacks a physiological basis. War offers no equivalent experiences to women, even when they transcend the passive heroism of renunciation to engage in activities such as caring for the wounded or those unfit for military service or making social or economic contributions to the war effort, activities that go far beyond merely passive endurance and sacrifice.

The mission of many women to maintain life through their helpful efforts reveals the deep opposition that exists between women and war. The law of war, its innermost essence, is *conquest through destruction,* while the law of the essentially female, according to its most original and most general function, is *the maintenance of life.* Newborn life must be more precious to the woman than to the man because nature has exacted its price in terms of suffering and travail from the woman. The fact that, for thousands of years of human history, the woman has not been capable of mounting significant opposition to war is explained by her secondary position from which her special sexual nature has been unable to free itself.

The degree to which the law-governed state protects individual freedom determines whether the social position of the woman rises or falls. As soon as the law-governed state is suspended, as it is in wartime due to the domination of military force, the woman loses equality or declines in status. Under only *one* condition could the demand for the equality of all citizens without difference according to gender be upheld: if the female gender were included in the general requirement to serve in the military.

This consequence has, to be sure, up to now been brought up only by opponents of equality, in order to construct an absurd argument. They have failed to take into consideration, however, the maternal duties of women, her difficult burdens of procreation, which are often regarded as a substitute for the male duty of military service.

There is no need for proof that the aggressive impulse that in men is accompanied by the inclination toward military actions is almost completely missing from the psychophysical constitution of the woman. The exceptions, the fact that in wartime a few women have come forth to fight on the front, proves, however, that gender differences in fact do not place absolute limitations on characteristics of individuals. Perhaps these exceptional women deserve respect for their commitment and their personal bravery – but only as unusually praiseworthy examples; they cannot serve as models for women in general.

To be sure, where the imitation of the accomplishments of male service in war has gained significant ground, as in Russian female battalions, this signifies a gross misunderstanding of what humanity should expect from women; it is the worst kind of violation of natural instinct. In addition, the highest valuing of physical bravery, courage, defiance of death and all other great achievements that accompany the military disposition of male nature at its best can do nothing to change the fact that war is the most fundamental evil that human society has borne for thousands of years.

The whole realm of war, which originated at a primitive level that does not recognize the human race as a whole but regards enemies as subhuman and of inferior value, stands in tragic opposition to the intellectual level of modern human nature. Even the high valuing of warlike masculinity comes from a time of primeval conditions and perceptions, and yet, at the same time, it is grounded and justified in a type of masculine nature that is still frequently found today. There is also, without a doubt, a connection between the impulse to war and a certain type of masculine sexual impulse. Even in the animal kingdom, this connection appears in fights among male animals although these fights present only an analog to a duel rather than to a war. It is the same sexual impulse that simultaneously gives rise to the dominant feeling of superiority of the male over the female and, as long as this type of male sexual impulse is common, how could there be any place for the woman to achieve equal rights or be regarded as a creature created equal to the man?

In wartime, the primitive condition of masculinity supersedes cultural forces and influences of recent origin. The atrocities that are committed in every war that go beyond legally waged warfare show clearly what power the instincts of primeval man can still gain as soon as the inhibitions of cultural life are discarded; and it is not by chance but because of impulses closely connected to the disposition of the warrior that in every war rape of enemy women is committed.

But even apart from such extreme unleashing of brutality – the suspension of every usual code regulating the genders, the destruction of married life and domestic loving relationships must suffer the most detrimental effects. War evokes destructive feelings of hatred and revenge and causes men to become accustomed to ways of life from which all cultural refinement has been removed. War leads to uncontrolled male sexuality, and this force is arguably the darkest shadow that war casts far into peacetime, and the consequence of war that brings most harm to the female gender.

Mentioned above are only a few of the most important reasons that women of all walks of life, if they take a standpoint consistent with their own natural and social tasks, must renounce war unconditionally as the most terrible scourge of the human race. There are many men who support this viewpoint as well, men who take an active role in the pacifist movement and all the efforts that go along with it; but if the struggle against war for the man is a matter of higher humanity, for the woman much more is at stake, namely the very conditions needed for higher possibilities of life for her own gender as a whole.

It may remain undecided whether war should be regarded as an unavoidable accompaniment of the human condition or even, as some think, as a kind of necessary chastening rod effecting the restoration of degenerated conditions of life. Whoever has firsthand experience with war knows only too well that it is much less "a school of courage and sacrifice for its victims" (Moltke) than a crucible of uncivilized barbarism, baseness, and corruption. In addition, we need not concern ourselves with the question whether war could ever be completely eliminated from the world by means of social reforms. One can even concede that the two greatest cultural achievements of women, their struggles against prostitution and war, are utopian goals – this concession does not lessen the value of these struggles in the least. After all, human society has struggled ever since it developed social organization against all manner of evils that it has never been able to eliminate completely, without ever giving up these struggles. But, it will only be when women in general comprehend that their mission in the life of society must be different from that of men, when they set their own values, oriented by the natural inequality of the genders, against the prevailing male values, that their entrance into political life will be able to open a new page in the book of world history.

Sexual Ideologies

During a severe illness, Saint Francis of Assissi long endured his pains in stalwart asceticism without seeking any relief. At one point he turned to one of his companions and asked if it would not be justified for him to express concern for his body. The companion replied, "Can you, Oh Father, testify to your body that it has always proved itself obedient in the service of the Lord?" And when the sick man answered in the affirmative, he continued, "Is it therefore not right and proper that you help such a friend, who has often risked death for you, in such an hour of need?" Thereupon cried Saint Francis: "Rejoice, Brother Body, and bless me, for as you see, I am eagerly responding to your wishes by hurrying to come to your aid to alleviate your pain." From this hour forward he complied with the orders of his doctor.

Under the rule of a dualistic philosophy that locates the meaning of life in a purely spiritual afterlife, a fanatical, striving ambition to liberate the soul at any cost from the fetters of sensuality was kindled; the body with its desires was viewed as the insubordinate, rebellious slave of the independent creature above sensuality, a slave that temporarily dwelt within the creature striving to conquer the flesh. The body was "the pigsty of the earthly house of flesh," as it was called by the mystic Gichtl, as well as "a dark prison of the soul, wherein the devil has his stolen castle."

In light of such views, it is a significant act to elevate the body to the position of a brother; within an interpretation of the cosmos, however, that locates the meaning of life in this world, this position seems self-evident. As a bearer of the soul – that is, the higher consciousness of achievement that transcends bodily needs – the body is granted exactly the same life span as the human creature and can claim an equal rank. As soon as the metaphysical underpinnings of the doctrine of damnation fall, the valuation of the impulses through which the human creature is connected to life on the earth will be changed.

Tired of all ideological principles, no longer influenced by the bidding of inherited values, and embittered by the grand words of ethics that are irreconcilable with facts, the modern individual seeks salvation in the discovery and recognition of the real powers that govern life – in both the outer and the inner worlds. The modern person no longer wants to bleed like a soldier in battle for an imaginary fatherland on the other side of the earthly world. And because the old devil no longer possesses even a stolen castle in the flesh, anymore than the old Lord God has a temple in the spirit, nothing now prevents the old slave from being made into a brother.

How does it happen then, that the movement for equality does not steadily move forward? It is because equality does not refer to libertinism, which in all ages disdains every serious approach to life in order, in secret, to draw as much pleasure out of earthly existence as possible. It could be that libertinism bears just as much guilt for the failure of equality as does oppression. Just as oppression harms human life with its chastening rod controlling the disobedient, libertinism promotes a harmful lack of constraint of human impulses. The opposition of interests within the human being seems to be accompanied, in spite of all our physical culture and sport, by the fact that the identification of body and soul in our thinking is as far from coming about as equality is from being fully realized.

The concept of balance in a psychophysical sense seems at first to be nothing other than health itself. However, it has a particular relationship with health. However invaluable, indeed however essential it may be, it does not rise to the level of a personal ideology. It is a starting point, not a goal. In the battle between the two great realms of value that correspond to the two sides of human nature, that is, the spiritual and the material, health does not possess a crucial power. The human being with an overwhelming intellectual drive accords it no importance great enough to outweigh the enormous claims of the mind. Anything encountered outside of that realm seems unimportant, inconsequential, of no value; for that reason, Nietzsche called the modern scholar the last ascetic. In a less flattering expression, one could say that this type, given to intellectual debauchery, is the libertine of the mind.

Usually the intellectual treats Brother Body worse than did Saint Francis; if the body fails or collapses, it is regarded as a disturber of the peace, and consideration of it becomes so burdensome that all meaning and worth is drained from life.

The human being in its primitive state, by contrast, anchored in the material, is just as disinclined to regard health as the highest good. Health signifies intact life, nothing more; those who possess it are not aware of it at all. The healthy person is like a rich man who wastes his wealth because he regards his treasures as inexhaustible. And so it happens that it becomes all too easy without the directives of an intellectually fulfilled life, for one to become lost without inhibition in the life of the senses, in which the body all the more senselessly rules because it is stronger in its elemental vitality.

For, unfortunately, Brother Body remains an ungovernable companion, which, when he abandons his instincts and is not at one with himself, does not know how to make the right use of his freedom. His inclination toward stimulation combined with the inability to set limits on himself makes equality seem questionable. Having barely escaped the bonds of Christian asceticism, he encounters a host of counterpressures that want to teach him mores, to demand avoidance of alcohol and nicotine, narcotics, and meat, eventually even to leave the so-called civilized world that has made him a sick animal, return to nature and once again go on all fours – yes, why not? And there seems to be no doubt: as soon as he is not led by the reins of codes, he stops displaying obedience to "the service of the Lord."

To be sure, the Brother Body of the female gender enjoys the reputation that he, from the beginning, has been living in a kind of pre-established harmony with the soul, such that being and duty do not contradict each other. Even if the female ascetic of Christendom speaks no less disparagingly about him than the male, it cannot be denied that the entire battle against the claims of sensuality in all times has been waged mostly by males. The reason for this is close at hand. If the body in general provides a constant impetus to conflict with the higher drives of the human life of the soul, where else than in nature, which is indifferent to the interests of the individual, would it be put in service of the interests of the species! Here the body appears as the "dark despot" that violates the spiritual powers. The male gender is dominated by this despotism because nature has given it, usually in greater proportion than to the female gender, the aggressive role in maintaining the species. Therefore, this is the starting point for all rebellion and enmity against it. In a deep sense, this relationship takes on the character of tragedy; it throws a gloomy light on the whole of human life, burdened with "original sin." Ordinary people look, however, in a venal way at the sore point of existence, taking comfort in the illusion that they can bargain with their souls. They even laugh at the despot and find everything amusing that falls into his realm. In this way, human dependence on the cruel moods of an incomprehensible lord seem less painful.

In truth, Brother Body does not behave in a brotherly way; he lurks eternally in the background, ready at any moment to attack the peace of the soul with some unforeseeable scheme. Should perhaps only an ascetic, certain of his mastery of his soul, be able to speak of his body as a brother?

Luther compared human nature with a drunken peasant who, if one helps him onto a saddle from one side, falls off the other – a saying that implies the worst conclusion. Yet Luther belonged to those attempting to reconcile body and soul; he did so by placing rational moderation in the satisfaction of bodily needs in the place of ascetic morality. However, Brother Body cannot be controlled by rational reason as soon as sexuality gains the upper hand. Then he succumbs to the same fate as the wood grouse that loses hearing and sight while mating; the voice of reason can preach ever so persuasively but cannot be heard when another power renders one blind and deaf.

During the entire development of culture humanity has sought in the most diverse ways to battle against the wood grouse in itself; all kinds of fantastic and extreme viewpoints have been concocted to serve the moral stance of human beings opposed to sexuality. They are merely symptoms of the difficulty of the long battles. If there is anything in the power of human beings that enables them to treat their bodies as "pigsties of earthly flesh houses," it is to be found in their attitudes toward sexuality. For that reason, nowhere other than here do God and the Devil wrestle so bitterly for dominance of the soul. In other words, we can liberate ourselves from the concept of "sin," not, however, from the conditions of the soul that religious thought condemns by means of this concept.

It seems that the drive that secures the maintenance of the species forms at the same time the means of its higher development, through which it spurs on the human being in various directions to its greatest achievements. That which is the greatest threat to the freedom of the personality claims at the same time the greatest power. Let us now follow these paths with the seriousness that befits their significance.

From the intellectual viewpoint, the sex drive is a different matter than it is in moral terms or as immediate individual experience. From the intellectual standpoint springs the need to liberate sexuality from every moral qualification, that is, the concepts "pure" and "impure," "good" and "evil." As a phenomenon of nature on which our entire physiological life is built, it cannot be subordinated to moral values at all. The drive that is the source of the eternal renewal of life, which has led the human species through eons of terrestrial existence, must in itself, set loose from its relationship to the events of lives of the human soul, awaken our highest respect. Without the continued existence of our species, what are all the achievements of human beings? Continued existence is the condition for our greatest hope, the hope of unlimited development that carries on the fruit of our work from generation to generation in an eternal chain; only through the power of the sex drive is its indestructibility guaranteed.

The evolutionary viewpoint grants sexuality a higher rank than it has ever before been accorded; this viewpoint regards as completely justified the view that the sex act is something holy, or at least something that in the consciousness of human beings of the future will be surrounded with an aura of saintliness.

According to this viewpoint, the circumstances of sexual matters in human societies as they have developed up until the present time are completely nonsensical, even pathological. If one regards the relationship of cultural humanity to sexual things with an eye to what nature would intend, to what would be in accord with nature, one faces facts that, at first glance, without considering the intricate processes that gave rise to them, are quite incomprehensible. How could the belief have come to dominate civilized society that views the most important and most holy natural drive as degenerate and barbaric, that makes it the object of shame and ridicule? We may as well admit that even among the most serious and perceptive of modern people the conception of the sex act as a holy matter is more of an intellectual judgment than a matter of feeling. Of the religious respect that the sex act as source of conception awakens, as long as it is so regarded, nothing remains when an individual is seized by the power of the drive that compels him or her to sexual activity. The feelings that accompany this drive enter consciousness accompanied by a mood quite far removed from the sacramental, respectful, or religious. The lack of connection between the higher regions of spiritual life and the elemental arousal of the sexual drive, unless it is created by feelings of love, constitutes the decisive failure of the modern psyche vis-à-vis sexuality. Have we not lost something irreplaceably valuable that human beings of earlier epochs possessed? Has Western culture not gone backwards, taken a terribly wrong direction away from the path of the natural and healthy through this divergence from the elemental laws of life?

There are peoples outside of modern culture for whom sexual acts have been cult practices based on religious ideas. In fact, such ideas were possessed by those peoples whose cultures provided the roots of the modern – and not only as intellectual theories, but rather as the expression and reflection of immediate experience. Diverse forms of religious prostitution belong to these practices, as does the Babylonian custom requiring every female to sacrifice her virginity in the temple of Astarte, the Greek practice of women serving as temple slaves in the cult halls of Aphrodite, the rites of forest and field that connected the sex act with the fertility of the earth, and many other such religiously based customs quite alien to modern feelings and understanding. All of these customs are based on a particular type and concept of sexual life – its unity with religious perceptions that invest it with a holy meaning and higher dignity than would otherwise be reachable by an individual.

However, the fact that the concept of holiness also contains its opposite, the impure, was evident already in a very early stage of human development regarding sexual matters. This was especially pronounced in certain strictures on religious practices, as this example shows: "It is a widespread rule that anyone undertaking a holy act or entering a holy place must be perfectly pure, and no impurity in this context is recoiled from more than the sexual." (Westermarck, *Sexual Questions*) The requirement that everyone who participates in religious festivals and celebrations must refrain from sexual intercourse beforehand even appears among peoples who otherwise are quite free of ascetic impulses, such as the ancient Greeks or the Islamic people, who require that pilgrims to Mecca remain celibate throughout the duration of their pilgrimages. However, the most clear-cut significance is seen in the meaning accorded to celibacy if it is required as a condition of a certain spiritual effect. For example, Muslims believe that the recitation of certain passages in the Koran can negate the power of evil spirits only if they emanate from the mouth of a man who is sexually pure. Abstinence intensifies the power of prayer, the very power of the spirit itself – such beliefs seem to be the basis for associating the performance of priestly offices with the requirement of sexual purity. Celibacy was assumed to bestow magical powers even at the earliest stages of human culture. When the role of the priest as a mediator with the divine was inseparable from the belief in magic, in the practice of shamanism, there was already the tendency to require strict control over sexuality. This view developed quite independently of mutual influence among the most diverse peoples. Within Western culture it grew organically from the basic nature of the religious consciousness in its relationship to sexuality and found its highest expression in Christian asceticism.

The attitudes alternating between sanctification and renunciation of sexual matters lead in two directions, both stemming from very early social and psychological factors, which can be traced in diverse combinations through the entirety of cultural history. If one does not want to go so far as to regard these two directions as symptomatic of the development of immanent tendencies, one can at least use them as helpful concepts with which to explain conflicts in sexual life.

The demonic character of the sex drive – demonic according to primitive ways of thinking because it introduces an outside power into the consciousness – engenders at early stages of thought the need to establish a relationship between sexuality and the divine, to sanctify it through sacrificial practices. What is hidden behind this need to sanctify is the same need that contributes to the origin of all religious concepts: the primitive human being's fear of unknown powers governing human life. In addition, the physical effects of sexuality belong to the phenomena that require purification, and everything that requires purification causes impurity, constitutes contamination, and so must be removed through sacrifice.

Primitive human beings felt possessed by hidden powers that had to be revered, placated, supplicated for grace through sacrifices, namely by giving to them whatever the supplicants themselves found especially valuable. In the sexual realm, this is the concrete manifestation of sexual activity, semen, produced by the human body – according to ancient belief even by the female body – which stands for sexuality in general, as indicated by vows of chastity. One form is for the masses through individual rituals such as sacred defloration carried out by the sexual act of the priest as a representative of the divine. The other form is for the divinely ordained, who must confirm their status through extraordinary, highly significant achievements beyond the reach of ordinary people. Is this view not already expressed in the fact that a precondition for involvement with the realm beyond the sensual is inhibition of the sensual element?

From this point onward, the directional lines of the processes of establishing sexual values clearly begin to diverge. The *affirmation* of sexuality that is proclaimed in the unrestrained satisfaction of the natural drive in noble cult practices and orgiastic festivals is opposed by the conscious *renunciation* of sexuality that aims at the repression and eventually the complete extermination of sexuality.

Two different worlds distinguish themselves within the human soul: beside the sensual being governed by irresistible forces of nature, there is revealed the human personality that opposes these forces with a power that it alone, of all creatures of the world, possesses. Through this ability, human beings believe themselves to be spiritual creatures connected to the divine, connected to God and belonging to Him. For this reason, the relationship of the priest to sexuality becomes ever more one of rejection. The battles he must wage with it and the difficulties that resistance creates for him only strengthen the belief that these drives must come from a realm producing influences that are enemies, warring against God. And, fed by the physical effects of chastity that operate most strongly in intense, passionate, and exuberant temperaments, the conditions of the imagination and metaphysical thinking create a system in which even the most important function of sexual life, procreation, is considered less valuable than the advantages of abstinence.

With the growing dominance of the spiritual principle that requires the renunciation of sexuality, the counterforce affirming sexuality declines, cut off by the connection to the divine in human beings and relegated to the low, animalistic, and earthbound. However, it disappears apparently and temporarily, only to rise victorious again in a later age in new forms and to maintain itself as a worldly spirit of power parallel to the religious. At first, however, sexual affirmation had to bring about a decisive, fundamental shift in order to return sexuality to its relationship to the higher realms of the life of the soul from which it had been separated by the process of spiritualization.

That which makes the idea of the sex act as a sacred practice unacceptable for people of our modern culture is its separation from a personal relationship, for the only condition under which sexuality can attain the level of a value of the soul in modern consciousness is through a relationship to a certain person, the erotic motive. Impersonal sexual intercourse, in contrast, as is practiced in prostitution, is viewed, precisely because of its impersonal nature, as reprehensible; indeed, it possesses not a trace of the element of feeling through which it can be connected with the higher achievements of the soul. The very factor, however, that constituted the special characteristic of sacred sexual practices, allowing them to be perceived as religious, was that they were impersonal. They could release human beings from their individuality by making them aware of their connections with nature as a whole, causing them to perceive themselves as tools of world history, which could happen only on condition that they remained separated from the sensations of the persons participating. Personal human connections between partners, before or after the sex act, could play no role; regarded in terms of cult meaning, these relationships had to remain completely impersonal. Indeed, in particular cases, if participants were supposed to act expressly as implementers of divine will, similar to a proxy siring of a son for a childless dead person according to the law of Manu, every personal demonstration of desire would be expressly forbidden. The motive for a sex act was not found in the person with whom it was performed; desire in a sacred sex act was not directed at one's partner, a certain individual selected from all others, for it was performed not out of love for that person but for the sake of magical effects. A moment of personal attraction would devalue the sacrificial act and rob it of its magical effects. The concept of such an impersonal act of sacrifice was the basis of religious prostitution; likewise, in the case of Assyrian girls who sacrificed their virginity on the temple grounds of the Astarte, no personal choice was allowed, and they were never allowed to couple more than once with the same man. He had in her life, as she in his, no further meaning. It belongs to the essence of sacrificial acts that personal interest is excluded; the holiness of the sex act requires that submission to a certain chosen person does not dominate the consciousness of the person submitting but rather becomes submission to a principle of existence that transcends the will of the individuals involved. Such a viewpoint was not only possible at a certain level of erotic development, it also led to the view that personal motives in ordinary acts of sexual intercourse played a subordinate role.

It is historically significant that Judaism strongly opposed performing sex acts as sacrificial deeds. The vehemence with which passages in the Old Testament inveighed against offering "sacrifice of one's seed to Moloch" and the bitter condemnation of every cult that practiced any form of religious prostitution show that the spiritualization of the concept of God has long wrestled against another concept of sexuality for domination of souls. Just as the invisible God allows no image of Himself so that He cannot be drawn out of the spiritual sphere into the sensual, He also demands a stricter division between the spiritual and the sensual elements than is compatible with sacred sex acts. These elements were not yet perceived by the primitive psyche as being in opposition; the spiritual in the human creature was not yet a power that strove to develop itself at the expense of the sensual. As soon as competition and opposition between sensuality and spirit began to emerge in human consciousness, the act in which the power of the senses is most strongly felt could no longer be the expression of a religious sentiment, especially when sensual power was regarded as demonic, the enemy of spiritual beings obedient to God. Those who wanted to offer themselves up to God needed the spiritual medium of reverence, which is incompatible with sexual arousal.

The justification of sexuality in Jewish morality was linked to the idea of procreation – in this form connected as well to the religious doctrine that God had given His chosen people the duty to be fruitful and multiply. If also in this connection personal motivation is almost as subordinate as it is in a sacred sex act, without the separation of sexuality from its sacred meaning the value of the personal bond that it creates could never have been developed.

The sensual experience which the sex act appears to be in consciousness could in Jewish sexual ethics achieve holiness only through the purpose for which God had established it. However, worshipers elevated into spiritual beings perceive themselves not only as tools of procreation, but also as bearers of spiritual qualities, as creatures whose lives possess worth in themselves. And this personal self-awareness grows along with the development of the concepts of God and the relationship of God to human beings, creating ever more glorious illusions until it arrives at its highpoint, the marvelous phantasmagoria of the son of God who offers himself as a sacrifice for the human race. Every member of the race born in bondage was freed through this extraordinary deed, every person was an object of love that inspired it and a participant in the divine that was brought into the world through him! The work of salvation is at the same time a declaration of human dignity; whoever pledges faith in this salvation is born again in the spirit as a person freed from the power of demons, released from the power of original sin, and clad with an independent responsibility founded in a person's individual relationship with God.

However, the development of personhood that led from Judaism to Christendom did not keep step with regard to sexuality. It belonged in its elemental expression neither to the divine spirit in human beings nor to the value of the personality that human beings now possessed, and it had lost the possibility of gaining holiness and justification by serving as a sacrifice in the form of an impersonal act.

Should it be taken as chance that among the holy books of that people whose morality renounced the impersonal sex act as sacrifice is one that is dedicated to the glorification of personally directed sexual love? Or have threads been spun in the darkness of the subconscious whose connections will become recognizable only at a later stage of development? From the perspective of the Christian ascetic renunciation of sexuality this holy book has been interpreted as a symbolic and prophetic portrayal of a spiritual relationship at the highest level, but from the perspective of the development of human culture, it occupies an only slightly less exalted place.

Indeed, one of the most important aspects of this development is the movement to incorporate sexuality within the complex personality. According to this movement, sexual desire is to be attached to a certain person, thus concentrating this most important influence on one object. And so there commences with the personal relationship of love a new kind of holiness and justification of sexuality in human thought. The sex act as a demonstration of love, an expression of devotion to a chosen person, is connected to the concept that the divine arises out of the realm of the spirit. On the basis of this connection, sexual feelings receive a completely new emphasis; desire sanctioned by one's own will is not viewed as impersonal sexual arousal caused by demonic powers because it belongs to the individual's complex web of personal feelings, and the satisfaction of a sexual impulse cannot destroy the consciousness of personhood.

There are deep psychological reasons why, in a world in which sexual love unfolded, the impersonal sex act lost, through concepts and perceptions from the realm of the higher life of the soul, the high status that it had as a phenomenon of nature. Some vestige of the old idea that the sex act must belong to a higher realm than personal volition to be holy did insert itself, to be sure, into the idea of Christian marriage, in which the sacrament divests sexual intercourse of sin, assuming that it serves the purpose of procreation. This view of the sexual in the Christian world is analogous to the heathen sacralization of the sexual, although the difference between the sacred sex act and the sacramental nevertheless is quite large. The sacrament remains as a personal vow connected to the strictest exclusivity; only personal volition has so little significance to the sacrament that the sex act can take on the character of an "act of duty," such that, even if it is forced through violence, it is not viewed as a violation of the rights of the person.

Even in sacramental marriage, which is expressly designated as a concession to human weakness, the sexual retains an element of impurity and sinfulness, a cause of bad conscience as soon as it appears together with the quality of lust that bestows on it the irresistible power of seduction. The Christian religion could not bring about the elevation of the sexual that would be necessary for the establishment of a new sexual order. Its prescripts tend to lead in the direction of renunciation; they require the choice of "chastity," which in the Christian sense actually means the complete absence of sexual feelings and limits itself in the masses to strict monogamy based on not acknowledging or suppressing the satisfaction of sexual needs to the greatest extent possible. The prescripts on sexual behavior laid down by later Christian teachers such as Alphons von Ligouri (who acquired a bad name because of his causative philosophy) were only compromises with real conditions developed within Christian morality. If one wants to find high, noble, "pure" thoughts about sexual matters then one must seek them in the words of the worldly rather than spiritual leaders of the Christian era.

Nevertheless under the rule of Christian morality the most wonderful transformation of sexuality, its unfolding into higher love, was able to take place. Some people have attempted to explain this as an unexpected effect of the cultural process in its multifaceted aspects. Yet, however incomprehensible it may seem at first glance that within a world of damnation and oppression such an extraordinary refinement and ennobling of sexual feelings was able to take place, there did develop in the tradition of Medieval courtly love a form of sexuality accompanied by the noblest of spiritual drives. There is no denying that it bore the traits of a fusion of religious and erotic motives. It signified neither rebellion against Christian sexual morality through the intrusion of the primitive, uncontrolled outbreaks that have often occurred from time to time during the history of Christian morality nor complete submission. Clearly enough, one can trace in courtly love a new growth in the other direction of development, that of affirmation.

If we trace back, in both directions, the tendencies through which culture determines the relationship of human beings to sexuality, we find two ideals of sexual life that, to be sure, are not completely independent of each other, but indeed are in opposition. On the side of renunciation is the Christian ascetic ideal of life, which in its absolute form has almost disappeared outside of the cloister, whereas in its conditional form it still prevails today in the doctrine that monogamous marriage is the single socially acceptable form of sexual relationship. On the side of affirmation is the aesthetic-erotic movement, which has played a significant role in the recent transformation and new ordering of sexual life.

Out of the formless, diverse drives of sexual life we have identified two ideologies in order to trace in them the general principles of renunciation and affirmation in their cultural manifestations – the ideology of Christian asceticism as the highest expression of the striving to exterminate sexuality from the personality, and the aesthetic-erotic as the highest expression of the striving to incorporate sexuality into the personality.

The conditions of modern life are favorable to neither of these two ideals; however, the way of life of the Christian ascetic lacks recognition even as a necessary transitional stage in development, because it is hostile to the affirmation of life and connected to certain illusory beliefs that have lost their persuasive power.

Modern views of sexual phenomena, the contradictions accompanying them, and their connections to religious, moral, and social concepts tend to overlook their deep significance. Sexuality in human life is by no means just a tool to maintain the species; according to all evidence it is just as inaccurate to regard it is a means of *development of the species*. From this misunderstanding stem the rage and zeal that sexuality lets loose in moralists, the unfulfillable demands with which it is burdened, and also the metaphysical meaning of asceticism in every worldview that seeks to lead human beings to a higher plane of life.

The objects of faith from which Christian asceticism drew the intoxication of overcoming the world are really only illusions created for such purposes. Illusions are likewise influenced by philosophical abstractions in Buddhism, which celebrated its triumph in the deluded claim of destroying the chain of natural events through planned extermination of all impulses of life and the destruction of life as metaphysical potency. The Indian yogi who attains the ability to transcend sensuality through the discipline of difficult postures and the Christian anchorite who mortifies his flesh by fasting and flagellation – these do not provide evidence for the truth of their illusions by the fact that their will power has reached such a sublime level of superiority; instead, they provide evidence for the strength of the spiritual drives that engender these illusions.

Outside of doctrinal faiths these illusions no longer play a role in the present day. And yet the Buddhist illusion of renunciation of the world was so convincing for one very influential thinker of the nineteenth century, Leo Tolstoy, that he made breaking the will to live the basis of his philosophy; and he could find no other expression for the moral passion that burned in him than Christian asceticism. To be sure, both Tolstoy and Schopenhauer proved through their lives that the power of their illusions no longer possessed sufficient strength to create a complete unity of thinking and being. Schopenhauer limited himself to constructing a theory of overcoming the world based on Buddhist ideas, without carrying it out in practice in his own life; Tolstoy, full of the pathos of sensation, but lacking penetrating strength of thought, struggled to live by Christian ascetic views, but was defeated by the clash between modern conditions of life and an antiquated philosophy.

Anachronistic attempts to hold onto and breathe new life into dead illusions of faith — not by believers who reject modern thinking outright but rather by those who discover new ways of thinking — make the objective evaluation of human phenomena very difficult. As long as Christian asceticism takes the sense of duty as its model, it engenders polemic; from this standpoint, we are inclined to regard it as a path of error that for many centuries robbed Western culture of free development of the affirmation of existence; it appears as the unwholesome power that opposed the happy and beautiful acceptance of sexual things in ancient times in order to sow in human minds a long-lasting condition of inhibition, insecurity, and guilt. It has removed the natural human drives completely from their rightful place and erected a tyranny of the spiritual over the sensual powers of life, which makes futile any attempt of society to regulate sexual matters.

However, in spite of the destructive conditions that accompany the ascetic sexual ethic, the concept of error is not applicable to it. The concept of error in relation to the cultural process in its entirety makes no sense. One can err by straying from a predetermined path to a set goal, but a path being built in the chaos of the uncharted designates every step as a necessary transition.

Even the heroic determination with which the ascetic struggles for control of the spirit in order to free himself or herself from all constraints must awaken admiration. The human being, divided within, filled with strong ambition for a higher plane of existence, devoted to the ecstatic imagination of an eternal life, creates through the sacrificial removal of all physiological needs from the self the conditions that empower the "soul," the spiritual and eternal part of the self, to become independent of the power of sensual drives. Saved again and again from countless errors and setbacks by long and unceasing effort, losing thousands of little battles, winning thousands of others, this struggle endows the history of the human soul with its peculiar and most distinctive character. The battle brings the intellect to its highest achievements by driving it upward to the heights of metaphysical speculation, where it seeks the solution to the enormous riddle of life.

It is the process of seeking, not of finding, which produces the permanent glory of Christian asceticism. Its illusions have lost their persuasive powers; as an intellectual interpretation of a certain condition of the soul they are no longer widely accepted. However, this does not mean that this condition of the soul itself has vanished. As long as the soul continues to exist, the function of the ascetic is necessary to spiritual development. The inner opposition that is expressed by means of the old formula of spirit and body, in the narrower sense referring to spirit and sexuality, has not been abolished from the world, and the pressure on the highly developed human being to have to "overcome" the sensual for the sake of spiritual powers is rooted too deeply in the constitution of the soul to be removed through a mere intellectual shift of values.

The Christian ascetic conception of sexuality is not the original source of that fateful division between the spiritual and the sexual drives. Christian asceticism was not the cause of the division between the two natures within human beings, the so-called divine and the so-called animalistic; it is only the latest instance of a division with origins far in the past – full of the greatness of this latest instance and at the same time absurd.

Clothed in fantasy, like all ideas of the primitive human being, explained through the relationship to demonic or divine powers that govern the concepts of causality of the primitive mind, the recognition emerged early on that refraining from satisfying natural drives could give an individual increased power that could be taken in new directions. An unbridled activation of the sexual will is not compatible with a strong ability to achieve other purposes; even uncivilized peoples possess this understanding, for they practice strict abstinence during wartime. To the same degree that spiritual demands, above all those of religious life, increase during cultural development, the suppression and overcoming of sexual impulses gains in significance. Human beings do not enter the sphere of the divine, their prayers are not heard (Iamblichus) if they do not remain "pure" through abstaining from all sexual activity – that is, to use modern terminology if they do not transform sexual drives through sublimation into psychic powers devoted to other purposes instead of using them up through the uninhibited satisfaction of sexual drives.

Therein lie the positive achievements of the ascetics, which cannot be explained away by intellectual interpretations of the cultural process. Even if one sees them only as benighted or primitive, one should recognize the fact that under their rule Europeans ascended to a superior position in the world. Even if the first cause of this fact was primitive vitality, it is still undeniable that this vitality emerged from under the domination of an ascetic morality, one whose most generous concession to sexual satisfaction was strict monogamy. The least that one must grant the Christian ascetic morality is that it did not destroy the vitality of subordinate peoples; it also has claim to the achievement that, by the highest development of will and intellect into a unified power, it helped create the superiority through which European culture has achieved its mastery over nature.

The intellectual motivation of the Christian aesthetic ideology locates the meaning of life in the hereafter and renounces the mortal world, a view that was not capable of derailing the life drive of the peoples of Europe, for intellectual reasons are not primary motivations; they can merely displace feelings, not exhaust their content, nor even touch their essence. Judged according to its intellectual motivation, Christian asceticism can actually be grasped as a symptom of exhaustion, as an impoverishment and weakening of the life drive; its effects, however, point toward causes that can be seen in its intellectual motivation. This movement displays that "heterogeneity of purposes" through which the original motivation of behavior leads to quite different results than were envisioned in setting its goals. These unintended results show us that the intellect is limited in its ability to interpret psychological phenomena fully. Asceticism intended to prepare human beings for the realm of Heaven, and instead it drove abilities already present in the human psyche toward giving meaningful content to life on earth.

What was the reality of the life of the soul that lay beyond the intellectual analysis of the ascetic? What psychological processes led the imagination of the early Christians to be able to interpret sexual matters as sin, the work of the Devil, a fall away from God? Such an extraordinary view, so counter to nature, such a misunderstanding and slander of the most important instincts of life would not have been possible if a logical process and a psychological process had not converged and led in the same direction. The ascetic used logic as a basis for the view that life on earth was a preparation for a purely spiritual afterlife of which the human being could only become worthy by overcoming all drives directed at earthly existence. This illusory belief springs from psychological processes that strengthen its influence to the degree that the claims of the spiritual life grow more strongly in the consciousness of the individual.

Let us consider the condition into which the psyche is directed through sexual activity. As everyone learns through experiencing this condition, an object of thought cannot at the same time be an object of sensual arousal. This means that, if attention follows either one of these directions, it can only be disturbed and distracted by the other. The more abstract mental work is, the less able it is to co-exist with the sexual.

The idea of competition between intellectual and sexual stimulation, the notion that the "brain" and "sexuality" are opposing poles, is accompanied by the concept that sexuality must be disturbing to the higher life of the soul. It is a physiological law that every stimulus is followed by a response. The degree of tension determines the degree of release; as high as a wave may rise, just as low does it sink. In the sexual sphere, where the organism reaches its highest physiological tension, the corresponding release is also the strongest. *Omne animal post coitum triste.* In human beings the physical reaction is followed by a reaction of the soul, and the result can be fateful. The process of sobering, the release of excitement, which is simply a result of physiological events, causes a type of physical recoiling or even disgust toward that which was just recently the object of the most eager desire – a situation analogous to hunger and satiety, which also can take form in the consciousness as over-satiety or regret. The negative feelings of reaction are interpreted as objections against their causes, which as a result seem wrong, sinful, repulsive to the higher nature of human beings. For the striving of the soul toward balance, which to such a high degree influences the devaluation of the worth of life – and the more sensitive the psychological constitution of a person, the more unbearable is the disturbance that the sex act brings with it, especially when spiritual ambition is predominant in the soul of an individual. This spiritual ambition does not tolerate the opposing power that accompanies it, even though it displaces it from time to time in order to give free play to primitive urges.

Thus, we gain insight into the reasons why at a certain stage of human development sexuality had to seem to the most highly developed individuals to be impure and reprehensible. It was the force that created conflict within them, that bound them to common and base forms of existence, and prevented their spirits from perpetually dwelling in the condition of that holy contemplative mood that signified preparation for the realm of Heaven. For such individuals, the physical pleasure of sexuality was ruined, and they did not yet know the sublimated pleasure made possible by connecting sexual impulses with qualities of the soul. Love was acceptable only as a condition of the soul completely free of sexuality. These sensitive souls sought to develop or transform sexual feelings into charity toward others or love of God in order with all their might and passion to suppress the disturbance of the soul's condition caused by sensual arousal.

For a person whose soul is so constituted, there is no other path toward liberation from the torments of an eternally unsolvable dilemma than the mortification of the flesh. Where this conflict exists, where there is no ability to love, mediating between the sex drive and the personality, even today one can find negative judgments accompanied by feelings of revulsion toward sexuality, even though it does not engender the martyrdom of complete mortification of the flesh as practiced by the committed followers of early Christianity.

All human beings seek the justification of their own viewpoints within the philosophies of the world that they develop. A person's explanation of the world is the intellectual commentary explaining his or her own self. However, the connection between the intellectual process out of which a philosophy emerges and the psychological nature of the individual doing the thinking seldom reveals itself through events that can be easily identified and traced.

In the case of a few modern thinkers, Schopenhauer, for example, and to an even greater degree Weininger, there have been attempts to trace these connections because their times drew attention to such questions. Thinkers from earlier times, whose personal stories were at best transmitted only through external evidence, provide no pertinent psychological information. It is also easy enough to realize that philosophical viewpoints are often based on a conflict between the claims of the intellectual life and those of the physical. Augustine speaks of this in his Confessions when he says, "It is one and the same soul that wants one thing with half of its will and another thing with the other half, and therefore it is torn apart by severe suffering." This passage was the first formulation of a condition of the soul that fifteen centuries later, representing a completely different human condition than Augustine imagined, was described in the famous words: "Two souls live in my breast; each one wishes to separate itself from the other."

This division into drives pulling in two different directions appearing in the consciousness as the conflict between spirit and body, seems at a certain stage of spiritual life to the person afflicted by it to be a condition superior to the unified viewpoint of the sensual members of heathen cultures. As soon as the overcoming of sexuality came to be regarded as an indispensable means of achieving a higher condition on earth and eternal salvation in Heaven, the human being whose constitution had no need for a hostile relationship between spirit and sexuality was devalued, doomed to go through the world as a being of second rank, profane and sinful.

In the transformation from a sensual creature to a spiritual creature, the human being went through three stages. The members of the oldest cultural era lived like wild beasts in a naive affirmation of existence in which spirit and nature still existed as an indivisible unity. At this stage sexuality was not a source of inner conflict because all conditions of life were unified. To be sure, social orders established norms governing sexuality, but they were not based on renunciation. The Greek and the Roman societies allowed the sexual forces of human nature free expression from time to time by lifting social regulations at certain festivals. At this stage of the life of the soul, it was also possible that sex acts could have religious meaning to cults because the personality had not developed to the point that it would have hostile reactions to sexuality.

Human beings at the second stage lived with inner conflict; in their psychological constitution there was no possibility of reconciling the realm of the sexual with the realm of the spirit, so they created a fictional world of pure spirituality to which souls might flee from the demands of sensuality. In order to escape the conflict they had to choose complete abstinence or remain, if they lacked the necessary willpower, caught in a chronic dilemma that combined the conflict between spirit and sexuality and the conflict between thought and being.

At the third stage of the life of the soul, however, there appears once again in a new form unity between spirit and sensuality, either as an inborn condition of balance between sensual and spiritual drives, as an organic, natural harmony of being, or as the striving of one for whom it is still possible but only through the application of the will to bring about personal harmony.

In temporal terms, these three stages correspond approximately to the three ages of culture. The epoch of antiquity, whose beginnings were dominated by the stage of primitive unity, ran its course and then ushered in the stage marked by the idea that conflict within human beings was the highest spirituality. This view was represented by Plato, Paul, and Plotinus, who rejected the material world as a hindrance and an enemy. The epoch of the Medieval Age that began under the domination of conflict led in time to the stage of synthesizing unity. Courtly love, a transitional phenomenon, was the first attempt to bring about a loving marriage between the sensual and that which transcended it, followed by the dawning of the modern age, during which there began to burn, even more decisively than at the turn of the eighteenth century, the light of full consciousness. The values of classical as well as romantic art required a psychological-physical constitution possessed only by individuals able to achieve a synthesizing unity.

The present, however, with its confused tendencies, its ambivalence and contradictions, unites these three types in countless transitional forms that crisscross each other and battle in directionless chaos for domination. Affirmation and renunciation are scrambled together; theory and practice are not in accord, human beings representing primitive unity, who even today are probably in the majority, are denigrated to a mean level. Human beings are in conflict, lacking any means of conquering it, lost ascetics who cannot come to terms with their relationship to sexuality any other way than by satisfying the "animal" inside, setting aside their personality. Those who represent synthesizing unity are impotent and without respect. The compulsion of social arrangements from bygone eras and pressures of economic factors cause many to have the most debasing type of sex life, which destroys the higher tendencies of their nature. In addition, everyone is threatened by cruel diseases that rule over individuals and their progeny – what words are capable of portraying the miserable situation into which the sexuality of modern culture has sunk!

Should the blame for this situation really be given to the dominance of the Christian ascetic worldview, as many say? And how long has it been since this view has had any significant power in real life! In times in which it had a much greater influence on people's thinking than now, conditions were simpler, more heathen and yet at the same time healthier, freer, and more honest than at present. The views of the ascetic are symptoms, effects, but not causes of the position that the individual takes toward the problems of sexuality. Its cause, as well as the cause of the generally prevailing disorder and devastation in sexual matters, is actually conflict.

Yet conflict is also a necessary transitional stage in the development of the consciousness of personhood or personality, that most excellent product of the Christian world. For the Buddhist ascetic, the impulse to overcoming was the *suffering* that is bound inextricably to every impulse of life; for the Christian, who values suffering as a means of growing nearer to God, the decisive goal is employing free will to raise the divine part of the soul to complete domination. An enduring result that emerged from this struggle was a heightened consciousness of personality, even at the cost of internal conflict. As soon as this conflict of the soul receded, the personality entered into a new relationship to sexuality. Evidence for this is given by the *aesthetic-erotic* ideology that emerged in history later than the ascetic ideology.

Even in its first teachers, the Christian ascetic ideology appeared in both an absolute and a conditional or modified form; even among these teachers there were radicals who took the renunciation of life to its most extreme consequences and moderates who did not renounce beautiful and noble qualities in earthly life as long as they were subordinate to spiritual principles. Asceticism in its absolute form was not required of everyone; the movement also included the conditional type, in the form of monogamous marriage, whose requirements were no less strict than complete celibacy. To the vow of inviolable fidelity in marriage, any transgression is as dishonorable and sinful as the violation of the cloister's vow of absolute celibacy. Exclusivity of sexual intercourse between spouses, under all circumstances, at any cost, with no regard of any other consideration, belongs to the fundamental laws of Christian ascetic marriage. "Not for the sake of the flesh, but for the sake of the salvation of men," Augustine tells women to be eager to "renounce all else but love of your husband – he must be chaste; marital fidelity is your mission, you must fight for it."

The purpose of this exclusivity in the ascetic sense is the same as that of absolute celibacy: liberation from the domination of the sex drive. Only the means is milder. A complete victory over the drive is not required of married people; however, their desire must remain for all time focused on a single person; the sex drive in general can no longer play a role in their lives. The constant disturbances caused by opportunities and temptations to sexual adventure to which the unattached are vulnerable are eliminated by those determined to be faithful – according to the basic intention of marriage as a means of liberation through voluntary bondage. Thus, Christian marriage, in spite of the low position at which it places the individual, nevertheless contributes to the development of personality if one sees its essence, as Kant does, as – "the freedom and independence from the mechanisms of primitive nature."

Sexuality signifies in Christian marriage only a tolerated element of the base aspect of human nature. It cannot be a realm of the culture of the soul, to say nothing of a means to beautify and enrich life, according to a view that limits itself to instructions as to how the faithful can purify themselves from the consequences of defilement, as the sex act is defined. After all, mutual faithfulness was not required for the sake of human personhood but for the idea of chastity, the victory over the sex drive! The possibility that this drive itself, through pure, benevolent, high-minded sensitivity, could be a force of beautification and humanization leading to harmony with the spiritual principle was not accepted by the Christian ascetic viewpoint as it defined the type of marriage that was sanctioned.

Without sensual warmth and aesthetic meaning, sexuality is a common drive, akin to the lowest attributes of human nature. Sexuality becomes beautiful only through its connection with cultural refinement, noble through the filling of the soul with feelings of love. The aesthetic impulse, above and beyond the cult, was not bestowed upon sexuality in the antique world until it was given personal content; ancient eroticism was completely aesthetic in contrast to the eroticism of the Christian era which was particularly characterized by psychological motivation. What Ovid explicated in his *Ars amandi* was a form of aesthetic-erotic experience that had nothing to do with the concept of love as a connection between souls; rather, it referred to base sexual urges, which, however, through association with ascetic metaphysical viewpoints, could be of service to the highest psychological achievements.

From the extreme situation of libertines with their gallant tradition of covering naked sexual adventures with a thin veil of aesthetic pretention to the most sublimely sensitive romantics whose views of love have such high psychological content that they approach the realm of religion, we can see that during the Christian epoch the affirmation of sexuality unfolded in the most diverse ways; the heathen's aesthetic enjoyment of the senses was not only condemned by asceticism, but it found in the psychological eroticism of romantic sensitivity a second opponent that contributed to its displacement and devaluing.

Eroticism permeated with a religious element, appearing in the first manifestations of the sanctification of sexuality through personal motives, carried the unmistakable stamp of the old conflict in the life of the soul. In courtly love the requirement of distance – distance in love always points to something unresolved and unresolvable! – which separates the knight from the lady of his heart, was a symptom of difficulties in the connection between the psychological and sexual realms; for this reason ordinary sexual intercourse between married couples in this epoch, according to the norms of marriage which reflect conditional asceticism, lacked the high claims of the soul made by courtly love.

In the great lover Dante sexual love reached its highest religious glorification but not its full realization, for he established no deep connection of the soul with his sexual partner in real life. Even the love between Petrarch and Laura reflected an eroticism that required distance; this love also reflected some influence of the Madonna cult whose rays cast an unearthly shimmer onto the form of Beatrice. The pious fervor stimulated by intoxicating images of the most holy Virgin Mary, which impresses her features onto beloved earthly women in order to elevate them above the earthly through the power of the most intense feelings, cannot be reconciled with the claims of reality. Nevertheless this fervor warms and illuminates evermore the realm of sensitivity where the sex drive dwells; heavenly love celebrates the triumph of her wedding with earthly love in that portrait of the monk Filippo Lippi and the nun with whom he conceived a child, portrayed as the Madonna with the baby Jesus – not as a document of his moral corruption but rather as the peaceful integration of sexuality and an artistic nature in one soul.

It is significant evidence for the unerring certainty planted within people by the reconciling unity stemming from their inner harmony that such passion, under the domination of a morality that stamps it as evil, can be expressed in all openness. In the matter of love, even in pious souls, sexuality does not separate itself from faith; yes, one could even pose the question whether forbidden love, in spite of all its conflict with religious and bourgeois morality, is necessarily accompanied by a bad conscience in the lover. The concept of sinfulness exists more in the consciousness of the outsider who judges the lover according to moral standards than in the consciousness of the person in love – an important point regarding the psychology of forbidden love and its position in human society! A guilty conscience regarding sexuality is a reaction arising from a divided soul; that it also appears in the soul of a unified individual as soon as the intoxication of love has subsided only means that the individual has fallen back into the ordinary state in which values other than love are dominant.

Like the ascetic, the aesthetic-erotic conception of sexuality has a subjective root; it arises from a personality in which sexual matters are closely connected to the soul, and therefore perceptions are unified – in other words: in such a personality, sexuality has taken the form of love because either the emergence of sexual impulses or at least the inclination toward their satisfaction is connected to psychological conditions. This is the characteristic that brings an individual to the third stage of development – to be precise, the stage at which there is no conflict within the person. A documented case of such a personality is found in German literature in Goethe's *Diary*, a work that portrays with both great artistry and candid realism the superiority of the psychological motive to the physical. It is the document of a constitution that has internalized the need to fulfill one's duty through both moral norms and conscious will power.

Physiologically such a constitution could be explained as the perfection of the cerebral apparatus. The nerve paths that stimulate events in the consciousness are connected to those governed by higher psychological processes that cannot respond to stimulation from outside without setting them in motion at the same time. Physical connections of nerve centers appear in the consciousness as the "unity of soul and sensuality," as sexuality of the soul.

The view of sexual activity as necessary but detested, as mere satisfaction of a drive, which of course the primitive person and the conflicted person, insofar as he or she is not an ascetic, both practice, insults the unified person who furnishes every sexual experience with a contribution from the soul, from the essential personality. Thus is created a sexual culture whose highest tendencies aim to make sexuality into an instrument of love, to give sexuality personal worth through love.

In its perfected sensual/transcendent form sexual love signifies the reconciliation of the spiritual sphere with that of the primitive drives in the consciousness of the individual; for such a person, there is no conflict between the sensual and the spiritual. When applied to love, the concepts of "pure" and "impure," derived from the ascetic conception of sexuality, lose all their meaning. As soon as those higher feelings and states understood by the word "love" are attached to sexual arousal, love seems "pure" whether or not it exists in a socially permissible situation, for even in this connection, its purity and justification lie in personal perception. This is the psychological foundation on which the aesthetic-erotic ideology of life, as governed by ascetic morality, maintains and develops itself.

However, in the course of the generations conflicted individuals gain the ascendancy again and again. After almost disappearing during the era of the Renaissance, which was dominated by people who were either primitive or unified, the conflicted type in the epoch to follow once again promoted ascetic morality. It did not emerge, to be sure, in its most extreme form as an absolute renunciation of life, but in its modified form it was promoted all the more vehemently. The ascetics had become

Protestants, and under the pressure from this opposition the Catholic Church once again turned toward its erstwhile obligation to promote asceticism. The Reformation and Counter Reformation had equally little to contribute to the aesthetic-erotic ideology. Reacting against the prevailing strict moralism, it took the form of gallant love – a conventionalized sexuality in which personal relationships became formalities based less on deep connections between souls than on a superficial culture of interactions that ordered the relationships of the sexes in an aesthetic-erotic way. Among the strangest practices that developed at this time was the establishment of cicisbeism. Perhaps a late echo of courtly love, the role of the cicisbeo, or recognized lover of a married woman, went one step further in the renunciation of marriage by replacing the secrecy that courtly love had required with public recognition, even requiring the lover to acknowledge his beloved publicly.

Gallant love, which in the seventeenth and eighteenth centuries governed sexual relationships in France, and to some extent also in the rest of Europe, modified by national customs, receded into the background along with the political decline of the social classes that had promoted it. Next it was the bourgeoisie, rooted in its strict rules of life and a belief in a deep, noble type of personality, which brought forth the aesthetic-erotic ideology in a new form as a bond between souls.

The culture of personality that owes to the Age of the Enlightenment its effects of ennobling humanity does serve asceticism but not in the sense of Christian renunciation, which represented a tyranny of the spirit unwilling to recognize any power in life but itself. Next, a freer power in the conception of the personality came to the fore – asceticism not as a means of overcoming the world but rather as a means of acquiring *inner atonement*, as a path to the harmony of the life of the soul. The former type was the absolute renunciation of sensuality; the latter was its affirmation as a binding power, an oligarchical connection in which the personality reigns in accord with physical drives. Here the term "ascetic" gains once again its original meaning: it is an "exercise" in the control of the life of the drives by means of higher powers of the soul, in their control, not in their suppression and extermination. It demands differentiation of the rank of the inner drives, a valuation of life according to spiritual needs, the highest of which, after unity with oneself, is securing the personality from the intrusion of primitive influences. If freedom in the external sense is freedom from external duties and obligations, then inner freedom consists of independence from uncontrollable effects of the primitive. One is internally free only when one's own personality is so organized that one chooses the higher drives over the lower, not through reasoned choices, but out of genuine inclination.

The most beautiful formulation of this viewpoint, the enduring gospel of the culture of personality, was provided by Schiller in his essay "On Grace and Dignity." What he calls grace is the expression of beautiful sensuality, and "just as freedom lies midway between the pressures of law and anarchy," he says that beauty is "midway between dignity, as expressed by the force of the spirit, and lust as expressed by the force of drives." The condition under which the aesthetic develops in human beings is "that condition of the mind where reason and sensuality, duty and inclination, are in accord." In the beautiful soul, grace and dignity are united, grace as the expression of a free inclination that develops emotion into the sublime, and dignity as the expression of the governing spirit. From the object of his or her inclination the lover requires dignity because only it can be the guarantee "that he or she is not merely required to satisfy a need but rather that one is freely chosen, that one is not desired as a thing but valued as a person."

The Schillerian concept of dignity as a component of the aesthetic-erotic ideology also contains the element of the ascetic insofar as one understands by asceticism not the voluntary suppression of the sensual nature but rather its mastery by the spiritual. Without this mastery, love cannot exist; it is the condition for the sublimation of the sexual impulse and its transformation into love. Thus, love does not appear merely as a synthesis of the sensual and the spiritual in human nature but also as a fruit of the battle for mastery of the spiritual; the psychological achievements resulting from the developmental process of the personality create the preconditions for psychological eroticism. It was an expression of asceticism when Fichte said, "All powers of a human being are attained in battle with oneself and through overcoming oneself;" likewise, Goethe, praising the superiority of the secret inner personality, expressed asceticism when he said, "From the power that binds all creatures, the human being frees himself who overcomes himself."

Here, where the lines of affirmation and renunciation meet, lie the most subtle problems of the culture of the superior personality. Perhaps even in the goal of metaphysical identity of the sensual and the spiritual, based on the Romantic view of life, there was a danger of overvaluing the sensual – the danger that is customarily brought up as an objection to pursuing the aesthetic-erotic ideology. The materialist belief system, in the vulgar sense of denying the spiritual world in order to give all meaning to the sensual, misunderstands human nature – a misunderstanding that even noble spirits such as Enfantin did not escape when she called "the flesh as holy as the spirit."

After all, it is a basic and natural fact of human developmental history that the flesh and the spirit battle against each other. In addition, the life of the soul based on attaining harmonizing unity is not to be understood as meaning that through an inborn balance an unshakable peace of mind can be created. Disunity belongs to the essence of human nature; the human psyche is put together like a kaleidoscope, and only in the rarest of fortunate cases is the combination of diverse components a thoroughly unified whole. Yes, one can even say that the individual life of real human beings can more often be understood as composed of combinations of dissimilar components than as the image of closed unity that is the basis of the concept of the soul. What creates the unchangeable nature of character is not a given unity but rather a given multiplicity although in every phenomenon that we call a personality this multiplicity is governed from an inner center. The individual's personality is self-created only insofar as he or she is able to achieve harmony by means of conscious self-discipline, creating a voluntary commitment to a value system, borrowed or self-created, that controls his or her drives.

Not conflict in itself but that which it produces is the

substratum of value judgment; its value or lack of value can be measured only by its effects. Thus, conflict for Goethe bore significantly different fruits than it did for, say, Schopenhauer. If in Goethe's life the overcoming of conflict as a path to harmony played the leading role, Schopenhauer's intellectual achievement was the explication and glorification of conflict in the sense of negating life. This philosopher never found his way out of a morosely negating attitude toward the world. He portrayed sexuality as the vile means of eternal renewal of a vile life; in contrast, Goethe's deepest words of wisdom to Gretchen as the embodiment of the sexual fate of Faust were: "Come, lift yourself to the higher spheres; if he has a presentiment of you, he will follow after." Within Faust, the striving for perfection through the reconciliation of two souls, precisely where the tragic conflicts of sexuality occur, does not lead to negation; the ascetic world-renouncing Faust, who wanted to be rid of this life, drinks out of the goblet of sensuality only the ability to submit himself to the primitive forces of life, to lift himself above the one-sidedness of a spiritual course of life and into universality.

In addition, nothing could more clearly differentiate the renunciation of eroticism of a Dante, in whom the need for distance dominated, from that of a Goethe, in whom soul and senses developed into a complete unity, than the relationship of both great men to their first loves. Both recognized in these women the power to lead them into the highest regions of life, but while in Dante this meant the untouched and unapproachable, a quickly fading beloved, who stimulated in him the unfulfilled yearning, carrying transfiguring power, in Goethe's case transfiguration accompanied sexual fulfillment – Gretchen, who pleaded for Faust at the Throne of Perfection, signified in his life the first experience with sexuality and at the same time was the agent of unity toward which his path was destined to lead.

The other great work of German art that concerns the problem of establishing a relationship to sexuality, *Parzifal*, moves, in contrast, in the direction of renunciation. Kundry does not sanctify and exalt sexuality through fulfilling a sexual destiny as Gretchen does; rather, she is saved through the one who opposes her and falls dead at the feet of the renouncer. In Wagner's *Parzifal* the Christian ascetic ideology celebrates its last triumph .

Or is it perhaps not the last one, but a renewed one? The closer we come to the present, the more genuine synthesis recedes behind images of unsolved conflict. Like the prophet of a new age, Goethe creates, through the wonderful totality to which he dedicates his own inner life, the aesthetic-erotic ideology, endorsed by his person and glorified by his art, his timeless creations that proclaim the justification and sanctification of sexuality through love. He is like a god who lifts a life of debasement up to Heaven with arms aflame. However, the generation of his grandchildren and great-grandchildren no longer possesses the gift of awakening the sensitive heart of the Bajadere. She is as little able to find liberation from the yoke of sexuality in reconciliation as were the creators of Christian asceticism.

II

Culture up to now has never done justice to human nature by incorporating sexual drives. Viewing the individual person in terms of his or her natural purpose as a mere agent of reproduction puts the individual in constant conflict with this natural purpose stemming from his or her sexual characteristics. Although the Christian view of life literally set Heaven and Hell in motion, it has not succeeded in establishing even a halfway successful organization of sexual life; instead, it has merely attached to it a guilty conscience, which brings along two companions, hypocrisy and indecency.

The guilty conscience hovers over the sexual life of civilized peoples like a curse that hinders them from establishing a natural and appropriate relationship to this part of life. The unconfessed, the suppressed, the secret – all are symptoms of a bad conscience. And according to the ways that human beings usually react to a bad conscience, the results are hypocrisy on the one hand and indecency on the other.

One could also consider hypocrisy as shame at the impure. Inadvertently, morality tends to encourage hypocrisy, the expression of the need of the average person to seek a compromise between the higher demands of morality and the lower tendencies of his or her nature. Of all types of hypocrisy, the sexual is the most common, as well as the most forgivable, for it reflects the striving to cover our lowest natures with the veil of a higher form of culture, the will, at least in appearance, to subordinate nature to culture.

Whenever the natural appears in its naked form, there looms barbarism in cultural life. In the realm of nature, there is but one governing power, the power of the primitive, unsuppressed by any opposing force; however, it does not acquire the character of the barbaric until it encounters culture, to which it becomes a contrary and opposing force. Thus, animal sexuality, like animal life in general, is free from the influences acting on human sexuality that were introduced by culture; if one wanted to try to free human nature from these influences, it would not become innocent and natural like that of animals but merely barbaric. Moreover, the guilty conscience evoked by sexuality in civilized people does not arise entirely from moral grounds; one can also identify something like a cultural conscience that reflects the human drive for higher planes of existence. Along with the decline of culture as a general phenomenon in modern life, a barbarization of the sexual has occurred; to be sure, hypocrisy has declined, but this does not mean that the situation has improved. The reduction of hypocrisy is by no means a sign that the human condition has become healthier. Rather, it indicates that a barbarization has even corrupted our view of the means that should be able to improve the conditions of sex lives within culture.

If the concept of culture entails the subordination of base drives to spiritual values and promotes a way of life incorporating an orderly control of sexual matters reflecting noble values, sexual culture may be understood in two ways: as a means of controlling sexuality within social life in order to constrain its primitive force, and as a means which the individual relates to this primitive force in his or her personal life. Viewed from either perspective, the culture of the present falls far short of its potential.

One must realize if one wishes to recognize actual conditions in this area without prejudice, that one is dealing with an *insoluble* problem because the sex drive in itself, stemming from nature, is in relation to the human conditions of life a *purposeless* phenomenon. It is said that Helmholtz asserted that if an optician had given him an instrument as imperfect as the human eye he would have given it back, and how much less perfect are the physical organs that serve the reproduction of the species! Nature has ensured the maintenance of the species through an enormous waste of reproductive cells and drives; across the world, untold millions of cells perish so that a single one can succeed at developing. Equal to this waste is the waste of the reproduction, enormous in relation to the remote possibility that it will bear fruit. The more the individual gains in importance, the stronger is the discord between species and personality in the life of the drives. Culture, which increases the value of the life of an individual because it fills it with heightened content, stands, for this reason alone, in opposition to the power of the natural drive that strives to subordinate the individual blindly to the species.

The exuberance of the drive, without influence of the possibility of conception, is so great in the human species that it vanquishes every attempt to subordinate sexual life to higher values. In animals, nature has limited the emergence of the sex drive to certain times and conditions; strict limitations regulate intercourse and conception. However, at other times the animal is free of the burden of serving the species and is not constantly subject to a purposeless and unrelenting drive as are human beings. With the loss of mating seasons, the discrepancy between the demands of the sex drive and the duty of reproduction is found in human beings to such a degree that unfruitful sexual intercourse, which merely serves the satisfaction of a physiological need, is unavoidable. A man who wanted to make unlimited use of his sexual capability for reproductive purposes could easily sire a hundred children every year. A community, if spared the effects of wars or epidemics, would suffer over-population after a few generations if every couple produced ten or twelve children. Therefore, unfruitful sexual intercourse has continued, despite all the religious and moral opposition to it during the entire history of culture.

Another incongruity of the sex drive as a natural phenomenon in the human species is that awareness of the intention of nature does not accompany the awakening of the drive in human consciousness. This lack is also spared the animals. In them, the sex drive and the reproductive drive are combined as one; they cannot avoid the consequences of their sexual behavior. And so the instinct of sexual attraction uniting the genders completely fulfills its mission when it awakens a lustful urge in the consciousness of the individual that does not need to be supported by any awareness of a purpose extending beyond the borders of the individual. The notions that the purpose of sexual desire is procreation and that conceiving new life is the purpose of the sex act, come from an observation that depends on a relatively high level of development of the intellect.

Procreation as a conscious aspect of desire for the opposite sex is not a component of the sex drive. Imagining progeny can, under the influence of a certain mental proclivity, direct sexual desire, but it does not call it forth; it has nothing at all to do with the emergence of the sex drive in the consciousness. In his analysis of the "sexual impulse," Havelock Ellis does not identify the drive as a drive for procreation. He finds that there is some confusion over this matter. "Procreation as a goal plays no role as part of the sex drive in any living creature. . . . it is the natural goal and objective of the sex drive, but the contention that it is a part of the sex drive or that it can define it in any way must be rejected as absolutely inaccurate."

Also, Albert Moll in his *Studies of the Sexual Libido* identified only two components of the sex drive, both unrelated to procreation in either feeling or thought – the detumescence drive, seeking release of the state of arousal, and the contrectation drive, seeking enjoyment of physical and psychological contact with another person. The phenomenon of the sex drive can be completely explained through these two components, especially in view of the fact that this drive can in many cases be directed toward a partner of the same gender, which makes no sense at all in terms of the procreative purpose – a fact that, on the one hand, is interpreted as a symptom of degeneracy (see Blüher, *The Role of Eroticism in Male Society*) and on the other hand as the very basis of all higher development.

In the dynamics of the human soul, one must regard the absence of consciousness of the purpose of sexual desire as a deficiency that during the evolution from animal life to human life evoked an undeniable chain of errors. For that reason, one would apply a completely false means of interpretation to the sexual behavior of the vast majority of human beings if one regarded deviation from the purpose of procreation as a symptom of sexual degeneracy.

Yet, Christian von Ehrenfels begins with this assumption in his *Sexual Ethics* when he asserts that the only "generatively right" man is the type in whom the only concept of sexual arousal is "impregnating the female body and planting seeds that will blossom in the birth of children." However, how can the general cause of the arousal of a basic primitive drive be an insight that can only be acquired by knowledge gained by a developed human intellect?

Those who, like Ehrenfels, attempt to make the sex drive "honorable" through associating it with the intention of procreation, are disregarding the facts of nature. Through rational reasoning, as a moral precept, which Christian morality requires; or as generative instinct, according to modern eugenics, this intention can be introduced to the sex life of an individual through instruction and admonition; or, most strongly of all, it can be promoted by social considerations such as the rights of inheritance and family lines based upon them. However, the drive to procreate, as a physical drive connected to the sex drive, like the drive for love in nobler natures, has not yet developed in the human psyche.

The special significance of sexuality in human life rests upon the fact that it is not only the means of procreation but also the fulfillment of love, and it serves the individual in that purpose as much as it does the species. Two opposing spheres of interest are here united. It is not only the case that sexual desires conflict with impulses of the spiritual realm, but their connection with individual love interests originating in the realm of the soul also creates an additional complication.

In spite of the pressure exerted by Christian morality in support of the notion that procreation is the justification of sexuality, the source of the refinement and ennobling of sexuality has not been found in that morality but in individual motives. The cause for it can without a doubt be sought in the psychological mechanism governing the relationship of the ego to the will to procreate. Love between one individual and another is in certain cases more powerful than the will to procreate because the expansion of the borders of the ego through love is an immediately experienced feeling, whereas future progeny can only be imagined. Also, in the Christian ascetic ideology the egocentric emphasis was quite dominant; the reward of eternal salvation was attached to the self, the continuation of the personality through thoughts of immortality overshadowed the value of continuation through progeny and bestowed on the interests of the species a secondary status.

Likewise, according to the aesthetic-erotic ideology, the interests of one's progeny are secondary. The child, described as the "fruit of love," not only casts a more brilliant light on the loving relationship but also bestows a significance on the particular couple that transcends their individual lives. A child awakens in beautiful souls the happy notion that conception by a loving couple creates a life that is more perfect and harmonious than a life created by dutiful submission or mere lust.

Ellen Key made this idea into a kind of dogma and article of faith. A sexual relationship as a means of enhancing life under the premise that lives created by great love "enrich future souls generation after generation" – that is, the belief that seeks to bridge the opposition between the interests of personally directed love and the interests of its progeny. However, noble love belongs to the realm of culture and not that of nature, which knows nothing of the idea of personality. Moreover, passionate love is actually no guarantee of the quality of its progeny, and the dogma of Ellen Key is to a great extent unproven.

The generative impotence of individual love becomes quite significant as soon as consideration of procreation is taken as one's main concern. On this basis, Ehrenfels constructed a condemnation of sexual morality in its entirety, which he called "cultural," noting that it was based on personal relationships. In his alternative "constitutive" morality personal attraction is no longer the justification for a sexual relationship, only the couple's ability to improve their race. This idea represents a complete renunciation of the motives operating up to this time, an abrupt change in the direction of our entire cultural process. A value system similar to Ehrenfels' constitutive morality existed in ancient Sparta. In that society, the interests of a progeny of high quality were so much in the foreground that all other interests were pushed back, even the exclusivity of female sexual submission. The strongest and most superior possessed all rights in both the male gender and the female; weak infants were put to death; young girls went about naked and took part in gymnastic exercises in order to strengthen themselves for motherhood. Nevertheless, Sparta did not thrive any longer than did Athens, and it is not the source of the eternal fame and glory of Greece.

As an example of how the fruits of constitutive sexual morality have developed in recent times, the Mittgard Union might be mentioned, an organization that aimed at practical application of this morality in a type of selective breeding program carried out according to eugenic principles. Followers of the Union planned to establish a settlement on a German chivalric estate where a thousand women and a hundred men, selected according to the strictest eugenic methods, would breed a racially pure, completely healthy tribe. Every man would have the duty to live with a woman only as long as it took for her to conceive. Then he would seek a new partner, which would be an easy matter considering the ratio of ten women to one man. The enthusiasm of the adherents of this Union could not be dampened by the fact that in such a human breeding farm, despite great care taken in selection of participants, unknown inherited traits would be present and would show the same tendencies toward latent qualities that are present in modern society at large nor by the fact that the offspring, as soon as they left the borders of their eugenic zoo, would be subject to all the destructive influences of the outer world. They were convinced that this was the way to create a superior race of heroes in a few decades' time.

All cultural influences of a noble type have contributed to making the sex drive a personal motivation, to humanizing it by connecting it to the higher experiences of the soul, and, indeed, in the constitution of a great number of superior individuals, this connection is immediate. Their inner nature is so oriented that, instead of all the temptations of the sex drive, such persons choose the claims of the soul and see in beloved persons neither a mere means of satisfaction of drives nor a mere tool of procreation.

Galton, originator of the concept of modern eugenics and its most prominent representative, has expressed doubt about the value of individual love for the interests of progeny. He defines eugenics as the science that is concerned with social powers that influence, mentally or physically, the racial characteristics of future generations, and he believes that the ideals of reproductive hygienics will in time be granted religious sanctity. In his designs for such a program, he speaks of an "honorable moral doctrine for good people who take part in the work of the world and know the dangers of sentimentality."

But sentimentality – insofar as one understands by the term the domination of feeling over reason – is inseparable from love. Precisely because love is directed toward a certain personality, it cannot easily be shaped by considerations outside of the person. And the opposition between the principles of eugenics and the tendencies of individual love will always lead to deep conflicts as soon as the health of a pair united by love does not correspond to eugenic requirements. After all, the phenomenon of sexual love consists of organically uniting the sex drive with the *personality* and not with any other complex of instincts and concepts. To release the sex drive from its psychological connection with the realm of the personality and connect it instead to the realm of the rational will to procreate would be a physical revolution that up to now has not been possible to bring about through intellectual means.

Christian asceticism, albeit in its modified form, has employed the most extreme means of religious pressure in its efforts to merge the sex drive and procreation in the human consciousness into a united function – to be sure, from motives that have nothing in common with the eugenic movement. Conception according to the Christian viewpoint signifies the creation of an immortal soul, sanctified by God, and the quality of that life is in the hands of God. Because in all areas of morality, actions are judged by their intentions, the intention to conceive must be joined with the sex act so that a claim for God's grace can be made for the resulting progeny. Instructive in this respect is the position of Augustine toward his illegitimate son, Adeodatus, whom he does not mention without adding, "my son in the flesh, conceived by me in sin" and stating that his son had no part of this sin – precisely because the intention to conceive was not involved in the act of giving him life. For that reason he praises as a special grace of God the fact that his child nevertheless was "well created."

No greater metaphysical significance than the relationship to the creation of an immortal soul has been seen in sexuality from any philosophical stance; if even this grand perspective is not able to establish a connection between the sex drive and the will to procreate, how could it be achieved through prescripts whose content is exhausted in the concept of health!

In the end, only an objective observer who seriously considers how great is the danger of harm to health under the life conditions of modern civilization will in the interests of health place all other concerns into the background. Such considerations and observations originate in the striving, represented in certain medical circles, to take specific circumstances into account and to place on health, in all aspects of life, a value of the highest rank. One may identify this viewpoint as the *utilitarian hygienic* ideology – if it is the case that a viewpoint that decisively avoids all higher spiritual claims can still be labeled an ideology.

While the ascetic Christian viewpoint regards the sex drive in and of itself as sinful and therefore places it under the control of a sacrament prescribing very serious duties, and the aesthetic-erotic viewpoint judges the drive by the form in which it appears, condemning raw desire in order to place sexual love in the highest rank, the hygienic-utilitarian viewpoint views the sex drive as a physiological need whose satisfaction belongs outside of the realm of ethical value judgments and in the realm of considerations relating to health.

This viewpoint, above all, is the one that places the problem of abstinence – the center of every sexual morality and sexual culture – in a new light. Abstinence before marriage was the demand of modified asceticism, abstinence before love that of the aesthetic-erotic viewpoint, according to the utilitarian-hygienic viewpoint abstinence is seen primarily as harmful to one's health. According to this viewpoint, however, the problem of abstinence is seen from a very one-sided direction. It is also incompatible with the demands of aesthetic-erotic culture that disapproves of sexual intercourse as mere satisfaction of a physical drive and with the views of the ascetic who damns it in no uncertain terms.

In regard to the dilemma found in the question of whether it is better for the individual to suffer harm to body or soul, the Christian ascetic would choose the body without question. Also, apart from any metaphysical significance attributed to abstinence, the danger of physical damage caused by nervous and hysterical-epileptic seizures, hallucinations and manic conditions is not a concern of Christian asceticism because it is at the same time the source of wonderful sensations. This viewpoint sees "wrestling with the Tempter" in every experience that strengthens one's faith in the supernatural and enriches our inferior mortal existence with the incomparable pleasures of spiritual power and superiority.

Modern people, however, regard as unbearable burdens the intensification of nervousness, stimulation of fantasies, and loss of peace of mind that result from abstinence because these conditions are incompatible with their utilitarian way of life. They see as detrimental the distraction of attention caused by an inwardly directed tension of the will, for they apply their entire force of will to external tasks in life.

One may ask how modern individuals should be expected to follow the moderate ascetic demand of abstinence prior to marriage. The modern type of conservative who supports this requirement does not realize that it places much higher, much more difficult demands on the average person than did the ancient type of strict conservatism. In the early Christian communities, conditions were uniformly organized according to an ascetic way of life; the strictness of their precepts on sexual ethics corresponded to their entire way of life. A person who takes on the duty to fulfill the same precept in the present day must develop much greater willpower and endure much greater renunciation and isolation than was necessary in earlier times; back then, this precept was supported internally and externally. Today, it meets with virtually unconquerable resistance from both sides.

In contemporary culture, threatened by morbid influences, the inner effects of abstinence are also different. The sublimation of the sexual impulse into higher psychological achievements requires a completely healthy and vigorous constitution; in people tending toward neurosis, the suppression of the sex drive causes pathological results that go against the interest of society "so that society does not gain a victory paid for by sacrifices, but gains no victory at all if it pays for conformity to its broad prescripts with an increase in nervous disorders." (Freud, *The Sexual Aberrations*)

It is, however, not so much conformity to a strict sexual ethic as it is impotence in the face of destructive influences of modern civilization as a whole that is to blame for an increase in nervous disorders and the reduction of the resisting powers of the body and the soul – but the result is the same! As soon as such influences gain the upper hand in a society, as measured by weakened powers of resistance in the average person, the values that inspire the strong and intact individuals to reach their highest potential cannot be maintained. Every norm that creates high tension creates a large cadre of unhappy, maladjusted individuals – this fact is not a reason to abolish such norms; but if the number grows until the average person belongs to the cadre, such a norm will be challengeable because it will ultimately do more harm than good.

One can raise the same objection made to the Christian ascetic ideology to the aesthetic-erotic ideology as a basis for sexual order: that it is appropriate to the natural make-up and the conditions of life of a small number of people but unattainable, for internal and external reasons, for the great majority. The overcoming of the sex drive through constant exercise of willpower in order to free the life of the soul from sexual pressure requires abilities that only a select group of human beings possess, and they can exercise them only under healthy, simple conditions of life. At this point, the insoluble nature of the sexual problem in the life of the peoples of Western culture becomes glaringly obvious. The utilitarian-hygienic viewpoint that finds decisive the claim that abstinence is simply destructive and concludes therefore that paid sexual relations are permissible has by no means abolished these problems from the world.

To be sure, the argument denouncing abstinence as harmful to one's health becomes weakened by the fact that it places itself on the side of sensual desires. As soon as the hygienically oriented view of sex life begins to offer directives for the practical behavior of an individual, the claims of the soul must take a back seat to physical needs if conditions cannot support a unified satisfaction of both. In the language of the bourgeois world, in which the double standard prevails, it is claimed that because the economic circumstances of a young man require celibacy long after his sexual maturity is reached, he should, according to prudent hygienic regulations, make use of the services of prostitutes. To what degree the hidden celibacy required of the protected portion of the female gender brings the same disadvantages is a question rarely asked. The moral assumption is made that the sex drive does not operate in the female nature until it is awakened by love of a particular man.

Windscheid goes so far as to assert (in *The Relationship between Gynecology and Neurology*) that "the sex drive, especially in the higher social classes, is not inborn in normal women, but acquired. It is abnormal for it to be inborn or awakened by a woman herself. Because a normal woman is not familiar with the drive before marriage, she will also not miss it if she has no opportunity in her life to experience it." Such a method of declaring individual situations unhealthy and abnormal if they do not conform to prevailing moral notions demonstrates how effects of moral prejudices can be influential even in the sciences; also notable is Windscheid's arrogance regarding class distinctions in his expression "especially in the higher social classes." Of course, the actual reason that sexuality seems subdued in young women of higher classes compared to those from the lower class is to be found in the power of the severe inhibitions created by their education and environment.

That the sex drive should be connected to higher expectations of the soul that require a loving relationship to be satisfied is a characteristic of females of a superior nature, whereas the male nature in general is free of this – although such a predisposition doubtless exists among some males as well. This differentiation explains the distinction between a prostitute and a man who uses her services. That which is considered physiologically normal in a man is seen as a defect in a woman. The consequence of these differing male and female natures is that the female gender, even though regarded by many as more primitive and "wilder" than the male, is in this regard more highly developed, for the connection of sexuality with higher experiences of the soul, its ennobling transformation into the erotic, actually is one of the highest achievements of culture.

That prostitution throughout cultural history has sunk ever lower in social prestige can be explained by the increasing level of development of the female personality along with the growing power of eroticism or sexual relationships emphasizing emotional bonds. In the Medieval era, prostitution, although lacking honor, was an ordered and regulated profession. At present, it signifies – not only due to moral prejudices that could fade over time – the deepest debasement of the participants.

Only through connection with the feelings of the soul does the sex drive lose its debasing effects on the personality. Indeed, how can it be explained by personal motives without considering its results? In a world in which sexual love is valued highly, sexuality cannot be considered a mere physical release. The most superficial male view of sexuality, which places it on the same level as other body excretions, can only be understood as the expression of a faulty psychosexual constitution. How little this aspect of the life of the soul in individuals corresponds with the culture of the personality is revealed even in a mind like Montaigne's when he says, "the pleasure of Venus in the end is only the pleasure of emptying our vessels, just as nature makes pleasurable the emptying of other bodily organs."(*Essays*) However, the act that signifies the fulfillment of the highest desire of love from the viewpoint of a sexual ethics that stems from a deepened and refined eroticism cannot at the same time be regarded as the mere satisfaction of a physiological need nor as merely "sinful." To nature, lust serves the fulfillment of her purpose – which is the reproduction of the species; culture, which bestows worth on the individual, transforms lust into a means of heightening the soul. Whenever these two types of meaning are lacking, only misuse remains, either through offending nature or offending culture.

Even though prostitution involves the fleeting sexual relationship of male and female partners, involving the soul of neither of them, it can nevertheless be regarded as an anthropological phenomenon – to be sure, only as far as it does not violate nature, which is possible only if it is limited to those persons whose souls are developed to the level at which this behavior is appropriate. Such an anthropological phenomenon is of course atavistic because it is an expression and symptom of a backward psychosexual nature. Prostitution for man and woman is actually sexual barbarism, not because it is found in all peoples living at the level of barbarism – which is not at all the case – but rather because it lacks any presence of the higher human soul, that ideal through which in the spirit of culture sexuality is humanized, transformed from an animal drive into a means of the fulfillment of love.

However, sex life in modern civilization is characterized less by undifferentiated sexuality than by prostitution as a mass phenomenon. Its steady increase has resulted in more serious consequences for both individuals and society as a whole than ever before. Through the pressures of the outward circumstances of life, many women and almost all men succumb to prostitution who otherwise would have kept their personal integrity intact. Through its general process of mechanizing life, contemporary civilization reduces sexuality to its lowest level by making its fulfillment subject to the laws of commerce and thus cutting off its connection to the higher realm of the soul.

It has already been a good while since the Danish writer Lambek (*On the Culture of the Soul*) asserted that we owe the decline of European manners to the fact that they require more time and attention than modern people have to expend. This is all the more true of modern love lives! The man who wages battle in the competition of civilized life in the intellectual or economic spheres simply has no time to create a higher culture in the sexual realm. He pursues fulfillment of his sexual desires through opportunities that demand the least possible expenditure of time or emotion. This was most tellingly brought out by an old physician doctor arguing for medically regulated prostitution as an expedient solution to a pressing need when he said, "The ambitious man of today has no time for courtly love ballads." (*Inquiry of the Austrian Society into Battling Sexually Transmitted Diseases*, 1909)

Not surprisingly, we encounter again and again the conclusion on the part of police physicians and physicians in general that state bordellos should be established. With state sanctioning and organization, prostitution would lose its most medically dangerous quality, its secrecy. Medical supervision could be extended to both sexes, and all the confusion and compulsion in this area of urban life would be removed from the bottom up.

These suggestions go along with the movement for the moral rehabilitation of prostitutes as practitioners of a socially approved profession – a shift from condemning to approving of a practice that modern health care opposes. Could this change really be possible within Western culture?

The rehabilitation of prostitution on the basis of the assumptions that it is a necessary institution and that prostitutes perform a necessary social function because they protect the family from the uncontrolled exercise of the male sex drive is an abstract logical conclusion that disregards all the deeper motives from which prostitution is condemned. Augustine himself addressed the social necessity of prostitution with his famous words: *Aufer meretrices de rebus humanis turbaveris omnia libidinibus*. And yet this idea over the course of time has never gained social acceptance. Opposing views cannot be held at the same time: if society grants the highest rank of female life to the roles of wife and mother, as well as virgin, the promiscuous woman cannot enjoy the same respect simultaneously. It is particularly significant that champions of the courtesan devalue the role of the mother (see Weininger), because no society can continue without setting a high value on motherhood. Such a transformation of values would be the end of any society that wanted to endure.

We have not even mentioned that the development of the personality that women in Western culture have achieved is very closely dependent on their behavior in sexual matters. Their progress toward equality with men is inseparable from the concept of personhood. Whatever attitude one may take toward prostitution, under all circumstances it signifies the absolute renunciation of female personhood. In order to measure how far this renunciation goes in a person who claims that prostitutes are necessary and useful members of human society, one need only look through the medical literature on this subject. There one finds, clothed in the guise of unbiased objectivity, expressions of startling crudeness, as in a description of a policed street in Bremen as "a sexual service installation at the highest possible level of cleanliness," or in the pronouncement of the police medical authorities that bordellos are established because society has a right to refuse to tolerate "anti-health sewers." There are many other examples. A doctor who faces the lowest depths of human nature on a daily basis may well be tempted to forget the rights of women as people when encountering those who hardly know where to begin to advance their level of human development – but the real issue should be their rehabilitation, that is, their potential for social equality with the rest of the female gender in terms of their rights to personhood.

Many people point to a culture like Japan, where the geishas, after working as prostitutes in tea houses for a certain number of years, return to the roles of wife and mother without losing bourgeois respectability. The enthusiastic glorification that Keyserling (in *Diary of a Philosopher*) bestows on the geishas seems at least to acknowledge that prostitution can, in an aesthetic culture like Japan, be divested of its inherent barbarism. This example, however, comes from a source outside of Western culture. Moreover, the geisha will not be able to maintain her social respect as soon as Japanese women, under the influence of the Western concept of personhood, are able to improve their status.

As medieval and barbaric as is the view that a woman who falls into prostitution has no opportunity for atonement or reform, there is nevertheless, within Western culture, no possibility for prostitution to be lifted to the level of a respected and orderly profession.

If J. Bloch is right, prostitution would also lose a specific attraction it possesses, if this happened.. He sees in it a practice providing an outlet for the basic instincts of masculinity, otherwise repressed by culture. "*Only* the prostitute can satisfy these instincts. The mean, crude, brutally animalistic qualities of prostitution clearly exercise a magical power of attraction over many men." The prostitute is, to her customers, a woman one need not take into consideration, the *ancilla libidinous*. Completely disregarding her identity as a personality or a social being, they generally regard her as solely a vehicle of releasing a man from his physiological needs or, indeed, from the pressures of civilized life.

From this view, one can conclude that the moral condemnation of prostitutes also springs from a psychological root. Flaubert, in a letter to the love of his life, wrote about the attraction to prostitution, explaining it by referring to the effects of opposites: "In the idea of prostitution there is such a complicated knotty confusion! Lust, bitterness, completely empty human relationships, excitement of muscles, and the jingling of money – it all makes one dizzy when one looks at the ground. And one learns so many things! And one becomes so sad! And one has such beautiful dreams of love! ... Yes, a man has missed something if he has never awakened in a strange bed, never seen someone's head on his pillow whom he will never see again, and never come out at dawn and gone over bridges with the desire to throw himself into the water – even if all this were only a shameless disguise, the temptation of a chimera, the unknown, the character of the damned. . . . "

Translating the language of the poet into the language of psychology, this passage means that feelings evoked only through a superficial arousal, without the involvement of higher motives of the soul, cause reactions that are expressed in depressive states – in Flaubert, the surfeit of life that is translated into the impulse of wishing to throw oneself into the water. Casanova may also serve as a believable source testifying for the depressive effects of soulless prostitution – believable because he was a completely worldly hedonist lacking any moral scruples. Recalling an evening spent with prostitutes, Casanova said: "Debauchery saddens the mind as much as it debases it." It is this psychosexual reaction that appears in consciousness as revulsion toward the object of desire and, disguised as a moral judgment, as "disgust."

In addition, the form taken by transitory sexual intercourse in modern life shows that it is leading in a different direction than toward state regulations. The growing spread of secret prostitution, not abiding by police measures, demonstrates that, in spite of all hygienic dangers, unregulated prostitution exerts the greatest attraction. The free forms of sexual relationships, in their many gradations, still harbor a residual possibility of illusion because they can conjure up the effects of adventures, conquests, personally selected experiences. A state-regulated, orderly bordello business, conducted in a sober, businesslike manner, without orgies or excesses, would soon go out of business – quite apart from men's distaste for medical control of their own bodies because it would evoke boredom and disgust.

However, the retreat into barbarism that the suggestion of state bordellos signifies, in spite of its association with utilitarian and hygienic purposes, is symptomatic; it is the most telling expression of the inner essence of the cultureless civilization that is divorced from all concepts of higher ways of living. Human beings have become machines, tools without souls, slaves to primitive powers that control them without even reaching their goals – nothing could be more in accord with an understanding of life that suspects all higher spiritual needs of sentimentality and distrusts them as relics from the past!

Just as symptomatic in this respect are movements that presumably for the sake of higher purposes seek to eliminate the rights of the person in the area of sexual life. The constitutive sexual morality, in the final analysis, sanctions the abridgment of the rights of the personality through prostitution. If the personality is deprived of rights for the sake of procreation or for the hygienic purpose of satisfying a physiological need, these constitute a difference in motive, but not a difference in the view of the personality.

The ideas of the utilitarian-hygienic ideology have only to a very modest degree the ability to create influences strong enough to reorder the life of the individual from the ground up. In their application to the average person, to the common level of human nature, they are not compatible with a deeper understanding of life. Like all such prescripts and rules of behavior, they make an impression mainly on those who are timid, powerless, somehow inadequate, but individuals of this kind are usually too weak to resist dominant circumstances. To be sure, such people can avoid bad consequences in the realm of their own habits, as in avoiding harm from the misuse of alcohol and nicotine, perhaps even syphilis, but they remain completely impotent against the destructive influences of civilized life as a whole. One might also ask if succumbing to hygienic hypochondria does not bring more disadvantages than advantages with it. The utilitarian-hygienic ideology leads all too easily to a tepid, sober, rationally constrained existence ruled by second-rank values. Health, respectability, moderation, self-control, and moderate change – all very praiseworthy and useful, but what a dreary person these create!

The orgiastic element of human sexuality that was spiritualized by asceticism into an ecstatic condition of the soul, passionate worship and love of God, and that was transformed by aesthetic eroticism into the sensual intoxication of sexual love is in this context emptied out; it is made as harmless as possible because a rational regulation of sexual intercourse is essential, according to either the eugenic or the hygienic viewpoint.

Such a view is based on a misunderstanding of human nature. The need for tumult, orgy, drunkenness is not driven out of human beings when hygienics takes the place of morality; this need is as difficult for hygienics to conquer as it is for ascetic morality. It is true that romantic emotion, the fire of passion, enthusiastic rapture do occur less and less in modern life. To some extent, the orgiastic element can be condemned as spiritless, anti-aesthetic excess, but the remedy is not found in the power of hygienics. The reaction against the boring monotony of daily life, the primitive rebellion against the overburdening demands of work that express themselves in such excesses, have all too deep causes in the human psychological constitution.

Even assuming that the utilitarian-hygienic ideology were compatible with the nature and needs of the majority, the value of the ideology lies in the willpower that it requires; it must reach beyond that which exists. An order founded on existing possibilities lacks the potential of creating new possibilities in the human psyche. Not through an appeal to the highest abilities of the individual does it seek its realization but rather through the recognition of one's inability to transform the self into something higher.

Who wishes to be satisfied with humanity as it is? The imperfection of ordinary human nature has always stimulated the moral passions of superior people. If this passion were extinguished, then the process of development would be robbed of its strongest driving force. More than ever, the human being is a work in progress and a being in transition, acceptable only through the idea that his or her imperfection is the preparation for a higher plane of existence. This idea gives the notion of development the great persuasive power that it possesses in the mental life of the present day.

One path of development gives social institutions the purpose of systematically improved possibilities of life; the other path is development through personal culture in which the intellectual attainments of the past are transmitted and enhanced from generation to generation. That which is valued by the utilitarian-hygienic ideology belongs almost entirely to the first path. Its potential lies in external conditions to which individuals must accommodate their lives; it is a social ideal, not a personal one. Only if individuals already possess healthy conditions in the natural soil of their existence are they able to develop the higher potential that lies waiting on the second path.

If one traces to the present the course of thousands of years of the zealous struggle of the human soul with overpowering natural drives, one may come to this conclusion: asceticism in itself, or "virtue" in the Christian sense, in overcoming the baseness of sexuality, has lost its cultural meaning, and asceticism as a means of inner atonement, as a condition of inner freedom, is inseparable from the concept of sexual culture. A higher spiritual level cannot be reached by "mortification of the flesh;" rather, the justification of the flesh to the spirit will only succeed if the drive is not regarded as an enemy or a despot. In this direction lies the unique meaning of sexual love. It incorporates hopes for an improvement of sexual conditions in the society of the future, for it is a phenomenon belonging to that border area where the sensual and the transcendent merge, and the lines of affirmation and denunciation converge in order to create new attainments of the soul and new conditions of inner life. To be sure, they also bear traces of the purposelessness that accompanies sexuality. But the human being as creator of a spiritual world would have no place in the natural world if it were not imperfect. Human beings, whenever they succumb to primitive forces, are more pitiable, more miserable, less capable than animals; in contrast, they are great, unique, masterful lords of the earth whenever they employ their spiritual power to conquer primitive forces and subordinate them to laws that human beings themselves create.

The Development of Female Eroticism

I

We have traced the progressive movement toward the forging of a connection between the sexual sphere and the personality. What has been previously said in this connection about the three stages or types of psychosexual development basically applies only to the man. The developmental path of female development in erotic matters has been largely unexamined.

The connection between personality and sexuality may be created by love experienced by an individual; at this stage of development, a sexual relationship seems justified in the consciousness of the individual only when directed toward a certain, chosen person, that is, only when sexual desire is accompanied by love of the person desired. According to the generally held view, this convergence in the soul is an inborn capacity of the female constitution while in men it usually occurs only in the course of sexual experience and even then often imperfectly. Therefore, female morality rests on an inborn condition of harmony; it does not emerge from wrestling with opposing forces as it does in men; but, analogous to aesthetic qualities in the female nature, is a product and a gift of nature.

Like so many other claims made about the female gender, when one examines their real origins, this one was constructed by male fantasies, by wishful thinking associated with male erotic desires. Yet another step removed from observation of the factual is the belief according to which unity of body and soul has always been a natural attribute of the woman. So says, for example, Emil Lucka in his book *The Three Stages of the Erotic*, in which he asserts that only the emotions of the man have a history; those of the woman do not "because she is eternally the same; he is always new and always problematic, never completed. He falls into confusion and sin, while she cannot err for her instinct is nature itself – she is unfamiliar with sin. That which the man has set down for her, she has silently accepted."[1]

To be sure – silence about herself has been an inviolable commandment for women during the entire history of civilization. She has kept silent for many prudent reasons, aware that she has been dependent on the good or ill favor, approval or disapproval of a stronger person. However, the assumption that female eroticism has had no developmental history because the female gender has always possessed unity of soul and senses, expressed in personally oriented sexual love, ever since the female gender existed – this notion cannot possibly be based on the observation of events in cultural history, for over time female perceptions have undergone some definite changes, although perhaps not as clearly identifiable as those of the male.

Women, quite in contrast to men who in all eras have expressed themselves a great deal about their relationship to sexuality, have been either forbidden or unable to do so and have kept largely silent on the subject. Because of this silence, the development that has occurred can only be understood through the evidence found in customs, institutions, and value systems. If we must assume that in reality the personal inclination toward love was from the beginning the decisive force in female sexual perceptions, what a martyrdom for women the whole, infinitely long epochs of human development must have been that preceded the era before love was recognized in choices of legal sex partners! What suffering must have occurred in the female soul under the veil of silence and quiet sexual submission! And was the man really so crudely constituted that his lust for the object of his satisfaction made him completely blind and deaf to woman's suffering?

According to assumptions we are presented with regarding female eroticism in past epochs, we should unquestioningly accept the view that, during ages when prostitution was approved and

---

[1] The essay "Sexual Ideology," which discusses the three types of sexual development appeared in the Munich magazine "Frauenkunft" several years before Lucka's book was published. (Author's note)

parents had the entire say over selection of spouses, female attitudes toward sex must have been completely different from those of modern women who regard forced submission to men they do not love as a severe injury to their innermost feelings of pride and honor. However much blame one might place on female impotence and lack of will, there are examples enough of the consciousness of personhood being sufficiently awakened in women that they have spoken up for themselves. And as soon as we accept the idea that a sense of personhood emerged as a result of a process of human development, it becomes self-evident that female consciousness must have developed in transforming from a collective sense of group identity into a sense of differentiated individual being. For this reason alone, women could not have possessed unity of body and soul in the experience of love from the beginning because the basic condition required, namely conscious personal differentiation, did not yet exist.

The same thing is true of primitive women as is true of primitive men – sexuality at the first stage is not a source of conflict. The opposition to it is not yet present in the soul, for it is born along with the claims of the personality. Just as the primitive man regarded the woman only as an object, as a means to an end, or as booty, the primitive woman thought of herself as the object of a man whom she regarded as her lord and possessor. All social arrangements of ancient times that related to the relationships between the genders point to the fact that individualized inclinations of love played a very subordinate role. One may therefore conclude that female sexuality at that time was based on a very different set of concepts and was assumed to be governed by very different motivations than would be compatible with modern ideas of womanhood. The establishment of group marriage, as practiced during the matriarchal epoch of human society, leads to the conclusion that female sexual feelings and connections were bestowed on only one beloved individual of the other gender but that *he* had a legally fixed number of sexual partners. Under such circumstances, anything like modern female eroticism or even a distant cousin of it, would seem like an amazing hysteron proteron. But even disregarding such ancient customs, which still belong to the realm of speculation, many customs even in advanced cultures would be unthinkable if personal devotion to a chosen man had been the major influence on the sensibilities of women. The role of the female slave is based on the assumption of a value system in which sexuality was closely bound with the idea of property. Whoever owned a woman had the right to sexual possession of her. And this concept extended itself to free women under certain circumstances, notably when victory in war turned women into the booty of conquest, objects to be confiscated. As long as property rights over a woman are in effect, the man receives fidelity and submission; his person recedes completely behind his role as owner. If the owner changes, then submission, without resistance, is transferred to the new owner. Like an object with no soul, for example, Briseis in the Iliad was transferred from one man to another; none of the parties involved asked about her feelings and we are told nothing about them.

That the concept of exclusive devotion to a chosen lover, associated in Western culture with an increasing emphasis on the overvaluing of virginity, was foreign to the female gender in ancient times, is demonstrated conclusively by the customs mentioned previously, as well as the temple prostitution of Assyrian girls and the Greek temple slaves. Moreover, in marriage in later times, it was only on the basis of the idea of ownership, not personal relationship, that exclusivity of the partner became the hallmark of the virtuous woman. The same primitive views of women are, even in the present, so prevalent in Asia that Flaubert could say, "The Oriental woman is a machine; she does not distinguish between one man and another."

Even in the early phases of Western culture there were primitive customs, such as the practice of many peoples of giving the bride to the wedding guests or the custom at the beginning of the Middle Ages requiring a host to bestow to his guests a female member of his household, sometimes even his own wife, as a sign of hospitality. These practices show such disregard for the feelings of individual women that they can only be understood if there is a complete absence of what to us today is the central essence of normal womanhood: sexual self-determination.

II

The development of sexual self-determination as the basis on which the woman was gradually able to overcome her position as an object in her own consciousness is the most significant sign of the distinction between primitive and advanced concepts of womanhood. Because of its many definitions, the concept of the primitive should be more closely examined. The primitive in the sense of the original, natural, or unspoiled has a positive meaning. This is not the definition pertinent to identifying developmental stages of the individual; in this context, the word primitive is intended to mean the opposite of a higher level of the soul, that is, the undeveloped, the backward, and the lacking.

In ancient Greek culture, the understanding of the female was not at all like it is in modern times. In spite of her bourgeois status, the legitimate wife was no more highly regarded as a sexual object than was a slave; both were mere objects without valued personalities. Her task of procreation gave the wife more respect than the slave, who was regarded as solely an object of lust. However, how little the wife was valued as a person is seen in the fact that she did not have the right to raise her own children. The only women valued as personalities were the courtesans, who were not only granted the means of higher intellectual development through interaction with learned men but even the opportunities to choose their own sexual partners. Even they, however, were not considered capable of the love of the soul, which Plato claimed existed in its highest form only between male lovers.

A different situation prevailed in Roman culture. The marriage relationship mirrored in the eulogies on Turia shows a highly personal identity of the woman, who in her devotion to her spouse goes far beyond the role of mere object, demonstrating the characteristics of a superior development of the self. And every exchange of poems between bride and bridegroom, for which Roman literature is known, reveals that a personal relationship was formed through a process involving elevation of the woman's status – evidence of which is also provided by elevation of the legal position of women that occurred at the time.

Nevertheless, these advances were only precursors of a development that can by no means be taken as typical of the general condition of the majority of women. In order to create unity of personality and sexuality in the soul the effect, both the female and male genders must change. Christianity, to which credit goes for the religious endorsement of consciousness of personhood in Western culture, makes in this regard not the slightest differentiation between man and woman. The same precepts about sexuality apply to the female Christian as to the male. In addition, although conflict between personality and sexuality grew in the highly spiritual male Christian, resulting in negative judgments of the female gender, the next result of Christian asceticism actually turned out to be a type of emancipation of the woman. Social norms shifted from regarding her as a mere possession of the man, a mere object, toward the woman becoming aware of her own self-worth, based upon the worth that religious doctrine granted every human soul.

Marriage was also not unaffected. The inner union of the souls of spouses, as required in Christian marriage, however, was not based on the individual inclination to love but on the effect of the sacrament, the divine grace that justified, purified, and sanctified sexual intercourse. This sacramental character of sexual submission in the form of married sexual duty had great significance in the psychosexual developmental process of the woman. Through it the female position as object underwent a substantial transformation. Sacramental marriage does not make a woman into the free governor of her own body, but in sacramental marriage the same can be said of the husband. Both become servants of higher purposes through divine will. There is still no recognition of individual personality in sexual relations, and yet, through the basic idea of sacramental marriage, the woman as a sexual being arrives at that stage – the second stage of her development – that will permit her to climb to self-determined personhood through voluntary devotion to love.

An additional influence came from Christian ideology. Many female Christians of high spirituality chose, despite the apostles' permission to become blessed through motherhood, ascetic celibacy as a path to salvation. Gradually more and more Christians, in their aspirations toward Heaven, strove toward a sublime state of existence. Devoted Christians of both genders developed enormously strong personalities and resistance to all inner and outer temptations. The faith that was their highest spiritual possession and the ascetic impulse, out of which the highest powers of the soul are created, became the particular content of the highest Christian personality, and at the same time, the soil in which consciousness of personhood as such would take root and grow.

Motherhood, in ancient times the primary reason to value the woman, still revered in the era before fatherhood had gained its full rights in the consciousness of the man, now was ranked below virginity. As has the conflicted male type of recent times, the men who chose a spiritual life in the early centuries of Christianity hated women's potential roles as tools of seduction and snares of evil because they saw earthly existence as nothing other than a false path and located true life only in the hereafter. To them, motherhood as a means of continuing an accursed existence was less esteemed than virginity, a path that could deliver up untainted souls to Heaven. However, this shift in values unintentionally increased the sense of personhood in the female soul. Whereas the mother was now only a means to an end, in contrast, the virginal saint had the same value as the man on the basis of the same achievement. So, over the course of the Christian epoch, diverse influences united in changing woman's consciousness of herself from a mere object into a being with a soul who could determine the purpose of her own existence and pursue it through her own actions. In other words, she could develop her own individual personhood. This was the preparation for the free and voluntary devotion to love in which the next unfolding of sexuality would reveal itself.

Of course, females' internalizing the belief that they are property, long so closely connected to the female sense of honor, continued to exist during the second stage of development but gained a different meaning due to the influence of new ways of thinking. One cannot truly understand the development of female sexuality if one does not recognize the influence of the idea of property, and, even more importantly, the *idea of legitimacy*. During the primitive stage, the connection to a certain man was forged under the influence of the *idea of property*, without the personality of the owner being in the foreground; during the second stage the idea of *legitimacy* in the form of divine sanction through the sacrament is primary in the consciousness of the woman. The concept is still not based on the man's identity as a unique individual but as her owner he enters into a higher relationship to the woman through the blessing of the sacrament, whereby God makes him equal to his spouse and gives both partners the same responsibilities. Great efforts of both church and society are directed toward fixing these ideas firmly in the self-conception of all females.

One cannot appreciate enough the importance of the effects that legitimacy and legality have had on a certain type of woman in respect to her attitude toward sexuality. For, in this type, social and legal precepts have such great power that they completely control her perceptions. Even today, when personal selection in love has gained the top rank in our moral views, one can often observe that the influence of rational factors, such as social suitability and parental approval, sometimes strongly influence the awakening of loving feelings for a selected spouse. The overwhelming importance of marriage to many women lies in the fact that their sexuality cannot function without inhibition and inner resistance if not accompanied by the sanction of legitimacy. In the final analysis, such women are quite hostile to free love as a way of life because if it prevailed then they would lack the motive that influences their sexuality most strongly. The tendency of the female organism to merge physiological and psychological influences easily into an inseparable unity also plays a role: the man on whom a woman bestows her virginity holds in her mind a lasting power. She feels inseparably connected to him and so she wishes to have her first sexual experience, decisive in her entire life, under the protection of legitimacy, which will also permanently connect this man to her. This is more or less what Spitteler meant in *Imago* when he wrote of the "mystery of the flesh" that "compels the woman to throw her heart after the body that with every fibre belongs to the man who changed that body, who transformed her from a virgin into a wife and mother. . . . Oh you fools who worry about whether the woman who desires to be your wife loves you! With all her heart! Laugh at her resistance, bring her to the altar, for marriage is stronger than hatred and longer lasting than love."

At this second stage, the type of the virtuous wife of the old school still stands. How much of an ideal model she has been, even if not dominant in reality, one can see in the literature of any era. Even in such a frivolous milieu as the court of King Louis XIV this model was viewed as the only moral one. The Princesse de Clèves in the novel named for her by Madame de Lafayette was so inseparably connected to her husband through the dutiful bonds of marriage that after his death she was unable to belong to the man whom she had passionately loved for many years.

It is the same type of wife that Fichte had in mind when he said, "The second sex is a step below the first one according to nature; the second is the object of the energy of the first. . . . Now, however, both are supposed to be equal as moral creatures. This would be possible only if the second sex went through a new stage, one quite unnecessary for the first. This is the stage at which she would acquire the sex drive that is natural to the man." On the basis of this thinking, Fichte comes to the conclusion that the woman cannot give herself to sexual lust in order to fulfill her own desire; it is the satisfaction of the man's desire that motivates her. "In the uncorrupted woman no sex drive expresses itself, only love, and this love is the natural drive of the woman to satisfy a man."

Here female love is not presented as free and voluntary devotion to a chosen man but as a drive to satisfy a man. Such a drive does not necessarily rule out individual personal relationships, but it lies in the nature of drives that they are mainly directed by characteristics of the species. If one examines the type of woman that Fichte is describing, one finds no trace of the feelings of the free personality. According to him, the human dignity of the female is based on her submission to a man, holding nothing back and losing her identity in his, once and for all. "Completely united with him, she acquires life and activity only through his eyes and his actions. She ceases to live the life of an individual."

If this description may be called subjective and exaggerated, there is no doubt that it fits many women, even those from the second stage, in whom eroticism involves not as much the person of a particular man, but the man as a bearer of the substance of her life. That, however, such a relationship involving complete suppression of the self must be based on the strongest legitimacy and legality is self-evident. What Fichte unintentionally brings out is the fact that women of the second stage are able to maintain their sexual identity and human dignity only in *legal* relationships; moreover, only in legal sexual relationships can the drive to satisfy a man unfold in the female soul without damaging her human dignity. For without legal relationships where would this drive lead the woman?

III

In the investigation of what is called the unity of soul and senses, the question emerges: is this a matter of development of an organic function that brings about a connection of external physical stimulation with inner drives as an achievement of the soul, or is it a matter of subordination of the will to rational considerations that are able to influence the moral sense? Only the first would be a truly endogenous unity, the consequence of the merging of the sexual impulse and the sphere of the personality so that the first experience would set the second in motion; this is what is meant when one speaks of the unity of the soul that is supposed to be the particular characteristic of the woman.

At the same time one must take into consideration that in general it is easier for the female gender to conform to the authority of moral values than the male – not because females are morally superior but because suggestibility belongs to the teleological nature of the woman, that is, it belongs to the characteristics through which the woman in primitive society adjusted to her expected roles. If one considers as well that the female mind is not accustomed to observing or analyzing feelings and that every such attempt is judged negatively, then one cannot deny that even divergences in individual cases are hardly possible.

In the second stage of female eroticism, in which the concept of legitimacy and the sexual impulses merge in the consciousness into a unity, one can surely doubt whether this unity is based on a physical function like sexual awakening through the personal attraction of love; to be sure, there are signs of this in the life of the soul of the virtuous woman, namely under the influence of Christian piety. The basis of this virtue and at the same time the female sense of self out of which, influenced by medieval thinking, the concept of female honor emerged, is exclusive submission to a chosen person – whereby, however, it should be noted, that the choice need not occur through the exercise of one's own will.

Marriages of duty, toward which such notions are directed, have been opposed in modern times because, to the extent that there is no love between the partners, they are sometimes regarded as no nobler than paid sexual intercourse; however, this interpretation overlooks the fact that there is an ideal connection between sexuality and the fulfillment of duty for women at the second stage. This connection is closely bound up with the concept of female honor; a woman's personal worth is not reduced through dutiful submission sanctioned by sacrament or society although it is reduced through voluntary submission, even if her primary motive is selfless love.

This viewpoint determined the life of the woman during the Middle Ages and has extended its influence to the threshold of our own times. Nevertheless, in spite of all religious and social pressures, personally oriented love has become more and more valued in the attitudes of civilized people – ever since it first appeared in the courtly love of chivalric culture, clad in the glory of the highest powers of the soul. Love stories also are the main subject of traditional novelists and they have maintained this place in world literature as a whole throughout recent centuries. However, if one looks more closely at this love, one sees that it is somewhat different from what one understands as deep love in the modern sense. It is true that these love stories often concern life and death, but this is less a sign of the depth of the unions of souls portrayed than of the passions of characters willing to set their lives on the line for rather modest reasons. How easily the love of Romeo shifts from Rosalin to Juliet! It is not the person of Juliet who decides Romeo's fate but eroticism itself that has an overwhelming power within his soul. For other authors of older literature love is even less connected to its object; it is easily transferred from one beloved to another. For example, Boccaccio says of Sophronia, whom Hegesippus delivers each night to his friend in his place, without her knowledge: "As a reasonable woman in this circumstance, she gives Titus the love that she had pledged to Hegesippus and travels with him to Rome." In the speech defending his behavior to the family, Hegesippus says that Sophronia should not be offended by the substitution because he gave her to Titus with honorable and virtuous intentions, although without her knowledge or consent. This revealing line of argument indicates how females of the second stage were regarded in those times.

A counterexample and at the same time a measure of the degree to which sensibilities in this area have become refined over five hundred years is found in Mörike's Painter Nolten. Suspecting that his fiancée Agnes is capable of infidelity, he has his friend begin an illicit correspondence with her in a disguised handwriting. When Agnes is eventually reconciled with her lover and learns of his deception, she realizes how virtuous and good he is and goes mad because her feelings are unable to recover from her involvement in the deception; even the mere idea of being connected to the soul of another man has incurably ruined her capacity for love.

In the historical process that the relationship between the sexes has undergone, their psychological state has grown ever more similar; they are parallel to each other in a human correlation based on their common membership in the species. However, this fact does not prevent the possibility that the same condition of the soul can express itself differently in the two genders. At the primitive stage the difference is greatest, but even at the second stage, the stage of conflict between gender and personhood, the symptoms of the same condition are very different.

In the previously mentioned book on the three stages of

eroticism, Lucka identified and discussed in detail a phenomenon called "metaphysical eroticism," which he claimed to be an exclusive characteristic of the male psyche and completely absent in women, with one notable exception. According to Lucka's argument, metaphysical eroticism has its roots in religious concepts. The Queen of Heaven, the Virgin Mother, adorned with the most treasured attributes of the female, a being who has stimulated the deepest experiences of femininity in people of many cultures and generations, merges the fire of erotic ecstacy with a real person. The feelings that she evokes combine the heavenly realm with the earthly and glorify the image of the woman into its noblest form. At the same time, however, there remains a conflict between the higher life of the soul and the sexual impulse that women presumably are not familiar with because they already possess the unity of soul and senses as an inborn quality.

Accompanying the presumptions of metaphysical eroticism, or the more familiar ideology of courtly love, however wonderful its results in people of that epoch whose souls were most highly developed, is an imperfection of the apparatus of the soul, attributed to faulty connections of the nervous system that directs disparate impulses within the brain. We may conclude that this imperfection also may be found in women of the second stage in spite of the lack of symptoms.

On the level characterized by conflict, love runs the danger of being damaged or lessened through sexual fulfillment, for love resists too much nearness in order to preserve the distance without which it cannot exist. All the presumptions on which courtly love is based can only be upheld under the condition that no sexual involvement destroy the ability to preserve illusions. Therefore the maintenance of distance from beloved women is an important condition of chivalric adoration, which is distinguished by the fact that it is usually bestowed on married women, who are difficult to win and kept at a distance, if only through outward, practical hindrances.

How would the chivalric adorer, whose soul in spite of all his nobler striving may not be completely free of male sexual aggression, be able to preserve the required distance if he were not supported therein by the reserve of the woman? Writings on courtly love are full of endlessly repeated complaints that beloved women are cold, strict, and unapproachable. These cannot have been composed out of thin air, or traced back to delusions; they must describe real behavior of real women. Should we assume that this female behavior was based on cleverness, strategies of love, or sophistication? Such duplicity would have required women of the time to possess a superior insight into the essence of courtly eroticism that, despite their sharp instincts in matters of love, cannot be attributed to them. Assuming that women of that era had no need for distance, the decisive symptom of incurable conflict, they would have sought the closest intimacy with all the determination of a unified soul – not unlike the situation that arises today when a couple attracted to each other experiences painful misunderstandings because one is a unified soul, one conflicted.

Not because of lack of feeling for her adorer does a woman refuse to grant fulfillment to his passionate desire, but rather because of the inability of conflicted eroticism to transform love of the soul into sexual love. "When courtly love flourished it happened that the noble lady in deepest secrecy would reward her lover with permission to spend a night in her arms, during which he was honor bound to ask no favor beyond kissing and embracing." (E. Otto, *Lives of German Women*) Unified souls would neither think of nor adhere to such an arrangement.

Thus, we may conclude that the behavior of the woman is based on a constitution in which the high claims of the soul in love have not achieved unity with the sexual. That this conflict in female eroticism does not exhibit the same symptoms as in male eroticism is easily explained by the different cultural positions of the genders. The sexual behavior of women was directed by the prevailing ideology of female life emphasizing reserve, moderation, and preservation of decorum; in short everything that belongs to women's natural defenses, as elevated to an ideal of education through moral precepts. All these ideals helped the woman faced with a chivalric adorer possessing natural male aggression and subject to needs of primitive sexual hunger nevertheless to maintain love as a spiritual property of the soul – despite conflict that was openly acknowledged.

Another motivation complicated matters. Intellectual ambition, which plays no role in the life of a woman, causes the productive man to value experiences according to his interests. In the male psyche there is resistance to the fulfillment of the senses because the natural condition that follows this fulfillment reduces his energy. Only the distant, unreachable woman is able to inflame male eroticism to the high level of the soul at which the elements of rapture and renunciation flow together into a new and overwhelming state of being and attitude. Women at this level, intellectually unproductive themselves, do not transform conflict into metaphysical eroticism; they are content, like the primitive woman, to be objects to men. However, they change the viewpoints of men, who come to view them not as objects *beneath* them but as objects *above* them.

IV

Divisions and delineations of developmental levels of the soul can be made only provisionally. They cannot be precisely traced in time or analyzed exactly by their characteristics. Of course personal love, an achievement of a higher differentiation of the life of the soul, can be found far back in human history. In fact, one can even find a starting point in the animal kingdom when attraction to certain traits in a certain creature go together with the drive to mate. The concept of development is valid only when applied to the unfolding of existing realities. That which in the human species is not present as an existing reality cannot be created through any known type of effort.

Thus, the development of eroticism in stages is only to be understood as the growth of an already existing human characteristic. Growth in terms of breadth refers to the inclusion of more and more individuals involved and growth in the vertical sense refers to increasing perfection of phenomena of the soul that effect such change. Recognized changes in value systems accompany the developmental process through mutual influences that appear as products and at the same time set the direction of the perceptions of the individual.

It is already widely known what great changes are occurring at present in value systems regarding matters of female eroticism. The battle against old-fashioned notions of womanhood, which is still fully supported by legal standards, is being led by women who view sexual equality solely in terms of the right to personal choice in love; in other words by women of the third stage. The identification of this value and the movement for its social elevation belong only to recent times, whereas as phenomena of the soul they existed in individuals long before. However, just as the fact that some men of past epochs provide individual examples of personal love of the soul does not disprove trends in the development of male eroticism, similar individual cases among women do not determine the general development of female eroticism.

Perhaps one may see in the figure of Heloise, the great heroine of sexual love, who with full awareness set her right to free devotion above the value of legality, the first representative of the third stage. With marvelous candor she wrote to Abälard: "Nothing have I ever sought in you but you yourself; I desire only you, not what is yours. I expect no marriage bond and no marriage gift . . . If to you the name wife seems holier and more honorable, to me being called your lover almost seems more enticing. . . . If today the emperor, the lord of the world, would offer me the honor of his marriage bed and let me rule forever over the whole world, I would pronounce it sweeter and more worthy to be called your paramour than to be known as his empress."

These words express the typical feminine thinking and feeling of the third stage; Heloise, student and beloved of a philosopher, possesses the mental capacity as well as the personal strength to acknowledge her feelings and to put them into words. Nor does she fail to voice a polemical expression of condemnation of women of the second stage: "She must consider herself a commodity who chooses a man on account of his money over a poor man, who desires a man himself less than what he owns. Certainly the woman who enters marriage for material reasons should be paid, not loved."

These words are all the more startling because they were spoken at a time when the sacramental, impersonal conception of marriage was the predominant view and extramarital sexual intercourse was generally viewed as a serious sin against a divine commandment – a view that Abälard himself delivered in an long, impassioned sermon condemning Heloise, the unrepentant sinner for the sake of love.

One can find in Abälard's words signs that he, apart from his fear of physical harm that exerted a strong power separating him from sexuality, was a conflicted man, if not a representative of metaphysical eroticism. His exchange of letters with Heloise is a documentation of – to be sure on the highest spiritual level – a typical relationship between the conflicted man and the woman with a unified soul. Although contemporaneous with courtly love, it differs substantially from the relationship between the chivalric adorer and his lady, the mistress with power to decide on the degree of nearness and favor she granted. In contrast, Heloise, overwhelmed by the need to succumb to her unified eroticism, without thought gave in to her lover's passionate wooing.

Born in the year 1101, she gave voice for the first time to the feelings that, many centuries later, would become the basis of a higher female morality, a new culture of humanity. She was compelled to break a long silence out of an all-powerful love that transcended all boundaries. In spite of the humility and subordination typifying her erotic nature, she rose so far above the female position as object that she was able to find expression for her experience as a subject.

On the path set and illuminated by Heloise, its first great representative, female eroticism gradually moved toward unity of the soul, to be sure delayed by moral detours that would be unacceptable to modern sensibilities. Developments along the way included the establishment of the cicisbeo, who brought courtly love into day-to-day life, furnished with full sexual rights, and the shift from marriages of convenience to marriages of love. The contributions of women's inclinations are difficult to determine, but if women did not have the power to defy claims of their families in entering marriages, they did have some influence over the form that marriage took. The cicisbeo was like a chivalric adoring lover with the difference that he acquired quite public spouselike status, serving to some extent as a second husband, next to the legal one, and tolerated by him without jealousy. This custom was described by Lady Montague in her letter from Vienna at the beginning of the eighteenth century: "Taking a lover here does not put one in danger of losing one's reputation, but rather it contributes to enhancing it, for ladies are judged more by the status of their lovers than that of their husbands. . . . Husbands are as friendly with their wives' suitors as if they were their agents, taking over their most tedious duties. . . . In short, it is necessary for women to have two spouses – one active and one in name only."

We know that, according to the views prevailing during the age of courtly love, love could not exist between spouses. Something like this old opinion is definitely involved in the custom of the cicisbeo; yet, choice in love, although not in legal marriage, enjoyed public recognition. One century later the recognition of marriage for love was completely established – at least in the viewpoints of the leading minds who made the nineteenth century an epoch of moral transformation.

Now women's claims clearly and unambiguously come to the fore; for we are able to learn from women's own writing about what goes on in the female psyche. The German women's novel of the eighteenth century (according to the exhaustive presentation of Dr. Christine Touaillon) provides evidence for the change that occurs. Sophie La Roche, who was in her early writings completely under the influence of strict adherence to legality, later approached the new view that found its decisive expression in the next generation in the words of Auguste Fischer-Venturini. In her works the standpoint of the third stage is presented with passion, logical precision and creative artistic power. In one of her novels the heroine answers a suitor, who has asked her to whom other than a man the beauty of a woman belongs: "I believe that it belongs to the woman herself – just as do her heart and her life. If she gives it to someone, it must be a voluntary gift; if it is not, there is no freedom left on earth."

It is symptomatic of the inner processes through which female eroticism unfolds that women, only when they perceive themselves as subjects, break their silence and speak up for their wishes and desires in love. This can, for deep reasons, only happen at the third stage, for not until this stage of love do women have the possibility of perceiving themselves as subjects; as long as the woman is a mere object of the man's and exists as such in her own consciousness, she possesses no voice of her own.

That which has the highest, most ideal rank in this type of eroticism is the "exchange of souls" through which every trace of strangeness melts into the warmth of the common unity of souls and the will to possess each other in the closest and most complete intimacy, to penetrate to the depths of the loved person's soul, in order to offer oneself in complete devotion, holding nothing back, becomes the power that determines the direction of the experience. "I will never be on my guard against you, never be suspicious of you," wrote Julie de l'Éspinasse to her lover; "I will not hide from you any sensation, any movement of my heart, and never blush to appear weak or full of contradictions before you." The suspicion that any motive such as gratitude, pretense, or even morality, could be involved in her relationship to him, she denies with the words, "All of those things are repulsive and only designed to defame and humiliate a sensitive soul."

In this kind of love each partner is subject and object at the same time, the woman and the man. The notion of property recedes behind the idea of voluntary devotion; no other motivation than mutual love justifies the bond uniting the couple. A slogan expressing the value system of the third stage is provided by Ellen Key when she says, "Love is moral even without marriage, but marriage is immoral without love."

It would be unjust to apply this slogan retrospectively to the second stage of female eroticism and to condemn the entire epoch during which the honorable woman saw the justification of sexual relationships in legality, unjust to apply the standards of the unified soul. If female sensibilities in sexual matters actually had not undergone a process of development then the conditions of the past would be incomprehensible, as in fact would those of the present.

A type of conflict can be observed even in some women of the third stage – conflict stemming from the relationship of the personality to sexuality: "The development of the independent personality is in many cases accompanied by a basic discord, an incompatibility between the tendency of female sexuality toward submission and the tendency of the personality that strives for independence. Such women are erotically disposed to seek in men precisely the qualities that they cannot tolerate in the other areas of their lives. . . . Their sexual nature requires the masterful superiority of the man, but their will toward self-determination resists submission, as soon as its consequences become perceptible outside of the erotic sphere." (*A Survey of the Woman Problem*)

Also this type of conflict can be explained as stemming from an imperfection in the organization of a person's character. The sexual nature of such women remains primitive while other aspects of their natures develop into full personalities. Thereby their personal fate is threatened, for happiness in love is usually impossible for them to reach.

However, even more threatened are the females who are still in their whole beings at the first stage. One can easily recognize a segment of the female world today characterized by primitive femininity that knows itself only as an object of a man and the man as a sexual being without personal differentiation, the basic stance that in the course of development has met with deep disapproval, been rejected by bourgeois society and yet exploited. A woman of this description, faced with economic need, easily falls into some type of prostitution, giving the rights to her sexual favors to the highest bidder. In the characters of those often described as born prostitutes, there is a complete lack of the sexual self-awareness present in the more highly developed female nature. However, prostitutes seem to be inclined to select from among their ever-changing possessors an *amant de cœur* who has no obligation to pay because his privileges are due to the female's attraction to him.

The stronger the sexual self-confidence of a woman, the greater is her resistance toward any form of sexual possession. Her repulsion toward such possession is intensified into deep disgust by the very idea that a woman could be bought and sold. The various developmental stages in the world of women would present irreconcilable oppositions so large that they would rule out any common connection between the genders. Women of the second stage, pressured by modern conditions into the conservative camp, could not be comprehensible to women of the third stage and would lose their orientation without the values in which their sexual predilections are deeply rooted. To be sure they believe themselves completely different from the prostitute type of the first stage, but through the self-preserving drive accompanying their virtue, they want to preserve themselves from vulnerability to the polygamous needs of the male, and so tolerate the belief that prostitutes are indispensable to men. Because their own predisposition is not toward the goal of a complete merging with the person of the man, they are not concerned with recognition of conflict in his nature.

For women of the third stage, however, internal male conflict and all its accompanying phenomena presents barriers to happiness. To the degree that they are able rationally to consider the conditions and effects of their own natures, they must battle against any appearance of primitive womanhood that calls into question women's position in the world. No matter how high metaphysical eroticism has lifted the woman, she can be caused to fall just as far by conflict in the male nature, for the same sexuality that defines the primitive woman as the object of satisfaction may be justified or disdained.

Of course these stages of development are facts of nature that cannot actually be fought against even though here as everywhere culture has established a ranking order. The astonishing aspect of the confused perceptions of the present is the misunderstanding and misidentification of the stages and ranks of development that has some people recognizing only primitive womanhood and others assuming women enjoyed their most recent advances from the beginning.

There is no greater misunderstanding of female nature than the view that the most powerful advantage of the female person vis-à-vis the male is the opportunity to sell her body without any emotional involvement. This is not to deny that this opportunity can give the primitive female, under some circumstances, a kind of power and superiority. However, the primitive female is not so constituted that she would likely be in the position to benefit from such a superiority, and an enlightened female cannot, under any circumstances, accept the negation of the personhood that is entailed. She is right in this view, for if there is a genuine potential for woman's nature to advance, it is through the development of her personality to the level of incorporating the eroticism of the third stage.

The Evolution of Marriage

It seems that the general view of marriage has declined more in the present epoch of cultural history than in any other. Again and again, one hears expressions of doubt regarding its value and the happiness it is supposed to provide. New ideas and claims continue to emerge that are incompatible with the basic conditions of married life, and few who enter into marriage know if they are doing more than going through a formality pushed on individuals by the state. Is marriage out of date for those who are free of conventional prejudices? Or is it a challenge set for the free person by our sexual culture?

To be sure, the question as to whether marriage as the sole legal form of sexual relationship, its assumed role in Western culture under the dominance of Christianity, ever fit human nature can certainly not be answered in the affirmative. The discrepancy between the power of the sex drive and this single legal way of satisfying it has always been so great that Christian marriage, no matter what punitive means are used to enforce it, has never been able to suppress other forms of sexual experience, such as concubinage and prostitution.

Even less could one give an affirmative answer to the question of whether marriage in its actual form is a joyful contribution to human life. Perhaps many, or even the majority of individuals are joyless creatures, and their marriages merely express their inborn characteristics.

Considering actual marriages, however, does not do justice to the theoretical significance of marriage, and without a look at its development in cultural history, one can hardly gain an understanding of its essence. If one can, generally speaking, maintain that every social institution can be understood only in evolutionary terms, by considering its ancient origins, this is especially true of marriage.

As a social institution, the goal of marriage is to regulate sexual intercourse in order to integrate it into a higher organization of life. In so doing, it appears as an essential component of culture.

Of course, various forms of marriage are found among the most primitive peoples, mostly polygamous, more rarely polyandrous, and sometimes even monogamous, like the only legally and morally sanctioned form in Western culture.

On the original customs out of which marriage as such developed, there are fundamental differences of opinion. Some insist that in the beginning complete absence of sexual ties prevailed (agamy). This assumption is not inconsequential, for it leads to the conclusion that the regulating of sexual relations through social norms did not spring from a basic drive of human nature, but that complete sexual freedom was the original and natural human condition. One thing, however, is certain: as far back as our knowledge of the history of peoples and their morality reaches, we find everywhere the traces of social regulation of sexual intercourse – even if it is sometimes based on completely different assumptions than are considered moral in Western culture. Even if we assume that at one time complete freedom prevailed, this would have been true at a stage at which human beings were not yet capable of regulating their lives in general through legal means. An argument can be made that regulating sexual relations is a function of the social drive, which cannot be separated from the original state of the human species.

Two motivations of unequal power have influenced the emergence of marriage. Only through these two motivations does it acquire the significance on which its social form was founded and which it still has today. They provide the impetus for the transformation of the primitive psyche into the person governed by cultural norms; their presence has long been an essential prerequisite to our understanding of the life of the soul.

We know that recognizing the actual connection between father and child requires a higher stage of development of thought and observation, and that men could not have possessed an understanding of fatherhood from the beginning of history. The establishment of group marriage, as Morgan tried to reconstruct through tracing a kinship system that still exists among a few tribes today, is dependent upon a completely undeveloped awareness of fatherhood; for these group marriages were relationships in which exclusivity of sexual relations was not prescribed for individual couples but extended to a set number of men and women within a certain tribe or defined community.

The opponents of Morgan's views present male jealousy as a reason for their doubt that sexual relationships at one time involved groups of women; according to Westermarck it would be "impossible to believe that there ever was a time when men were not subject to this powerful emotion." Even disregarding the fact that today millions of men live in legal polyandrous marriages without such possessive jealousy, group marriage belonged to a time when neither the *consciousness of fatherhood* nor that other crucial motivation for jealousy, *the idea of property,* had been developed in the male psyche.

After all, the concept of property is a relatively new product in human thought. If we take a brief look back into the beginnings of cultural history, we can see that the original social contracts were not based on private property and ownership of land, but on persons and on purely personal relationships. The unity of this organization was formed by the *gens*, a form of social community based on familial organizations that in earliest times were matrilinear. At the time when the *gentile* social order emerged, marriage between *single* couples was unknown and the determination of paternity was uncertain; only later did membership in one's maternal lineage give way to the rights of the paternal line, until finally with the continued development of property the entire *gentile* contract was replaced by rights of land and private ownership, and eventually the state constitution took over completely.

With the transformation of relationships of ownership and in the principles of the social contract came decisive transformations in the sexual order. Next to the consciousness of fatherhood the idea of property ownership played the most important role. In the earlier epochs of human life existing only as a vague awareness, the concept of property grew along with developing means of production and gradually became one of the strongest motivators of people and the most important basis on which all later societies were organized. As the idea became connected to the growing awareness of fatherhood in men, it acquired negative consequences for women. The woman became an object to be possessed, changing from a person into property of the man who also came to extend his property claims to complete possession of his children, despite the greater natural right of the mother to them.

If on the one hand marriage serves women's need for protection, because her economic and social position can only be secured through a legal connection to a man, on the other hand, marriage, based on the man's exclusive ownership of the woman, also protects fatherhood. Even in its present form, marriage bears traces of the view that women are mere tools for men to use to become fathers. In its barbaric form forced marriage through kidnaping brings this viewpoint out most clearly. Forced marriage seems to have a special meaning in the development of the consciousness of fatherhood. A man who mated forcibly with a woman outside of his own tribe was required to validate the children she bore through special customs like the male childbirth bed; while the later and more civilized method of acquiring a wife, purchase, contributed to developing the view of women as objects to be owned.

It is significant that this form of marriage was a very strong factor in developing the male view of women as property. No matter whether a man purchased his wife by exchange of another female relative, a certain number of horses and cattle, service to his father-in-law or simply a sum of money – the woman through this process became a material object, and the man who rightfully acquired a woman by purchase could treat her as he saw fit.

At the evolutionary stage at which the man was owner, the woman his property, the form of the *patriarchal marriage* emerged, under which the man had the right to sexual freedom and the woman was strictly required to be absolutely faithful to her husband. One can see in this situation the increased association of the consciousness of fatherhood with the feeling of power that accompanies ownership. In practice, it was a polygamous era in which the barbarian view of fatherhood completely determined the social position of the woman. In patriarchal marriage, as practiced by the Semitic peoples, women as spouses did not enjoy higher status than other people, whether free or in bondage, who existed in serflike dependence upon the power of the male head of the family. Patriarchal marriage in Greek society, and even more in Roman, displayed a tendency toward monogamy, for a man was legally permitted only one wife, who enjoyed the same legal rights as a couple's children. Adultery was forbidden only on one side, for while the man had the right to put his unfaithful wife to death, extramarital relationships on the part of the man were punishable only if they involved married women. The husband also had the right to treat female slaves in his household as his concubines.

Only at the highest and most recent level of family life, the *monogamous*, are sexual relationships based on the equal expectation of marital fidelity of both partners. Whereas in the patriarchal family female monogamy was enforced through severe control and oppression of women and men had the right to polygamy, now the bond through which lasting marital fidelity is guaranteed has become a *mutual* commitment of faith. Marriage is conceived of as a complete and lifelong union, and in principle, the man and the woman are virtually equal in personal rights, although complete equality of the two spouses has never been achieved in practice. Male and female adultery are the same before the law, and the concept of ownership of a person has been extended and changed so that not only does the woman belong to the man, but also the man belongs to the woman.

This concept has effected a complete transformation of the position of the genders and of the essence of the marital relationship, for marital fidelity of the man does not have the same physical meaning as that of the woman and her high value in monogamous marriage is therefore based on completely different assumptions.

As early as the era of the Roman Empire, progress in marriage clearly occurred in shifting the woman's status as a piece of property in the direction of her becoming an individual with rights. In the *confarreatio*, as the patrician marriage was known, as well as the *coemtio*, the marriage of the plebeians, the Roman woman was the property of the man; subject to his legal rights over her, known as *manus*. As social relations were liberalized, however, a freer type of union, the *usus* marriage, became more common. It was entered without a religious ceremony. The woman simply moved out of her father's house and into her husband's. She had to demonstrate her freedom from the power of *manus* by separating from her husband for three days each year to show her independence. In the *usus* marriage the legal connection between partners was considered to be *affectio maritalis*, or the voluntary will to be married. Either spouse had the power to dissolve the union if the voluntary will of either party had been extinguished.

The legal status of Roman marriage is a model for the transition from rigid unions to marriages reflecting a climate of social freedom. The originally undissolvable marriages of the patricians and plebeians were changed into dissolvable unions and finally the very free *usus* marriages were in the majority. During the Roman Empire *concubinage*, which had been forbidden, was also legally recognized and marriage with slaves, freed individuals and foreigners was allowed, although children of such unions had no rights as citizens.

At least to a limited extent, marriage bonds thus became linked to equal rights, and therein a new social function of marriage may be seen. If marriage was originally a union solely serving the interest of the continuation of the species, gradually it came to serve the personal material interests of the partners more and more. Through their unions, spouses established family relationships that extended their own property and elevated their social standing. With the establishment of the monogamous family based on private property and the extension of rights of inheritance to female descendants, marriages became a determiner of social class. The requirement of equal birth and equality of property that guaranteed the partners various social advantages and increased and strengthened their personal power through marriage has been associated with marriage in the consciousness of society ever since. Even today, acquiring power through familial and economic bonds is an important component of marriage as a social institution. Such benefits have even been extended to offspring in the so-called morganatic marriage.

The current concept of mismatches is based on ancient views

of marriage. Among the Germanic tribes marriage between a free and an unfree person resulted in a loss of freedom; according to Saxon law it could be punishable by death. Among the Romans, in contrast, during the time of the Republic there was a long battle between the patricians and the plebeians over whether marriage had to be between social equals. It ended with the victory of the plebeians.

During the course of the evolution of marriage the requirement of equal birth and associated concepts regarding the female person were advanced by both the Germanic tribes and the Christians – two cultural powers that, united with the Romans, contributed to the long, difficult, and complicated process of forging the system of legal rights in marriage that emerged in modern times.

In the original form of Germanic marriage the position of the woman was closely related to that prevailing in ancient Rome. The Roman head of household exercised property rights over the woman known as *manus*, called *mundium* by the Germans. *Mundium* gave the husband the rights over his wife as well as his children and serfs. He could discipline them, sell them, or put them to death; he was, however, not permitted to separate from his wife at will without providing definite reasons.

Nevertheless a difference appeared in the Germanic view of the female gender that had undeniable effects on the later development of relationships between the sexes. Josef Unger discusses this detail in his excellent book, *Marriage as it Developed in World History*, saying, "Whereas among the Romans the grounds for the tutela mulierum – the guardianship of the woman – the imbecillitas and infirmitas consilii, was her assumed *intellectual* weakness, the sexual guardianship of the Germanic tribes, which decreased along with family protection in general as the protection of the state was strengthened, was rooted in the woman's *physical* vulnerability, in her *bodily* inability to defend herself against aggressive attack." The intellectual talents of women – if one is to believe the famous words of Tacitus – were held in especially high esteem by the Germanic tribes, an esteem that led to a view of woman as a higher being. The contradiction between this viewpoint and the low position that the female gender had in reality is obvious throughout the entire Medieval period and evidenced most strikingly in the era of courtly love. In spite of this unresolved conflict, courtly love was not without influence on married love. Quite early there emerged the tendency to regard marriage as an *inner* unity of spouses achieved through emotional motivation. At this point the Germanic view and the Christian converged and together brought about a new basis for the significance and importance of marriage – its inwardness.

According to the viewpoint of all ancient peoples up until the dawn of the Christian era marriage was a legally ordered bond between two individuals of opposite sexes for the purpose of creating progeny. A meaningful personal relationship on the basis of mutual attraction and inner unity was not a part of such marriages. To be sure, in certain particular cases in ancient times, love between spouses was glorified, as in the Greek saga of Admet and Alkeste, but such unusual couples were individual cases that had nothing to do with the legal status of marriage. Evidence of true married love is also provided by the *Eulogy on the Turia* (published by Eugen Ehrlich in the January 1917 issue of the "Tat"), in which a Roman husband praises the devotion and superiority of his deceased wife. He describes therein how she, led by the prevailing view of marriage as an institution for the purpose of procreation, offered to give her husband a divorce so that the household she would be leaving through her death could be given over to a fertile successor. Quite filled with love for her as a person, he relates his response to her, "I was so disturbed that I lost my senses; so horrified was I by the idea . . . that you could think of separation from me before fate had forced it, that you could actually conceive of ceasing to be my wife." Precisely because this view of marriage as a bond created by mutual love that could be terminated only by death differs from the prevailing view of the Romans, is the *Eulogy on the Turia* of such historical significance. It shows how far the development of individual feelings was in advance of the development of societal norms.

As a spiritual principle the unity of man and woman in marriage was not recognized until the Christian era. According to the Apostle Matthew, Jesus was asked by the Pharisees if it was right for a man to separate from his wife for any reason, and he answered that "a man shall leave his father and mother, and cleave to his wife, and the two shall become one flesh" – whereby he invested these words, a quotation from the First Book of Moses, with a much deeper uniting power than they had in their original sense. In addition, the Apostle Paul sought to elevate the inner meaning of marriage significantly by asserting that the relationship between husband and wife in marriage was symbolically equivalent to the relationship between Christ and his people. He said, "Husbands, love your wives, just as Christ also loved the Church, and delivered himself up for her his people for whom he sacrificed himself," and "But just as the Church is subject to Christ, so also let wives be to their husbands in all things." He also harkened back to the old words: "For this cause a man shall leave his father and mother, and cleave to his wife and the two shall become one flesh." However, he also associated the passage with a deep sense of mystical unity of being, an inner process that cannot be understood by everyone, for he added expressly, "This is a great mystery."

Herewith marriage was for the first time proclaimed as an individual connection of soulful inwardness with the power of a religious confession. Neither the interests of progeny that in the beginning had given marriage all its meaning and content, nor the bond of membership in a familial community with its external social advantages that emerged in more developed cultures, stands in the foreground: rather, here marriage is an inner union between two creatures of opposite genders with the sense that neither the man without the woman nor the woman without the man can acquire completion. From this point on, love becomes a new component of marriage.

II

It is important to note that the great secret or mystery of the profound merging of creatures through love was at first only an idea, at odds with reality, harbored by high, prophetic minds; in practice its establishment could not be brought about for many centuries.

Thus, the idea of love as the foundation of marriage, like concepts of social utopia, remained unrealizable in the next one and a half millennia of human development. The ascetic direction taken by the leading minds of Christian thought was not compatible with a mystical conception of the unity of the genders through love. It had similar effects as the Christian devaluing of women as tools of sensual lust and the devaluing of marriage as a carnal and therefore despicable unity of male and female. The church father Tertullian, one of the most severe despisers of women, also taught scorn for marriage, even at the possible price that the human race would die out thereby, and Justinus the Martyr asserted that the idea was simply incomprehensible that sensuality could be transformed into morality in marriage. In such attitudes the views of the conflicted person are undeniably present, the type who is torn between the claims of sexuality and the higher life of the soul and unable to reconcile them in a harmonious way. Saints of this type sometimes go so far as to extend their shame to their own parents because the sight of them is a reminder of the "impure" act to which they owe their own lives! And such ideas that typified the conflicted types of early Christianity also appear in the last great representative of this type in European culture, Tolstoy, as reflected in his view of marriage. He advocated absolute asceticism and condemned the modified form found in monogamy. His mystical interpretation of the words of the Gospel, "But I say to you that anyone who so much as looks with lust at a woman has already committed adultery with her in his heart," expresses the fateful essence of the psyche of the conflicted person. This viewpoint is deeply rooted, but it is not applicable to real marriages – even in light of the interpretation of this passage as simply an expression of strict moral standards. Over the centuries the same attitude has led to the same ways of thinking; for Tolstoy as for Saint Gregory of Nyssa marriage is "a product of weakness, a result of the sinful nature of human beings." The condemnation of sexual intercourse is accompanied by the condemnation of the idea that marriage is a morally based institution.

From this negative view of marriage in the church is derived the requirement of celibacy for priests and – an apparently contradictory consequence! – the elevation of marriage into a sacrament. The simplest explanation of the idea on which this elevation was based is that marriage is an unholy affair, but unavoidable due to the nature of human beings, needing justification through the divine blessing which it acquires, according to Christian teachings, through its role as a sacrament. As soon as marriage acquired its identity as a sacrament it also had to be regarded as an unbreakable bond that endured into eternity.

However, individual love was not regarded as a basis of this unbreakable, eternal bond. Unger in the above mentioned book correctly points out that canon law regards marriage from virtually every other viewpoint than from that of love. In the unbreakable sacramental marriage the bond that unites the spouses is not guaranteed by mutual attraction, but by the sacrament. According to the viewpoint of the church the declared will of those entering marriage is subordinate to the act of priestly consecration, for only thereby do the participants receive divine grace. It is not their own inadequate wills, not their undependable hearts, influenced by fickle senses, that bind them from then on but rather it is divine will. Therefore marriage must be sustained even if attraction based on free personal inclination no longer exists; men and women are not united in sacramental marriage to fulfill desire or satisfy inclinations, but to fulfill a duty that divine will requires of them in the interest of the maintenance of the species. To be sure marriage is valid only when sexually consummated, but sexual intercourse itself, according to the doctrine of *debitum conjugale*, acquires a meaning quite apart from acts of sensual lust occurring outside of marriage. That which would be "immoral" in a marriage for love, namely continuing to practice sexual intercourse in the absence of mutual inclination, is fully acceptable according to the concepts of sacramental marriage, because it is viewed as fulfilling a marital duty. This viewpoint teaches the wife that patient submission to the sexual will of the husband is a duty pleasing to God, and it teaches the husband that the fulfillment of his sex drive serves the divine will for procreation, as blessed by the holy sacrament. Through the connection of sexual drives with religious concepts this form of marriage greatly increased the significance and depth of sexual relationships, a change that would play an important role in the future development of matrimony.

Viewing marriage as a sacrament caused an ennobling of sexual relations that, at a certain stage of human development, came to regard human feelings as expression of the highest morality. This view rests on a foundation, without which it would perish, of fervent piety governing all moods and sensations, to which all other interests must be unconditionally subordinated. Mere love with its immanent desires cannot compare.

Thus, amazing as it may seem to us, the Christian viewpoint came to place the highest value on love as an ungendered phenomenon of the human soul, but devalued love as soon as it entered the sexual arena, with the exception of sacramental marriage. In that epoch when sexual love began for the first time to acquire romantic magic, that is, in the epoch of courtly love, marriages were formed, as long afterwards, through agreement of the spouses' parents or relations as mere arrangements of convenience, without the partners necessarily even being well acquainted beforehand. The attitude of the time toward marriage is best illustrated by the famous words of the Countess of Champagne as she presided in a courtroom proceeding in 1174. Asked whether there could be love between spouses, she said, "We hereby assert and affirm that love does *not* extend its rights over married couples because love between a man and a woman must be mutual and voluntary, compelled by no outside necessity, while married spouses, on the contrary, are united by mutual duty and duty-bound not to reject each other. Such a judgment, which we have reached through mature consideration and through securing confirmation thereof from a great many other women, is in all times an unshakable and unbreakable truth."

With fine understanding of the perception of women of the inner essence of love, this judgment honors the free and voluntary qualities of love as essential conditions. However, the idea that love and marriage can have nothing in common with each other has not continued to prevail as an unshakable and unbreakable truth.

Slowly, but more and more clearly during the course of

cultural development, there was a movement toward merging love and marriage into a union, in the sense that love should be the motivation for entering marriage, and marriage should be the realization of love. This change that took place in the modern consciousness was seen as soon as the distinction between the marriage of convenience and the marriage of love was made.

The marriage of convenience should not be confused with the marriage of rationality, as commonly occurs. The marriage of rationality consists of the voluntary union and merging of identities of two people who enter marriage on the basis of mutual agreement. It differs from a marriage of love only in that it is not formed on the basis of passionate attraction, but rational consideration by both parties, and therefore it is upheld by a sense of duty than by immediate feelings of love. For couples in love whose love does not endure over time, the later stages of their marriages are likewise based on duty. Marriages of convenience are defined as those that are not instigated and sealed by the two parties themselves, but because of external considerations of usefulness with no consideration given to whether these unions are advantageous to the parties' inner selves.

The further that we reach back into cultural history, the higher we find the regard for marriages of convenience, for married alliances, as originally formed on the basis of agreements between parents or other relatives, which could hardly be based on anything but economic and social factors. The marriage of rationality that encompasses a personal relationship between the two partners is already at a higher level; one can view this type as the transitional form between the marriage of convenience and the marriage of love. This type was the declared ideal of marriage up to the middle of the eighteenth century; passionate love as a basis of marriage was not highly regarded at that time. The closer we come to the present in cultural history, however, the higher we find the regard for the marriage of love, until finally it became so dominant that even notorious marriages of convenience, as, for example, those between reigning royal figures, were regularly claimed to be marriages of love. This is, of course, not to say that convenience even today does not provide a significant reason for many marriages, only that love in the general moral value system is more highly regarded.

The historical change that has occurred in the rank ordering of motivations for marriage is summarized by Müller-Lyer (*Phases of Love*) according to the following schema: Epoch I: economics, children, love; Epoch II: children, economics, love; Epoch III: love, children, economics. If the higher ranking of economic motivation over reproductive, as claimed by Müller-Lyer, prevailed at one time, there can be no doubt that the erotic motive has risen in importance in the present. Thus, one may conclude that the historical development of marriage in our culture reached its summit in the form of marriage for love as both a physical bond and bond of the soul between two people of opposite genders on the basis of a merger of life that attains the highest state of inner emotional unity.

However, it almost seems as if at this highest point of development the concept of marriage itself begins to dissolve. If the content of marriage is love, its essence completely and absolutely based on free and voluntary personal devotion, has not marriage as a societal bond and an enforcer of norms governing sexual relationships according to laws and duties, become a contradictory institution? As long as two people love each other they will regard living together as a desirable condition on their own, but if at some point they cease loving each other, the external compulsion with which the law seeks to guard the marriage bond can no longer maintain a marriage in the true sense because its content, love, no longer exists.

Through such reasoning the Romantics justified their rejection of marriage, a viewpoint held by many of the leading minds in Germany since the beginning of the nineteenth century. Marriage also encountered opposition from yet another side, from the standpoint of those envisioning a new social order. If marriage as a social institution is the expression of the concept of private property extended into the sexual arena, then it must change whenever relationships involving property in general undergo a significant change. Just as marriage evolved from its original freer forms when private property entered history, it should be expected to cease to exist as an arrangement based on the exclusivity of sexual ownership at such time that private property ceases to exist. This viewpoint was represented by the Saint-Simonists in France; they advocated unconditional freedom for the female sex, as Enfantin expressed in these frank words: "The new moral order calls the woman to a new life. . . . Every man who wishes to lay claim over a woman by mere legal means is no Saint-Simonist, and the only position of the Saint-Simonists regarding woman is the declaration of their inability to hold authority over her." Also Fourier saw in his phalansterium a system of sexual relationships in which the exclusivity of ownership was completely abolished in order to make room for a kind of time-limited group marriage reflecting human nature in its true form without the necessity of justification through hypocrisy, or indeed, any justification.

Vestiges of such utopian constructions that view human nature and its basic drives in a very one-sided manner, that is, primarily from the sensual side, can be found to some extent even at present. Some people think that as an economic institution marriage is becoming superfluous and eventually its role as protector of motherhood will be served by educational and social welfare programs. Further, they predict that marriage will be replaced by relationships that endure only as long as mutual attraction lasts, and that society will not regulate whether they are monogamous or polygamous. A worldview that completely does away with the concept of property ownership cannot justify the necessity for exclusivity in marriage.

At this point a question arises: what is the difference between a marriage of love and a free relationship of love? Is there any real difference other than the marriage certificate that legalizes the relationship and enforces certain external precepts? Is there an inner difference that would make the marriage bond superior to a mere love affair even if the duties of the couple toward their progeny were taken over by social welfare institutions?

This question gives rise as well to the need to forge a definition, a description of the content of marriage. Older and newer definitions shift back and forth from emphasizing the purpose of procreation to emphasizing companionship. The latter type locates the essence of marriage in the couple's shared life journey; sometimes placing great weight on the importance of economic union, on social rather than sexual significance, or on the entirety of shared life interests. Marriage, according to one older definition, is not only a *societas bonorum*, but also a *societas vitae*, not only a merging of goods, but also a merging of lives. According to other views, the main purpose of marriage is the conceiving and raising of children. The encyclopedists taught that marriage, according to natural law, bestows a general duty on both genders to carry forth the human species, and as means thereto both spouses have domain over each other's bodies. Likewise, Kant defined marriage as "a union of two persons of opposite genders based on mutual possession of each others' sexual attributes." To be sure, even today there are some legal scholars who regard marriage solely from the viewpoint of the state, voices who advocate definitions of marriage that include no purpose other than reproduction. For example, the jurist Rosenthal (in the periodical "Die Neue Generation") identified as the sole basis and purpose of marriage "to reproduce the species, to care for and educate one's progeny; marriage thus defined is therefore the legally recognized union of individuals of opposite genders for the purpose of procreation." According to this definition the only difference in kind between a married sexual union and any other sexual relationship is to be found in the intention to reproduce.

The logical consequence of this view would be to dissolve all childless marriages; if the content of marriage is the intention to reproduce, a relationship that does not fulfill this intention cannot be maintained. Indeed, we do find this principle carried out in ancient law, as for example, among the Jews. However, even the Catholic viewpoint, according to which only the intention to reproduce lifts sinfulness from sexual intercourse, does not recognize infertility as grounds for divorce and therefore does not identify the content of marriage as reproduction alone.

Also Nietzsche, whose formulations of new moral norms were voiced by the character Zarathustra, gave a definition of marriage that did not go much beyond the idea of procreation. Zarathustra says the following: "Marriage I define as the will of two people to create one thing that is greater than the pair who create it. Marriage requires respect for each other and respect for the force of this will. This is the sense and the truth of your marriage."

Here the conception of the purpose of marriage as an arrangement to benefit progeny merges with the idea of development that Nietzsche expresses in these words: "You should not only sew seeds to grow forward in your progeny, but also seeds to lead you upward in your own growth." Here he unites the longing for the superior being or "superman" with the will to marry. As fine and inspiring as the perspective is that is opened up with this view, after consideration, one must unfortunately conclude that, strictly speaking, it does not offer a practical goal for marriage partners because individuals cannot control the inherited traits they carry through any effort of the will. Also, it is known that inheritance does not proceed in a straight line from parents to children. In many cases the influence of traits of grandparents or even distant relatives is more powerful than those of the parents themselves. If someone seriously wanted to exercise such a will in this area, he or she would need to take pains to examine not only his or her own traits and those of the chosen partner, but also both of their relatives of the third and fourth degree – such a method would be likely to produce so many concerns that through it two people would never be able to guarantee in good conscience that they were suitable for marriage.

In addition, children usually are not in the foreground of the conscious minds of two lovers seeking a socially sanctioned, lasting sexual union. No serious argument can be made that the selective will of nature with regard to progeny is expressed in erotic attraction. In fact, it is precisely those possessed by deep love of the soul who seek to overlook or even justify the faults and frailties of the chosen person, or even to transform them into attractive qualities. This fact is the very reason for the Zarathustran notion that love cannot be the most desirable basis of marriage because it too easily leads to decisively wrong choices.

The inadequacies and contradictions among the various definitions of marriage lead to the conclusion that marriage cannot be explained by any single motivation. Three factors play a role, and their interests are not completely the same. The significance of marriage differs depending upon which of these three factors is most prominent. If occasionally under especially favorable circumstances all three can be satisfied, in most cases one dominates.

For the state marriage is an institution that benefits procreation; the state is interested in the sexual relationships of its citizens only insofar as they involve the production and nurturing of the young.

For society marriage is a union, founded on economics, charged with the task of providing secure child care, protected by family bonds, associated with the notion of the holiness of the domestic hearth.

For a person as an individual marriage is the enduring form of a love relationship with a chosen member of the opposite sex with whom one wishes to share one's life.

From these three viewpoints emerge the three differing components of marriage that can lead to conflicts to the degree that social and personal interests clash. Indeed, the social component of marriage, the economic-familial, is often quite at odds with the individual component; this component not only places limitations on the personal choice of a beloved partner, but may in fact place demands on personal relationships that run counter to the essence of love. It belongs to the essence of love that it be voluntary and without compensation. It is this tendency that is meant by the expression "selflessness" in love. However, working against the tendency toward selflessness is the requirement placed by society and family on the female to demand from the man as a price of sexual submission a whole array of social and material benefits that accompany marriage. In addition, the duty to give up her right to self-determination for these material benefits, as required by the legal norms of marriage, significantly reduces the personal freedom of the female individual.

It is thus easy to see that the criticisms of marriage stemming from the modern women's movement first of all had to be directed against all such requirements. The goal of the movement's struggle should thus be freeing marriage from its state and societal roles.

Released from the bonds of law and convenience, marriage should be able to fulfill its highest ethical potential as a union of love. With more value placed on the development of the individual, the female, conscious of her own personhood, will strive to recognize no other value in marriage than a personal relationship whose content is love alone.

Yet, we ask again how a marriage of love differs from a mere relationship of love if it no longer entails a lasting duty defined and placed upon it by state and society?

III

The idea of releasing marriage from the external bonds of duty in the interest of freedom in love is always met with the same main objection, that love as a sexual emotion is a transitory condition and therefore it cannot be the basis for an arrangement that will serve the interests of offspring as well as those of the spouses, an arrangement that must absolutely be reliable and enduring.

It is true that love as an emotion is not a permanent condition. If the interests of procreation and individual attraction of love were the same thing, as is claimed by Schopenhauer's metaphysics of love, it would have served its purpose if reproduction were fulfilled. To be sure love often endures after the birth of a couple's first child, its presumed metaphysical purpose, but in a great many cases love gradually diminishes after sexual fulfillment. Most modern proponents of free love regard love as transitory, and in general love justifies the claim "that the same powers that cause two paths to converge in the next moment cause divergence which increases from then on. The divergence after some years increases to the point that the relationship dissolves and both parties agree to release each other to select new partners." (L. Gumplowicz)

Is there not, however, something lasting in some cases of love that sets them apart from the transitory and transforms them into an enduring condition? Is every happy marriage only a gift of chance, only a winner in the lottery of life that is as little dependent on the inner worth and will of the personality as a winning lottery ticket? – A union that begins to unravel at the first conflict instead of growing in unity and understanding through conflict can hardly be called a marriage. It is nothing more than a sexual relationship whose duration is determined by chance factors.

Those couples who reach the agreement before marriage that they will live together only as long as their mutual love endures do not know what marriage is in the deepest sense. No marriage can be based on such an agreement.

The basis of marriage is not love alone, but rather the commitment to *the endurance of love.*

This commitment to endurance is, according to Meyer-Benfrey in his book on the moral foundations of marriage, the decisive difference between marriage and other sexual relationships. However, because he is of the opinion that love cannot be influenced by the will, he limits his claim to asserting that the commitment to the endurance of love is to be understood only as the *inner wish for endurance.*

At this point the problem of marriage encounters one of the most difficult psychological issues, an area that up to now has been as mysterious as the essence of love itself.

Contrary to the general view that the conscious will has no power over love – which Duboc in his *Psychology of Love* also maintains – it can be argued that the will to endurance can contribute quite substantially to maintaining love over time. Strictly speaking volition in love has not more but also not less influence than volition in human emotions in general. There is such a thing as conscious control of feelings just as there is conscious control of thought; inner processes in both cases rest on leading the will in a certain direction, on resolve within the personality. *Entering into a marriage means wanting to commit one's personhood to an enduring love.* Only under this condition can one truly carry out the decision to unite oneself completely with the life of another being.

If one separates marriage from its components external to the individual spouses, its nobler status and nature, compared to other sexual relationships, consists only in the achievement of volition that leads the individual beyond the egoistic borders of the person. It is this achievement of volition that, apart from economic and reproductive roles, creates a purely personal union. In traditional marriage the concept of duty directed volition, while in the marriage of love it is directed by the concept of voluntary devotion.

A definition of marriage could best be phrased thus: *Marriage is the will to create a sexual relationship formed by love into a merging of lives that brings two people of opposite genders into a union of souls.* Marriage also involves the decision to accept the fate of a second being outside one's physical self and to bear it without reservation as one's own.

This commitment need not be injected into love in a rational way, but the deeper and more inward love becomes, the more clearly the commitment proves to be fundamental. Marriage is the realization of love in the sense that it identifies and plans to maintain an achievement that belongs to the essence of love but is vulnerable to unreliable and unpredictable changes in erotic impulses if it is not guided by rational control. The transitory psychological heightening that love achieves effortlessly but cannot maintain is transformed into a lasting condition through the application of volition in marriage.

The will to permanence is served by – fidelity, a word that has fallen into disuse and lost its appeal for many. Marriage is completely based on fidelity; it loses every meaning as soon as fidelity is lost. Investigating the value of marriage means investigating the problem of fidelity in the life of the soul. In a time in which superficial people see the meaning of life in the enjoyment of the senses, and more serious people in the fulness of inner experience, the value of fidelity must be in decline, for it severely frustrates the drive for variation in sexual partners, a drive that brings with it so much potential pleasure, by limiting potential erotic experience to one partner. To be sure fidelity, while denying extensive erotic experience, may compensate by offering intensity.

It is a widely held belief that the meaning and significance of fidelity is different for the two genders – female fidelity is a guarantee of the genuineness of paternity and so the consequences of infidelity of one's spouse are much more significant for the husband than for the wife. This view of infidelity is the oldest and the most primitive; it originated in ancient times when the significance of fidelity in love was not recognized because exalted love as a sexual phenomenon held no place of honor. Nor was the hygienic benefit of male fidelity recognized, either because there were no venereal diseases or because their connection to sexual intercourse was not known. If one used preventative methods to reduce the danger of infection, the danger of the genuineness of paternity arose because female infidelity could also be promoted by prevention techniques.

In truth, fidelity in love has the same value for both genders. If love is the consciousness of unity of the ego with a beloved person and sexual union is the expression thereof, why should there be any difference in the behavior of the two partners to each other? Some people claim that the psycho-physiological constitution of the man is such that love for him as not as inwardly and inseparably connected to sexuality as it is in the woman, and therefore a man can have a sexual adventure that will not damage the fidelity of his soul to his beloved woman. This notion justifies the male right to infidelity not by men's freedom from the reproductive role of women, but by men's faulty constitution. It is also associated with the idea that at times male physical needs are more powerful than all psychological ties. From the point of view of the higher sexual culture this quality of the male constitution is a serious drawback. If this quality cannot be abolished from the earth by moral precepts, perhaps in individual cases the question of physical fidelity may be subject to agreement of the partners, even though only determined maintenance of absolute fidelity defines the true concept of marriage. Reprehensible in all cases is betrayal that violates marriage, not just exclusivity, which, if accompanied by no lessening of love, need not always signify infidelity.

Objection to marriage because its requirement of fidelity limits personal freedom is not valid. The marital bond is not a limitation of freedom to the true spouse, but the fulfillment of an inner need. Such a person sees in the commitment to a lasting unity with the beloved person only the realization of that which is compatible with his or her inner being. It should be added of course that not every person is suited to this noble form of marriage.

This single deviation from the ideal marriage is enough to

demonstrate that marriage has not steadily developed on an ever higher course, and marriage in reality at all stages of history has been imperfect.

To the concept of marriage in the modern view, that is, as only a marriage of love, belongs a type of love that is not completely identical with erotic attraction as such. It is a feeling of deep inner connection to another soul that is much more lasting than erotic attraction. Often people equate every kind of erotic attraction indistinguishably with love.

In his discussion of the aesthetic meaning of marriage Kierkegaard identifies the difference between romantic and marital love – a distinction that Lester Ward later applies in his *Pure Sociology*. Ward reaches the conclusion that human beings "in ideal circumstances attain happiness through marital love; marital love as the creator of general happiness cannot be improved. It is full and strong; it is lasting and it ends only when life itself ends . . . ." According to him there have been many gradations along the way toward ideal love. The current condition of marriage mirrors all possible prior stages; the type of feeling which is called ideal marital love is undeniably on the upswing.

The quality that distinguishes marital love from romantic love is the connection of the former to the sense of duty. Marriage must be built on both love and duty – strictly speaking it can omit neither one nor the other. No relationship of love is so perfect that it can persist under long-lasting unfavorable circumstances without the support of the sense of duty. The contrast between love and duty is erased by marriage; marital love differs from romantic love at the point at which the will for permanence and the will to fulfill one's duty merge in the mystery of love. Goethe wrote to Käthchen Schönkopf: "Whoever loves, wants to be bound to another" – a deep truth that contains the purest expression of the attitude of marital love.

Thus, one may see in the marriage of love the realization of that which the sacramental marriage strove to make out of sexual relationships by connecting sexual drives with concepts of the highest spiritual nature. In its process of making psychosexual connections deeper and more inward, the marriage of love takes a step beyond the sacramental marriage. Both forms can be in their inmost essence only lifelong, undissolvable unions based on monogamy. The marriage of love must be based on the principles of permanence and of exclusive devotion.

It would be a great misunderstanding to conclude therefore that this undissolvability must be enforced by an external law, as the Catholic Church requires of the sacramental marriage. Precisely because the lifelong monogamous marriage is an inner, mutually supported bond of love at the highest moral level that a human being can reach through his or her sexual nature, it is attainable only voluntarily and is impossible to attain by coercion, like any high moral achievement whose value and essence depends on individual volition. Legal measures have the purpose of creating certain arrangements that enable people to live together in society. The form of the legally undissolvable marriage is nothing other than a condition of the social order. In contrast, the religious view allowing divorce but not remarriage has the effect of spawning illegitimate sexual relationships. Also the power of faith has never prevented, in cases in which disharmony between spouses is insurmountable, the transformation of a sacramental union, by means of legally enforced undissolvability, into a forced marriage – with all the negative consequences that accompany a relationship that has been inwardly extinguished but is maintained only by external pressure.

If we take a look at the history of the undissolvable marriage, it becomes obvious that resistance to this institution, established after a long struggle within the Catholic Church, has never ceased. The Reformation abolished the sacramental character of marriage and transformed it into a union that could be dissolved "due to any guilty influence, equivalent to adultery, that is destructive to marriage." To be sure Luther retracted his opinion that marriage was merely "an external, worldly institution, like any other human arrangement." Nevertheless, it was a lasting result of the Reformation that the norms regarding marriage in most European countries came to handle marriage as a state matter independent of religion. The state took over the task of controlling marriage as a legal matter, and the result of this view is the secular or civil marriage that requires no religious validation and that, according to various legal stipulations, is dissolvable.

IV

Two distinct tendencies can be identified as the fruits of the developmental history of marriage that has unfolded over the last thousand years. They are the tendency toward *inwardness* that reached its highest and most complete form in the marriage of love, and the tendency toward *worldliness,* whereby the external form of the civil marriage was established, through which state and society recognize sexual relationships that meet certain conditions. However, neither tendency has achieved its ideal form. Neither the legal nor the social conditions of marriage are suited to promote its inner realization through love. On the contrary, the external conditions of married life are so unfavorable that one is almost tempted to say that love can more easily last longer than death than marriage can. One need not be a pessimist to assert that a happy marriage is extremely rare. It cannot be denied that the majority of marriages based on love do not live up to the promises made by the two spouses. The failure of marriages based on love, not to mention the weakness of human nature in general and the unreliability of erotic attraction in particular, can be explained by the fact that most people have no idea how to maintain love. They live their married life as if love were a beast of burden to be laden with everything difficult and distasteful in life. The legal and social conditions of marriage encourage this view, for they are tailored only to marriages of convenience, which are permanent but based on convenience according to conditions at the time of marriage.

If love is considered primary among motivations for marriage, if follows that this primary position must be maintained in marriage. The commitment to the endurance of love requires that upholding love in married life should be supported above all other motivations, that among all issues that arise love should be treated as most important, and that every other interest should be subordinate to it. Love should be valued above all else, and not allowed to be threatened or damaged in any way. Daily life with all its countless problems, trivialities, and irritations that govern married life, is the most merciless enemy of love. Nothing is harder for love to endure than the stresses of living together, burdened by all kinds of bad habits and circumstances, the shabby intimacies of endless monotony that destroy all illusions. It often happens that married people who have grown far apart from each other through day-to-day life and who suffer a hard blow of fate that demands self-sacrifice and mutual assistance, once again become aware of their original connection, and love which the dull monotony of married life had robbed from them, is reborn through misfortune.

Modern life, shaped by the current conditions of civilization, does not provide a favorable soil for the realization of the marriage of love; in fact, all its influences are hostile to the will toward permanence in love. Premarital sexual life is anything but preparation for married life. Marriage itself, conceived as the highest moral achievement of the human sexual nature, places such high demands of self-mastery, sacrifice, and consideration – qualities that modern life does not encourage – that a completely different culture of the soul is required than contemporary life provides.

However, even if we assumed that the marriage of love could create all the internal and external conditions for its realization, it would be as the sole socially sanctioned form of sexual relationship just as inadequate as the old form of marriage, with all its social and familial burdens. That the lifelong monogamous marriage based on free choice in love enjoys the highest rank in our social and ethical value system does not mean that it must be the only form of sexual relationship that can be acceptable to social norms. Such an assumption would repeat the mistake made when Christendom took the extreme step of declaring sacramental marriage the single acceptable form of sexual relationship. Not because the premises of this form of marriage are false is it unable to eliminate chaos in sexual relations, but because it makes rules for average people based on the assumption that they possess the characteristics of those of superior nature.

In the deepest book on marriage and love that the German people possess, Goethe's *Elective Affinities,* we find the first attempts to address the problems of marriage in a new way. Because the path toward secularization through the state has established the dissolvable civil marriage, in theory there is no longer any reason to have a single recognized form of sexual union. The state could in principle establish a "small marriage as well as a great marriage" as Nietzsche called the concubine system alongside marriage, or in other words, an easier and a harder path to marriage, thereby establishing an actual temporary marriage. The danger that then the "great marriage" would fall out of use, is not to be feared because even today committed marriages are upheld only by those capable of doing so.

In the course of its development marriage, as we have seen, has become more and more complicated and therefore more and more difficult for married people. As a social institution for protection of the woman as for protection of fatherhood under the ruling influence of the male rights to property marriage was originally a simple and unified form of life based on a clearly identified task, procreation. With the second component, the interests of family, the difficulty emerged, that under strictly ordered relationships and among people of undistinguished souls neither the establishment of marital unity nor the task of procreation is particularly motivating. In contrast, with the third component, the interests of the individual, which requires a personal involvement through inner belonging and equality of the participants, that element enters marriage that works against the other two components and causes them to recede more and more. This opposition is expressed most pointedly in the well-known saying, "Marriage does not ennoble love, but love ennobles marriage," which implies that a marriage that has ceased to be a union of love should no longer be seen as a moral relationship.

Yet there is a barrier to bestowing practical validity on this viewpoint: namely the established social meaning of the two other components. During the long history of culture marriage had the power to ennoble sexual relationships without love playing much of a role. Even in the present marriage is governed by the trinity of ancestry, tribe, and personality. In the majority of marriages the greatest influences are played by economic advantages, combined with social and familial factors. They are the forces that still exercise the greatest power persuading individuals to marry even if they run counter to the interests of love or even the interests of procreation if the health and fertility of a certain marriage is considered.

On the path toward *worldliness* that marriage took through the intervention of the state, lie the tasks and possibilities, the external conditions for entering marriage in the sense of newly won realizations and needs. This direction can be traced in manifold social impulses. As long as the state stands for order in the life of human communities it also has a strong interest in regulating sexual behavior. For the state the number of marriages and the physical suitability of the spouses for reproduction are much more important factors than the duration of marriages or the personal relationships of love between the partners. First of all, the state, as much as it can, must facilitate marriage and support it through economic advantages – a task that it up to now has completely disregarded by allowing private and familial economic barriers to prevent marriages, whereby the chaos of premarital sexual behavior has grown, a development that is to the detriment of the state.

Indirectly economic advantages would also support the marriage of love if young people were allowed to marry at an age when the personality still had the ability to adjust. However, according to the nature of marriage it cannot be realized through legal strictures and will always remain a creation of individuals. The marriage of love lies on the path of inwardness, which does not cross the path of secularization. History shows that the attempt to merge these two tendencies into one form by advancing the state role through moral-religious concepts such as sacramental marriage has been a failure. The legacy that the past should transmit to the future is to be found in the separation of these two tendencies – at the same time also in the awareness that the idea of monogamous marriage is one of the most valuable achievements of human society, paid for by enormous individual sacrifices over the millennia.

Whatever forms marriage may take as a result of its liberation from the coercive powers left over from a dying epoch, they will have to develop through *organic* growth out of this idea. That can only happen if the tendency toward secularization with all its characteristics does not cross the tendency toward inwardness. Therein lies the actual difficulty of creating new social norms for marriage. An incomparable possession of the culture of the soul, more costly than every external order, is inwardness and nothing that reduces it can be regarded as progress in human culture.

On the Essence of Love

"And if I have prophecy and know all mysteries and all knowledge, and if I have all faith so as to move mountains, yet do not have charity, I am nothing." These are the words of the Apostle Paul in that immortal hymn to love, the thirteenth chapter of his First Letter to the Corinthians, which proclaimed to the world a new power as the highest power of life.

The ancients honored justice as the highest power of law and the highest virtue. It was an extraordinary event in the intellectual history of the West that, through the intellect, the great power of love could be discovered. Justice, which is based on decision-making, can be learned and recognized; love, however, can be seen only in its effects – what it ultimately is, Paul's praises of the glory of love does not reveal.

Love as a governing principle has not been untouched by the current apocalypse of tradition and the dismantling of our inherited values. Quite different powers are regarded as the moving forces of history, and there is no lack of attempts to create values for the individual *"più che l'amore"* (d'Annunzio).

Only in one area does love still receive high esteem and recognition as a supreme value – that is, in the realm of sexual relationships, whether in the form of free unions or of marriage. For this reason, love shall be discussed here, for insofar as love shapes sexual culture, it belongs to the subject matter of this book.

If someone simply uses the word "love" in our day, one usually means a sexually fraught condition of the mind. However, the word itself is used for such a range of diverse meanings that a closer investigation is needed. The first distinction to be made is between sexual and non-sexual love, although it is difficult to identify the essence of this difference. Those things that belong to the essence of non-sexual love cannot be separated from sexual love. Everything that can be said of the one can be said of the other, except that sexual love is connected to impulses from the sexual sphere and is therefore a more complex and more enigmatic phenomenon of the soul. Nevertheless, precisely in sexual love, although only at the highest level of the soul, the original phenomenon on which love is based emerges in its clearest and most vivid form. Thus, it is necessary to gain insight into the nature of love in general in order to understand sexual love.

The goal of an investigation into love must mean deriving the laws that govern this experience of the soul. However, the laws of attraction, based on very individualized factors, rooted in individual differences, are as subtle, as incomprehensibly complicated as these differences themselves. Our entire knowledge of the soul's experience of love is superficial and based on crude empiricism. In this area, methodical experimentation is virtually impossible. Observation of others cannot penetrate into the deepest connections, and self-observation, which is indispensable in internal matters, is also quite inadequate, for self-observation disturbs the condition of the soul because reflection distorts one's own intentions, volitions, and consciousness. Moreover self-observation is perceived as something painful, unpleasant, and inhibiting, and therefore anyone in love avoids analyzing the condition of love.

Like alcoholic intoxication, the euphoria of love is incompatible with the dominance of rationality that is necessary for self-observation, and not only in regard to the object of love but also to the condition of being in love can we apply these words of Balzac: "The more one thinks, the less one loves."

The observation of the person who has returned to the sober, so-called normal mental state has, like the observation of an outsider, the disadvantage that there is not enough data available; in fact this person may even lack access to the most significant moments. In short, the reason that love, even though it has such an immeasurably large influence in human life, has remained mysterious and unexplained a topic of knowledge lies precisely in the fact that its most important effects take place in the subconscious. Because conclusions about the subconscious can only be made through external or self-observations of symptoms, we ought not to have very high expectations of attempts to explain love, certainly not of those lacking a metaphysical dimension.

Even in primitive stages of life lacking any trace of sexual differentiation, attraction and repulsion are influential powers. Without doubt, these elemental forces have been present in all stages of the human life of the soul. However, only at a certain stage of a person's life do they acquire the significance that gives them the character of love or hate. Love as a cosmic power that holds the universe together, as claimed in ancient philosophical writings, does not deserve the name if love is merely an expression of the sex drive that briefly brings together two creatures who are inwardly indifferent to each other.

A similar misuse that has added to the confusion is the tendency to speak of "self-love." The idea that a person loves only himself or herself – a reference to the condition of exclusive concern for the narrow interests of the individual – is, however, an unclear claim because love and egoism are conflicting qualities. Thus, we must dispute Teichmüller's assertion in *The Essence of Love*, that defines "the essence of love as joy over the activity of one's own soul." According to him, love is, "in its essence, enjoyment of the self" even though it appears to be enjoyment caused by the existence of an object outside the self. In so-called self-love, one's own self is the object of inner experience, but precisely in this experience one can realize that the condition that is created through this type of inner experience in actuality has nothing to do with the essence of love. For, in general, love can only be a condition of the soul directed toward an object outside the self; the situation in which the self is occupied only with itself is in sharp contrast with the condition we refer to as love. The object of our investigation is love, understood as a certain relationship between subject and object, self and the world outside the self.

In its immediate appearance, love seems to be joy over the existence of a thing or a person, a feeling tinged with the desire to connect the thing or person to one's own being. Thus, Leibniz described love as "taking joy in the happiness of another." According to him, to love is to "consider the happiness of another as one's own." Mendelssohn calls love "a willingness to be completely satisfied with the happiness of another." Here, the element of euphoria in love is explained. However, this euphoria is only an accompaniment; it is not the sole cause of the elevated consciousness that is part of the condition of love. It is not the wish to attain pleasure for oneself through connection with a second being that leads to love but rather the attraction of the actual person. Love is a condition that, as it runs its course, brings with it much suffering as well as many joyful sensations. Anyone who has experienced love knows enough to fear love as a great misfortune to the extent that the substance of love is desire.

The eudemonic philosophy in general regards the relationship between activity and its accompanying sensation of desire in a superficial way because it overlooks the fact that all higher directions of the will aim at definite goals and not merely at the attainment of desire. The eudemonic explanation of love is thus the most inadequate. An unhappy lover, that is, a person who cannot become connected to the object of his or her love, will not be turned away from the fruitless striving for love through the satisfaction of desire brought about by some other person.

The element of euphoria in love has also led to a very one-sided conception of love, the currently widespread viewpoint that the assumed opposition between love and egoism is supported only by uncritical and superficial analysis. If a devoted lover is merely obeying his or her own need in making a sacrifice he or she desires to make, or if at least the sacrifice is the necessary means to satisfying desire, then how is this love different from other goals of enjoyment set by the individual's striving for happiness? Nietzsche expressed the problem of selflessness in love by posing this question: "One person is empty and wants to be full; another is satiated and wants to be emptied – each is driven to seek another who can serve his or her desire. And this situation, understood in its highest sense, one labels, on both sides, love – why? And love is supposed to be something that is not egotistical?" Earlier, Stirner had similar thoughts. He refused to accept the idea that there is a difference between love and egoism. He maintained that he loved humankind with conscious egoism, asserting, "I love them because love makes me happy... Because *I* cannot bear a troubled furrow on a beloved brow; therefore, for my own sake, I kiss it away."

That which is here put forth as the basic phenomenon of love in truth does not even touch on its essence. The mere need for satisfaction does not elevate the individual above the sex drive on a physical level, and in the intellectual realm, it brings forth impulses of friendship that by no means have the character of that elemental, passionate awakening of feelings accompanied by mutual connection that love has.

However, even if we include in the concept of love less enthusiastic conditions of the soul, we must make it clear that so-called selflessness in love does not lie in the *exclusion* of egoism. Love is not the condition that is opposite to egoism because it includes painful self-revelation and self-overcoming – quite the contrary, for the lover does not need to overcome the self to set the interests of the beloved person above his or her own. The interests of the beloved are not distinguished from those of the lover who perceives them as his or her own. The lover does not become "selfless" but expands through widening and extending his or her personal perceptions beyond the opposition of self and non-self. The self is not sacrificed when the ego retreats; it is not denied or suppressed. Therefore sacrifices made by the lover are not accompanied by feelings of regret. Everything that happens because of love is perceived as voluntary and joyful. The Christian precept is right in identifying the "joyful heart" as evidence that an action that an individual takes that goes against his or her egoistical interest is undertaken in love and not out of compulsion. If one compares this situation to narrow concentration on the interests of one's own person, apart from any community, it becomes apparent how far apart love is from the egoistical mindset, even if the bonds created by love are grounded in a need. To be sure, Stirner kisses away the troubled furrow on the beloved brow because *he* cannot bear it, but the important thing is *that* he cannot!

Nietzsche takes as a starting point the need for *completion,* likewise a basic element of love. As long as we think egoistically, we can only value what we are ourselves and we will seek in the outer world only the confirmation and glorification of our own essential being. As soon as we love we are able to value what is in opposition to us as if it belonged to us. We experience a particular desire to imagine and acquire a different way of being, to make it our own by giving ourselves over to it.

Hegel therefore identified the first moment of love as involving the realization "that I do not want to be an independent person just for myself, and if I were I would feel lacking and incomplete." These words contain a deep truth; the state of isolation which satisfies the egoistical person is a deficiency and deprivation for the lover. For the price of removing egoistical isolation, the lover accepts the danger of willingly taking the suffering of others onto his or her self. Not only the ability to experience the *happiness* of another as one's own belongs to the essence of love; equally important is the ability to experience the *suffering* of another as one's own.

According to the ideology that sets love at the highest rank among the values of life, namely the Christian, the substance of love is not joy. What Christendom defines as charity is basically sympathy with the needs of others, suffering with them. The Apostle Paul never says a word about love originating in lust or love being a lustful condition, but he does say, "Love endures all, believes all, hopes all, bears all." The commandment that the law of Moses provides on this subject, "Love your neighbor as yourself," means, first of all, that we should not regard the suffering of others as something that does not concern us.

At the same time the commandment of Moses points clearly to another element of love that is much more essential than feeling the pain or joy of others – the striving for unity. The commandment contains the requirement of identification. It asserts that one's neighbor should have the same place in one's consciousness as oneself. There should be no difference between one's reaction to the interests of oneself and those of others. This is the same striving for unity that is found in the Indian adage, *Tat twam asi*, or "You are you," which proclaims that through community in life the separation of subject and object, I and you, which we perceive intellectually, should be removed by our feelings. However, in Indian philosophy the change that erases the difference between subject and object does not have the character of love. What Buddhism understands as Nirvana has no place for love because the consciousness of the person as a subject has been extinguished.

The person, the subject, the ego, belongs essentially to the problem of love, as seen in the Christian concept of divine love which conceives of God as a person. In the ecstatic erotic fantasies of the early Middle Ages, which introduced the sublime passion of burning divine love, the relationship to God came to be expressed as a personal emotional devotion. The language in which, for example, Augustine speaks with God in his *Confessions* is exactly the same as was later taken over by Romantic sexual love. "Beloved and sublime God," cries Augustine, "inflame and enchant us, intoxicate us with your fragrance and delight us with your sweetness; cause us to love you." The actual ecstatic experience, the *unio mystica*, when one's soul pours itself into God and one feels that God is poured into one's soul, this transformation of the consciousness of the self, is the ultimate experience of love.

Without this feeling of unity out of which the particular uniqueness of love can finally be understandable, sympathy with the joy or suffering of others will not grow into love. According to Hegel, the decisive meaning of love is the sense of unity. He writes, "Love means the consciousness of my unity with another so that I do not feel isolated and my selfconsciousness gains by giving up my sense of being for myself alone in exchange for my unity with another and the other's unity with me." Here lies the incomparable and unique meaning of love: the individual is freed from the isolation that his or her consciousness of ego has created and elevated above the egocentric perspective of experience so that a transformation and expansion of the ego occurs, such as no other experience of the soul can bring about. What is praised as liberating in love consists of this expansion of the personality effected by transcending the borders set by the egocentric mind. That such a liberation can be won only at the price of dependence on another person is correct from the point of view of the self-conscious egoist. However, those who regard isolation as a limitation and who view constraint of the inner life through the law of individuation as fetters see in the loosening of this law a wonderful opportunity. Goethe called voluntary dependence the most beautiful condition – "and how would this be possible without love!"

If love leads us beyond the egocentric perspective that consciousness of the self brings with it, this means that love changes the direction of the impressions that place our own person as subject and center to such a degree that a different object may move into the center and acquire in our consciousness the same or in certain circumstances even greater significance than our own self. This change is special and incomprehensible because love, a condition of the soul related to mystical-ecstatic experience, does not create a mere intellectual identification; the transformation that love causes in the consciousness of the self reaches much deeper to affect the original experience through which we perceive and grasp our own egos.

Love is not based on processes of recognition and evaluation of other people whom we encounter in our business lives or in personal relationships. We accord people the same worth and value as we do ourselves in a sense, but that which results from rational evaluation of people is no more than respect, deference, involvement; that which results from the recognition of similarity with another person is called friendship. Respect and friendship, under favorable circumstances, accompany love, but they are not the conditions for love, and they do not constitute the essence of love.

Without the special and specific relationship to what we call the ego, the essence of love is inexplicable. However, it is just as impossible for our rational perception to comprehend the ego itself, which we perceive as immediate and always present in our consciousness. Over the course of the history of philosophy, the ego or self has been viewed in quite a variety of ways. At times, it is defined as something original and real, as a substance, then as something derivative or insubstantial, even as a fiction that can never become substantial. Older philosophers regarded the ego or self as a spiritual thing; in contrast, to the modern scientific viewpoint, it consists solely in the unity of consciousness, in the continuity of perceptions and images that are unified in the mind of the subject and focused on as a center. The self "thus signifies only the subjective pole of the consciousness to which the object stands opposite as a necessary correlate." (Drews)

If love changes the egocentric perspective that is accompanied by the consciousness of the self by placing an object at the center, this change makes the feeling of identification that is unique to love comprehensible. The ego, conceived of as the immediate consciousness of the organic unity that every individual represents, experiences a complete transformation through the internalization of a complex of perceptions whose content is the object of love. We can only say that we love when we are changed so that an organic part of our own self becomes one with the beloved, without the beloved ceasing to be an object, for only then do we have all those extraordinary illuminating experiences that transcend the borders of the ordinary life of the soul, those experiences that we recognize as the effects of love. A complete removal of the relationship between subject and object does not take place, however, in the consciousness of lovers. As an activity of the soul, love is based on the condition that the subject maintain his or her independence as inner essence and the object maintain his or her independence as a being who exists in the external world.

Love is the complete transformation of the consciousness of the self through which the individual becomes capable of forming an organic unity of the soul with a being who exists in the external world.

The specific effect of love consists of an expansion of the consciousness of the self, going beyond the boundaries of the ego, which under no other circumstances can happen in ordinary life. Herein lies love's incomparable significance, nobility, and uniqueness, as well as the sense of "salvation," that is often ascribed to love. In truth, love does save the individual from the isolation in which he or she is imprisoned by the consciousness of self. Whenever an expansion of the ego occurs to place an object, whether a person, thing, or idea, at the center of consciousness that we call the self, this occurrence is an act of love. What distinguishes a person's profession from merely earning a living is the love of a "thing," the identification of a person with a type of work. To place a thing above one's own self means nothing other than to identify with it, to fill one's sense of self so completely with it that the self is extended to make the thing a component of itself.

Because love causes a complete transformation of the consciousness of the self through growth, enlargement, expansion, it is also accompanied by an intensification of all activities of the soul, especially a growth of the euphoric potential in life that is connected to the functioning of the self. For that reason, joy is one of the essential components of love.

Although the original phenomenon of love, identification of the subject with an object of the external world, was not strictly limited to persons as objects, love attains its full form only among persons, for only a person can strengthen love by loving the subject in return. The isolated individual finds himself or herself in the consciousness of another, and, perceiving the self as part of another person, also possesses a heightened life through that person. Hebbel had this meaning of love in mind when he said, "Love means conquering oneself in another person."

II

What distinguishes sexual love as a psychological condition from love in general is, besides the passionate zeal and force that color the emotions in a particular way, a certain type of desire that, to the extent that it originates from the sexual sphere, is unique. The connections between sexual impulses and higher activities of the soul, out of which love emerges, can vary considerably. Frequently the sexual component develops gradually out of a relationship of pure friendship. In such cases a pair of lovers, if they think about the origins of their relationship, can identify a stage when their feelings for each other were "pure," that is, based on inclination free of sexual desire. How the transformation occurred however, is usually impossible to explain. Even more mysterious is "love at first sight" the "*coup de foudre*," or stroke of magic. This is the fundamental riddle of love. It has an analog in sympathy and attraction outside the sexual sphere, which can also draw people inexplicably together, but the analog provides no satisfactory explanation.

Because the natural goal of sexuality is procreation, we may wonder about the effects of this goal and whether the individual choice of mating partners, which cannot be explained by sexual desire itself, is based on hidden factors of which the participants are not consciously aware. According to this line of thinking a subconscious cause creates an attraction between a man and woman, based on their suitability to produce offspring who would benefit from their combined characteristics. In this point, the normally opposing sister fields of metaphysics and natural science converge, for both locate the basis of the stirring of attraction between two particular individuals outside of these persons themselves.

The best known metaphysical discussion, based on keen psychological observations, is provided by Schopenhauer's essay, *Metaphysics of Sexual Love*. As a sexual phenomenon of the soul, love is discussed only in the form of sympathy; in its combination with sexual impulses, he identifies it only as the state of being in love, that grip of passion that unites two persons of opposite genders on the basis of their deep but inexplicable, unmistakable attraction.

All sexuality, claims Schopenhauer, is one-sided; therefore every individual needs another one-sidedness that is opposite of his or her own, in order to create the complete human being through neutralization of opposites. Although lovers believe that through their choice of a partner they are serving their own happiness and their personal satisfaction and "speak ardently of the harmony of their souls," in truth it is only the will to life that is using them to create new human beings. The purely personal matter of choosing a mate, as expressed in the trivial saying, "Every Hans finds his Gretl," in Schopenhauer's view gives love no importance; to him all the excitement that seeking a partner creates is beside the point. Only in the subconscious seriousness of the deep penetrating look with which two young people of opposite genders regard each other does Schopenhauer see "the meditation of the genius of the species on the new individual the pair could create . . . This new individual is to some extent a new (platonic) idea. Just as all new ideas strive with great force to come into existence and eagerly seize the necessary raw material required by the laws of causality, so too does this particular idea press eagerly and forcefully toward its realization. This eagerness and forcefulness is what the passion of the two potential parents for each other actually consists of." Because, however, egoism is so great in every individual that it would prevent submission to such service if its true nature were known, "nature can reach its goal only by planting a certain illusion in individuals through which they think that they are achieving a benefit for themselves that is actually only a benefit for the species."

The idea that the instinct of the species carries out a kind of trickery on the individual is a favorite notion of Schopenhauer's. It is the basis for his entire theory of sexual love: both partners in love are duped by a metaphysical practical jokester who uses nature to carry out this trickery of natural instinct on the human race.

However, if it were true that the sole purpose of the attraction of love were the creation of a person with certain characteristics, love could not last beyond the birth of this person. Moreover, the custom of marriage for love has been limited to certain places and times and has actually prevailed only during brief interludes of human history; therefore, the creation of particular individuals cannot be dependent upon the passion of love.

Schopenhauer thought that the significance of matters of love could only be explained by regarding them *sub specie aeternitatis*, that is, not from the point of view of individual happiness but only as serving the interests of the species. In this light, love has meaning and value only as a principle of creation. Only because the secret purpose of the passion of love is the precise determination of the characteristics of the next generation does it possess the importance that the naive mind grants it; as a personal matter between two participants, it can claim no widespread interest.

However, if human life as such is thus labeled insignificant, the personal fate of a mortal individual unimportant, what importance then does human reproduction have? Why should future generations be of more worth than the present one if their task is once again only to sire another completely unimportant generation and so forth into eternity? If life as a principle of being has value and significance, but the individual has no other purpose than bestowing this empty and fleeting life onto the next creature, then we should have no interest in the existence of any future generations and the seriousness and zeal with which particular lovers bring about their unions should be as unimportant to the species.

This metaphysical explanation of sexual love is lacking because it gives short shrift to the personality of the individual; however the natural sciences hardly do any better. They also regard the function of love as unimportant in itself, as serving the interests of offspring, not the lovers as parents. Love is defined "as the intuitive recognition of the most complementary conjugal partner at a certain time" and "as the secret recognition of the best choices for the purposes of the species" (Lomer, *Love and Psychosis*). This viewpoint makes the lover the servant of the selective will of nature. Another explanation grants that at least some of the impetus to love serves the individual interest, insofar as the attraction of love is regarded as a sign that union with the beloved person will guarantee renewal of the self in reproduction.

Hermann Swoboda says: "We have good reason to assume that in the feeling of attraction to another person of the opposite sex there is as much knowledge as can be brought to bear through eager research; if someone willfully insists on the choice of a certain partner... then it may well be that only through union with that person is a real maintenance of the self possible."

The determiner of attraction in love is no longer viewed metaphysically as the striving of a creature for a certain unbounded individuality but as a material cause, cell plasma, which is the means whereby an organism is able to carry on life and attain a kind of immortality. Just as gender-differentiated cells constitute the morphological principle in the animal kingdom, they also are said to have the potential that will lead to the discovery of the individual best suited to produce perfect offspring.

A theory from natural science that goes one step further can also be hypothetically applied to human eroticism. One can identify reactions in the lower organisms that are caused by chemical stimulation. The causes of such stimulation are the sense of smell or other specific senses whose functions do not play a role in the consciousness of higher organisms. Such chemotropical effects, not directly perceptible by our conscious minds, are said to underlie relationships of human love just as they do sexual attraction in all other sexually differentiated species.

As far as observed evidence goes, individual erotic attraction in human beings does point to an unknown physical agency. The particular sensation of desire that physical contact, the sense of touch, awakens under certain circumstances seems to justify the assertion that a physical or chemical connection between two people is the primary cause of sexual attraction, even if we know nothing about the nature of this substratum of relationships. In a book on the nature of love by Magnus Hirschfeld, which primarily discusses the sensual side of sexual love, what we perceive as love is defined as a certain type of vibrations, "which are caused by specific external stimulations of nerve receptors in our bodies." According to Hirschfeld, love and the sex drive cause "a movement of molecules that courses through the nervous system in a specific way, similar to the movement of heat, light, or electricity moving through a body, and about which we can say a great deal, without being able to identify its exact molecular structure."

This theory does not delve into the relationship of these chemotropic influences to the presumed evolutionary purposes of erotic selection; to all appearances, it ought not because experience tells us that children conceived in love are not noticeably superior to children conceived through the sex drive alone, nor are they more similar to their parents.

In any case, the consciousness of the lover is absolutely directed toward the interests of one certain person. In the first stages of sexual love, in which the aspect of the soul is dominant in the attraction, sexual motivation is subordinate; it does not appear as something present at the beginning, as a primary cause but rather as something added and secondary. If barriers to sexual union present themselves, it often happens that love remains on the second level and the relationship does not develop further than an association forged by purely personal motivations to enjoy inner togetherness, an intimacy of souls. Indeed, the need for togetherness is so dominant in the higher stages of love that Lester Ward even identifies the essential difference between natural and romantic love in the fact that, in romantic love, passion is satisfied through the presence, not the possession of the beloved: "It appears to consist of a series of repeated sensations of the nerves that take place when the object is near but that are interrupted and blocked when it is distant."

Goethe portrays the relationship between Eduard and Ottilie in *Elective Affinities* thus: "Only the nearest proximity could quiet them, but it could completely put them at peace, and this proximity was enough; not one glance, not one word, not one gesture, not one touch was needed, only pure togetherness. Then they were not two people; they were like one person in a state of consciously perfect comfort, satisfied with themselves and with the world."

This portrayal reminds one of the interpretations of love in the form of a myth that Plato set forth in his *Symposium*. The human being originally was a double creature that was split in half by Zeus because of its pride over its perfect nature. Thereafter, when two such creatures come together into one being they seek to recreate the original unity; and the attraction that drives them to do so appears to them as love.

The common ground between this meaningful but humorous account, which Plato puts in the mouth of Aristophanes, and Schopenhauer's very serious metaphysics of love, separated by two thousand years of human thought, is the idea that through love the ideal type of human being, the complete human being, who appears one-sided as an individual, is created once again. This desire for and striving toward the whole is for Plato the essence of love – in essence it is nothing other than the highest level of expansion of the self.

Plato's discussion refers to the "harmony of souls," a phrase mocked by Schopenhauer because to him the idea is the product of a teleological illusion. It appears that the specific idea of a harmony of souls evokes strong resistance from many commentators, for example, Krafft-Ebing, in a scientific explanation of the phenomenon of love, also seems to feel compelled to express his rejection of the concept. His elucidation is not based on the interests of the progeny; rather, he limits himself to discussing love, in which he finds the sexual motivation dominant, as the primary or first cause. For the researcher, says Krafft-Ebing, the "bond of the hearts" or the "harmony of souls" of which lovers dream, is not at all "a mystery of souls, but in most cases traceable back to certain physical qualities, which in some cases may involve the soul, through which the power of attraction of the beloved person is evoked. One speaks then of the fetish and fetishism." Erotic fetishism develops when certain qualities of a person or even the objects they use, acquire powerful associations that awaken images of the whole personality. Like Binet, Krafft-Ebing seeks the source of every physiological attraction in the individual magic of fetishism and finds in fetishism the explanation for "the individual sympathies between man and woman, the preference for a certain personality above all others of the same gender."

Indeed, this is less of an explanation than merely a circumvention of the problem, for the mechanism of falling in love, inspired by certain qualities of a person's body and soul, is not explained.

The question remains: why do certain characteristics exert the magic of fetishism? Why is desire stimulated in certain individuals by certain qualities? Why do these qualities have an *erogenous* affect, that is, why do they stimulate erotic sensation in certain persons while leaving others quite indifferent? Krafft-Ebing asserts that it is a well-known fact that experiences of the soul which govern these experiences are directed by chance. The simplest explanation, he says, is that falling in love occurs when the sight of a person of the opposite sex coincides with a sensual stimulation and this sight enhances the stimulation. "Impressions of sight and feelings become associated, and the experience becomes more substantial to the extent that repeated exposure to the same image awakens the optical image in memory."

In this simplest case – the only one, by the way, mentioned by Krafft-Ebner – there is no connection with the particular individual nature of the person in love and the desired person; a completely external chance circumstance, lacking any deeper motivation, governs attraction stimulated by one person and experienced by another. This type of experience is not exactly the most revealing, not what one would select from all the diverse situations of sexual attraction, in order to gain insight into its nature.

Are there really no regular patterns to erotic attraction? Is the personality of the participants so irrelevant that under favorable circumstances any given man could fall in love with any given woman? If so, how do lovers ever arrive at the peculiar illusion that their feelings involve a harmony of souls?

One must first of all try, out of the apparently random diversity of cases of erotic attraction, to identify the cases in which certain specific characteristics can be identified. The instances of erotic attraction governed by chance, which cannot be explained by personal qualities of the participants, as described by Krafft-Ebing in his selected simplest case, naturally defy all rules. Such cases are open to all possibilities; blind Cupid chooses to force people whimsically and at random under his yoke. His victims are ordinary people whose souls, at least in the erotic sphere, are not greatly developed. Such experiences are, however, not the soil in which love's illusion of the harmony of souls can thrive. They hardly distinguish themselves from mere sexual adventures in which distinctive characteristics of the body, much less the soul, scarcely play a role. That this type of eroticism is the most ancient and the most common, one can well imagine; Gottfried Keller said, "when a truly healthy man meets a similar woman and each is inclined toward the other, a healthy love never fails to follow."

To be sure, more sensitive people also experience similar attractions caused by external chance circumstances, recognized or unrecognized. Such attractions cannot be explained by the participant's tastes, mental needs, or moods. However, even in people whose souls are developed to a high level, the illusions of the harmony of souls or mystical merging of essence do not easily form. Rather these sensations remain irresistible compulsions in the conscious mind, intimations of a dark primitive world that has taken over one's heart. Recent literature is rich in portrayals of this kind of eroticism. Often a man is the one snared by the force of a strange power and only with difficulty can he resist a certain woman after being blinded by a passion that leaves behind a dangerous trace that can never completely disappear.

It is this type of erotic experience that most clearly points to the influence of inexplicable origins, to a physical agency in nature not yet identified. It is a well-known fact that certain people possess special powers of erotic attraction that seem to have neither external nor internal causes. One could regard the erotic gifts of such people as analogous to the so-called *vis comica*, the gift of comedy, through which some people stimulate irresistible laughter simply by the way they speak or move, by their expressions and gestures. Parallel cases of eroticism occur only in special stimulating ways in which certain people present themselves, in indefinable nuances of behavior that have erotic effects. Because, however, this *vis erotica* has its strongest effects in physical contact and appears in individuals whose natures are not at all predisposed to love, one may assume that their powers of attraction are based on an unusually large amount of an as yet undiscovered physical agency; just as a particular lack thereof dooms others to erotic impotence.

The entire force of this physical agency can be recognized only in those cases in which it appears independent of the qualities that a person who has succumbed to another's *vis erotica* would otherwise hold dear, in those cases in which the affected person regards himself or herself as the victim of a blinding, irresistible power approaching insanity. The effects of physical attraction may also exist when the psyche is exerting no attraction, even, in fact, when there is an undeniable repulsion of the soul.

Not much understanding of a phenomenon is gained if one traces its origin back to unknown processes of an equally unknown physical substratum. Because, however, there is no known experimental method to investigate this hypothetical substratum, we must content ourselves with merely assuming that it exists, an assumption that offers at least some assistance in understanding the elements of eroticism.

Except for this unknown agent, the existence of which we can only assume from observing its effects, the transmitted impressions of the senses, especially those of sight and hearing, play a major role as physical requisites of eroticism. They are more comprehensible to us because they appear attractive to the consciousness even though they are not the same as general aesthetic merits. They need not give the impression of great beauty and physical perfection that erogenous experience awakens in some cases. Most people prefer a certain type, and while not all individuals of this type cause a strong reaction that leads to falling in love, they are much more likely to do so.

A certain regularity can be observed in the operation of sensual pleasure as a cause of erogenous effect; individual taste seems to be oriented toward opposites and in the realm of the physical to strive for removing the one-sidedness of the corporal nature of the individual. This principle explains the attraction between small and large people, thin and heavyset, and pairs displaying other physical contrasts. This effect of opposites belongs to the best known dimensions of erotic attraction; if it, nevertheless, is not universal and predictable, the cause thereof is to be found in the unknown physical agency that presumably stimulates erotic attraction.

These two factors of erotic attraction, which are by no means always mutual, explain the diversity and apparent chaos of erotic attraction. In addition, physiological requisites of eroticism are complicated by two contradictory factors: attraction based on affinity and attraction based on polarity. This means that not only is difference attractive, but also similarity, the latter in the sense of *confirmation* of one's own nature, the former in the sense of *completion*. The following rule can tentatively be advanced: to the extent that intellectual factors play a role in attraction, attraction is based on similarity in depth of understanding and level of intelligence; to the extent that attraction comes from the heart, opposites evoke pleasure, perceived as completion, as between natures who are strong and weak, hard and soft, forceful and mild, rigid and adaptable. If, however, physical attraction derives from the characteristics of the participants, there must be a deeper explanation of the connection between the personalities of individuals and their erotic effects, as exerted and perceived.

III

In his book on love Stendahl identified four types: passionate (*amour passion*), gallant (*amour goût*), sensual (*amour physique*), and vain (*amour de vanité*). This division corresponded more to the situation in France of his time than to love in the present; what he called *amour goût* and *amour vanité* belonged to a transitional form of sexual culture, not to the actual domain of love as an experience of the soul. The same can be said for sensual love if it lacks duration and intimacy and fails to transcend its basic level to invest a sexual experience with aesthetic value.

Among these types, only passionate love earns the name of love in the narrower sense; for only it attaches to the identification of subject and object all the accompanying elements that in their perfection attain the most intimate union of physical and psychological domains of life.

Stendahl calls the process of the soul that evokes the birth of love *crystalization*. According to him, this process begins with admiration, followed by tenderness, followed by hope. These phases of the heart correspond to the beginning of crystalization. Stehdahl explains the process by using an analogy. If an object is dipped into a saline solution, glittering crystals gradually form on it until it is completely covered. To this process, Stendahl likens the mental process characteristic of love that attaches new beauties to the beloved person through every perception. Thus, the lover reaches the point of finding the object of love beautiful without thinking about the ideal of beauty; for "in love one merely enjoys the illusion that one creates for oneself."

We learn nothing about the relationship of this illusion to its effects from Stendahl. Yet the most salient characteristic of crystalization is individualization, specific rapport with the unique nature of the beloved. The effects caused by appearance are traceable to this rapport; we interpret physical appearance as an expression of personality. If we attempt to perceive the beauty of a person as the symbolic expression of that person's ability, then what evokes individual pleasure is the symbolic aspect of appearance insofar as it mirrors a certain uniqueness. We perceive facial expressions and movements outside of the erotic realm, and we do so according to rules of perception that are not generally applicable and yet govern our behavior toward the other person, especially at the start of a relationship, before greater familiarity with a person's qualities alters our initial interpretations and influences them to one degree or another. Our sensitive perceptions of persons of the opposite gender are stronger than those we have of members of our own, and they are stronger yet when awakened by influences of a sensual type or through certain psychological-intellectual stimuli to erotic arousal. From this moment on, fantasy begins to play a role. It constructs an image of the beloved object from the needs and presumptions that emerge from our subjective natures, an image that seems to correspond to perceived characteristics of the object. These symptomatic characteristics awaken associations with our own personality and bring latent wishes to the light of consciousness. The symbolism employed, a matter of personal taste, cannot be rationally understood; however, precisely in its subjectivity the nature of our own being is expressed. If the person who has the characteristics so important to us exerts such a strong attraction that in the end we perceive him or her as something that belongs to us and from a certain point on cannot be separated from us, the reason is that through that person a piece of ourselves has actually been made real. In this person has been realized the *subjective sexual ideal* that every person carries within as a projection of his or her own nature, a wish formation created by one's own psychological constitution (see *Female Eroticism, The Subjective Sexual Idol*).

Certain symptomatic characteristics that one can call *erogenous characteristics* operate on the individual as "magical fetishes" because they awaken in his or her imagination the immanent image that, if ever so shadowy and unclear, is the object of his or her secret yearning. The more aspects of the image are supplied by erogenous characteristics, the more completely they are confirmed; the more vivid and lively they are, the more inwardly connected the lover feels with the object of his or her attraction, and the sooner arises the illusion that one's "other half," or alter ego has been found, that a wonderful and secret "harmony of souls" exists that has filled the lover with intoxicating happiness. The immeasurable pain that seizes a lover whose feelings are not returned or who must separate from the beloved can be explained by the fact that such an unhappy lover has been deeply wounded in the center of his or her consciousness, in the self that has merged with the beloved person into a unity – for the essence of love is precisely the identification of one's own self with the self of another person, that modification of the consciousness of self through which we are capable of creating an organic union of the soul with a second creature.

The laws of these processes, their determination through the particular nature of every individual, emerge completely only in sexual love, for this is in its relationship to the object completely and totally dependent upon one's own individuality. Also in this point, it differs from every other type of love, such as love of parents, whose relationship to the object is not at all or only slightly determined by individualization because in most cases it is extended over several children. In this kind of love, identification is not created by personal motivation but rather through the feeling of connection and belonging bestowed by nature. One can say the same of the love for children and one could even maintain that these types of love are the more perfect, the less they are determined by personal motivation, the more dominant in the relationship is the feeling of natural belonging.

The situation of sexual love is exactly the reverse, for its particular distinction is personal motivation and its perfection results from the growth of individualization. In its basic form, it is also based on a natural connection – that of a man and woman brought together in service of the purposes of the species.

In no other kind of love, no matter how highly developed, is the image of the other person a second self, perceived as the other half of one's essence. This exchange of souls belongs only to highly developed sexual love, and its special significance is undoubtedly dependent upon the particular people involved, not the purposes of the species. The lover is thus not made into a fool by the species but by his or her own self, which attaches its own subjective wishes and needs to the beloved object without possessing any assurance that the impressions it is following are accurate.

"The combination of qualities that make up our own special person, different from all others and that give rise to the content of the self-image mirrored in our consciousness engenders, to some extent as a byproduct, more or less sharply outlined, a complementary image that we project onto the outside world and seek to realize in individuals of the opposite sex." (*The Subjective Sexual Idol*) This creation by our subjective person determines the image, in our thinking and perceptions, that we have of what a man or a woman in general is; real experiences form only the raw material; the blueprint has been created by our individual natures. Fitting our need for completion, the composite idol that everyone's fantasy creates from members of the opposite sex displays the traits that will lead to our own completion, in certain respects even a reversal of our own natures. It appears in the psyche like the complementary color of our eyes. This subjective idol plays a decisive role in relationships of love, and its transmission through projection onto a particular real person is assured by erotic signs.

The opposition on which the image of completion rests is thus not to be taken so generally as to suggest that everyone seeks the partner with the fewest possible similarities to him- or herself. Often it is assumed that the strongest attraction arises between the most masculine man and the most feminine woman as sexual opposites. Such general oppositions are, however, much too superficial. Without the subtle penetration into the individual constitution of the personality, the erogenous effects of contrasts or opposites cannot be explained. Richard Wagner made the keen observation that the love between Lohengrin and Elsa was not based on absolute difference completely remote from their own selves, but on a certain part of their natures, which contains in itself the definition of what is necessary to reach completion. In addition, when Schopenhauer says that every individual needs the complement of his or her one-sidedness in order to recreate the human type through neutralization, he is not referring to an absolute polar opposition, as between God and the Devil, but to a relative opposition through which qualities emerge, which in combination with certain other qualities perfects the human type.

It is, however, not the human type that concerns lovers, but their own individual fates, the pressures of the one-sidedness and loneliness attached to their individuality, from which they hope to be released by love. Removal of one-sidedness, neutralization, self-completion – these are just various names for the reality of sexual attraction to the soul. Wherever we perceive the symptoms of qualities that we need for neutralization, there we find the conditions for the beginning of what Stendahl called crystalization – the formation of a wished-for creature, of an idol defined by erogenous signs. The imagination makes use of perceived information and builds further with the raw material provided by subjectivity.

The idol emerges most clearly in the daydreams of the lover, whose fantasy plays with possible experiences in which he or she imagines the beloved speaking and acting according to his or her own innermost wishes. Here one's self-observation can best recognize the formation of such idols, especially if one notes a discrepancy between the traits of the real person and actual memories of that person acquired by experiences. However, in daydreams, the feeling of love overshadows conscious awareness, and wishes overshadow real memories which only return in a painful or resigned waking state.

Indeed, these processes do not merely occur in the realm of eroticism; we tend to give our imaginations plenty of room to attach hopes, expectations, and dreams to anyone with whom we interact. However, in erotic relationships the workings of the imagination have much deeper significance; in fact, one can even say that without its participation there would be no great passions in love.

The role of imagination in love, as well of that of subjective idol formation, is touched upon by Dante in the wonderful confessional text that he called *Vita nuova*, which discusses his love of Beatrice and the relationship of his muse to love. Dante traces the mastery of love over the soul back to the power that the imagination bestows upon love, and in spite of his unconditional devotion to his beloved, whom he calls the mistress of his soul, he nevertheless writes about the possibility that her image, which never left him, was "only an arrogance of love" designed to gain control over him. We find this self-observation, developed into a complete insight, in a modern poet, Grillparzer, who was destined to be unhappy in love because of his erotic constitution. He writes, "I believe to have discovered that I love in my beloved only the image that my imagination has made of her; as a result, I have made reality into an artistic image that delights me through its correspondence to my thoughts. I am repulsed all the more strongly by even the smallest deviation of reality from this image."

So great is the power of imagination in eroticism that the mere depiction of those qualities that have an erogenous effect on a person can, in some circumstances, inflame passion. The era when romantic sexual love moved souls with the full magical force of a new psychological attainment has provided us with numerous literary documents of such awakening of love from a distance. When the sexes were kept apart from each other by severe moral strictures, the awakening of love by description was a component of wooing in indirect fashion, and even today, it is often the first causal factor.

People to whom love is the main concern of life are such practical and self-serving experts in the science of erotic signs that their success in love is partially based on the accuracy with which they can exhibit or feign to exhibit erotic signs. All great conquerors in love, male or female, understand the applied psychology of love; they arrive unawares at the laws of love. They know what strings to pluck in order to set in motion the souls of the persons they want to impress. They know that the erotic imagination, once touched, continues to elaborate on an awakened image from within itself; their skill consists mainly of refraining from interfering with the great magician in this work. A certain distance is an important aspect of the creation of love; the imagination must have its creative room. And if Nietzsche claimed that the strongest effect of women on men is the *actio in distans,* or action from afar, this is less due to the nature of women themselves than to the nature of eroticism.

Does this mean that sexual love is just an illusion based on deceptive images? Does it mean that the lover, who directs all of his or her passionate desire toward a certain person, blinded by traits whose authenticity is not guaranteed, loves in this person only an illusion that is a reflection of his or her own self? Is love only an auto-suggestion that tricks lovers into indulging in the idea that they have found their "other halves," belonging only to them and created expressly for them?

There can be no doubt that love can be deceptive and unreliable. Deceptions and disappointments in love are such ordinary, everyday phenomena that we often do not even think of the full extent of their painful effects. There is no more disturbing drama than the fading of passion, when, soon after a couple is committed to each other, they awaken as if from a magic spell. Bound in closest intimacy, they are then taught by experience how little their loved ones really resemble the images of them that they have created. In addition, sexual feelings themselves create an intoxicating condition ending in physical release. This release brings with it the danger that the physical could extend to the psyche and that every time intoxication dissipates, passionate love could also be diminished.

How can this be? Is love not defined as the expansion of the consciousness of the self through its extension over a second creature? If all its high and noble effects are mere figments of the imagination, if love actually has no power to unite real couples in the deep intimacy promised by love, what value then has the praised transcendence of the boundaries of the self?

IV

Human beings in love are different than they are in their ordinary states; the vitality of their bodies, minds, and souls is heightened. Under the influence of the erotic charm of the beloved object, the lover is transformed to a certain degree; the influential force that the beloved emits works in sensitive natures so strongly that they are taken over and controlled; they conform to the wishes and views of the beloved without being aware of any deception. (We are not speaking of the deliberate deception and falseness rife in eroticism at the lower level.)

To the same degree that the object of love is transformed, so too is the subject. In mutual love both partners go through the same experiences of the soul and both are subject as well as object. In this way, two lovers see each other in the heightened form into which they have mutually changed each other. For them, there is no possibility of distinguishing what their normal conditions are and what belongs to the attraction of the erotic.

Those wishes and assumptions that the lover directs toward the object of love we have called the subjective idol, and the characteristics that it bestows on a certain person, erogenous signs. Qualities of the body and soul function as erogenous signs. In the perfect form of sexual love, the strongest striving for unity between material and spirit, body and soul, sensual elements and erotic elements of the soul are not separated. For this perfect love, body and soul form an inseparable unity; love takes the body, the symbol of the soul, the visual appearance, as the expression of invisible essence.

Not everyone possesses the same degree of accuracy in perceiving erogenous signs, but the happy formation of a relationship of love depends on this perception. The lack of such accuracy, the imperfection of erotic physiognomy, brings dangerous possibilities of deception with it. Yet, every heart touched by the deception of blinding external qualities succumbs to the possibility of being led astray. Certainly, people whose external characteristics attract the imagination of others, as happens with all attractive people, can easily be the cause of false interpretations. Nowhere are erogenous signs less reliable than in the face of great beauty, which seems to promise just as much inner splendor as outer and to set the viewer under a spell that clouds his or her powers of judgment. Beautiful women and handsome men frequently cause deception without intending to deceive. They often do not know themselves how different the image they project is from the one they have of themselves, do not realize the effects of their own characteristics. So it can happen that the inner tenderness of a female appearance or the vital energy contained in a masculine form is to blame for the worst errors of erotic choice when they are associated with an inner life that does not correspond at all to outer appearances.

Nevertheless, there are cases in which the aesthetic moment is decisive, not the completely unpredictable force of erotic attraction with its attendant deceptions. The interpretation of erogenous signs is generally reliable, for without doubt there is a correspondence between the external and the internal person whose nature to the practiced eye is also visible outside of the erotic realm.

Much more likely to lead to error are those elemental influences that stem from the physical agency not yet fully understood. These influences are independent of the psychological nature of their possessors, so deception is a great danger because the inner process of the origin of love in some circumstances occurs on the basis of real physical attraction. The resulting delusion can reach such intensity that the lover can misinterpret every quality of the beloved object. At this point, the attraction of love can simply be likened to succumbing to a magical spell.

This is precisely how, with incomparable poetic mockery, Shakespeare portrayed love in *A Midsummer Night's Dream*. When Titania, victimized by the scheming trickery of the sprite, admiringly caresses Bottom's donkey head, the audience reacts with mixed laughter and horror at the fateful deception with which love threatens the human heart.

Excursus on the Imaginary Self

I

Among the various sources of deception that stem from erotic attraction, there is one that has its origin in the image of the self. Only a small number of the processes that make a human being into an individualized creature are illuminated by self-reflective consciousness. As a result, a person's unique nature, insofar as it stems from the subconscious life of the soul, is of necessity hidden from the self. What appears to the rational consciousness as the self rarely conforms completely with what the real person is, the sum of his or her actual drives and capabilities. Only imperfectly, only by arduous efforts and diverse experiences can recognition of the primary foundation of one's own nature be achieved.

A person's real self is reflected in activity and behavior. What a person thinks and says about him- or herself, the reflexive self, is not reliable unless a certain degree of insight into the primary core of the self has been attained. In most people, however, there is a gap between the reflexive self and the real person that they do not realize is there. On the level of naive consciousness, all of us have the immediate certainty that no one knows us better than we know ourselves, that our self-image is accurate, complete, and the only one that is right. At the next level of awareness, we find that we possess two different selves, the one in our own consciousness and the one that others perceive. We are often quite sensitive to the gap between these two realms; we find it unjust that others do not understand our "true natures." Only at the third level, true self-recognition, can one comprehend the gap between the reflexive self, that is, the image we have of ourselves, and the real person. However, this happens so rarely that it plays virtually no role in human affairs.

Much more frequently, it happens that the imagination completely disables our power of self-observation and furnishes the reflexive self with all the desired qualities corresponding to its subjective taste. Then the reflexive self is completely identical to the imaginary self. The fantasy image often has almost no traits in common with the real person; as a result, all confrontations with reality merely lead to chaos and confusion. Such people believe themselves to be subject to dark forces of fate; they regard their own experiences as quite inexplicable, and assume that they are caused by higher powers – providence in favorable cases, demonic forces in unfavorable. Because of the dominance of their imaginations, they are incapable of perceiving the distance between their imaginary selves and their real selves or of comprehending the effects of this gap in their lives.

Nevertheless, the imaginary self does exert great suggestive powers. An individual does not act like the real person, who can only be discovered through many different experiences and interactions. Rather, it is through his or her self-image that a person achieves stature, impresses others, or exerts persuasion and charm. This is most true in erotic relationships because the imaginary self is stimulated by attraction to a beloved person. Erotic attraction intensifies awareness of the self and especially the imaginary self, and this intensification increases the power of attraction. Mutual effects result: one person receives an impression from the other; this impression strengthens his or her imaginary self so much that it not only reflects but doubles the impression perceived.

Through the imaginary self, the erotic experience becomes a comedy of disguise; the persons involved perceive each other as beings quite different from what they are in reality. They wear masks without knowing that they do. Each party wears the mask of the imaginary self for show and sees the beloved person in the mask of an idol that they project through the magic lantern of their own inner selves. A complicated intrigue of shorter or longer duration is played out until the partners take off their masks. This tragicomedy does not end with the death of the heroes, but the death of their masks signifies the death of the attraction of love.

The illusory quality of the images of the object of love is not visible to the lover until it is joined to an unsuitable person; the extent of the power of his or her own illusions still remains hidden. The greater the distance between the real person and the reflexive self, the greater is the danger of deception. One can say that the inner and outer harmony of life in an individual is proportional to the relationship of the reflexive self and the real person. The more the two coincide, the more unified and reliable is the personality and the less likely is disappointment. In matters of love in particular, the correspondence between the reflexive self and the real person is one of the greatest advantages; where that idol of the self, the imaginary self, is completely missing, and along with it the self-delusion that causes so many false moves, the danger of deception is greatly lessened. However, erotic attraction is also lessened. Dull individuals who lack feeling and imagination are not the heroes of passionate adventures of love. For people like Casanova, happiness comes not only from their *vis erotica* but also from their richly adorned imaginary selves.

If one considers the many possibilities of deception in love, one can hardly resist the impression that love itself is actually an illusory condition, an intoxication of the soul whose value and significance in human relationships has been greatly overestimated. Why is it that our self-consciousness values the unfounded inclinations of love so much more than respect based on rational reasons? Does this value stem merely from ignorance of the true nature of love? Do we become swept up in the illusory belief that our deepest and truest essence has had a profound effect on someone when actually only our minor and chance characteristics have caused that person to idolize us?

No matter how unreliable erotic signs are, how numerous the errors that result from subjective judgments, it happens nevertheless that they are confirmed by experience. *The confirmation of erotic signs* occurs when we *in reality* find in the beloved person the qualities that we assume are there, based on our own natures. To the extent that we are disappointed in these assumptions, our attraction grows cold or even turns to hate according to the law of opposite reactions; to the extent, however, that these assumptions are confirmed, attraction deepens and grows into a lasting process of increased togetherness. When it happens that the real person surpasses the immanent image in decisive aspects, togetherness can become an inexhaustible source of ever renewed attraction and everything that love promises is realized.

According to its nature, love is directed toward an object that appears as a part of the self and at the same time leads toward a completion beyond the self. The relationship of person to object is determined by the nature of one in combination with the other. What the lover seeks above all, what gladdens him or her the most, is the confirmation of the presumed qualities in the person who is the object of love. The stronger the feeling of inner unity through such confirmation, the sooner does the real person take the place of the imaginary idol. The wonderful ability of the lover to perceive and understand the innermost hidden essence of the beloved person rests on a pre-established relationship that involves the whole self and an intuition through which the whole self needs the loved one as its other half to create a whole.

That such an experience is caused by a real person in the real world is of the same decisive meaning in love as is the realization of any other striving. As little as we are satisfied by fulfillment of our goals in mere dreams, can we be satisfied with love of a mere idol. The idea that our feelings are not attached to a real person but to a product of our own fantasy would completely destroy the happiness that love brings with it. In order to achieve fulfillment, the lover accepts flaws in the beloved object and tolerates them for the sake of belonging to a real person. Thus, one may say: the goal of love as an experience of the soul is identification with a real person – the means thereto is the formation of an idol that can come into existence only with the assistance of the imagination. Without idolization the feeling of inner union and essential belonging cannot emerge because only through these feelings are the borders transcended which separate the egocentric self from all other persons. Mere esteem, which involves no idolization, brings about no transcendence of the borders of the ego, no identification or oneness with another.

Of course, this relationship between the idol and the real person as beloved object in the lovers' psyche is often quite difficult to untangle. If we consider a bond of love between two people, who can say which is dominant: the precise knowledge that they have of each other or the illusion that each creates of the other? If we regard the tendencies of love in its highest expressions, however, we shall see that striving for such inner nearness, such complete devotion, can only be satisfied by the union of the souls of two real persons.

II

Although the conscious content of love cannot be transmitted by teaching nor conveyed through communication, although love cannot be learned or taught like intellectual subjects, love, at its highest levels, as experienced by the most diverse people of both genders, has strikingly similar aspects. The person gripped by love experiences it not only as a feeling but also as belonging to the world of ideas. Such individuals spontaneously report similar ideas about the essence and effects of love although, of course, they differ according to the degree and extent of the erotic experience. The formation of every relationship rests upon these concepts or ideas of love; it is they that determine the spiritual level, the richness of the soul's involvement, the fullness of inner connection. That they emerge *spontaneously* from the sensations of the lovers is characteristic of the condition of love. To be sure, sexual impulses also emerge spontaneously in every individual and lead to similar results; however, sexuality comes from basic drives and causes behaviors led by drives, while the ideas associated with love are purely intellectual; they are ideas in the subjective-psychological sense.

The ideas of love in this sense set the goals that determine the thoughts and actions of the person in love, whose consciousness of the self has merged with another person to create a unity. As soon as the realization of these ideas enters the realm of possibility, one can no longer call them illusions; the ideas of love then attain the same rank as other ideas people commit themselves to bringing to fruition.

The following quotations provide inductive support for this point of view. The fact that they are taken from the letters and writings of prominent people could give the impression that the concepts of love are produced only by the artistically productive imagination. The superior talents of these people enable them to express the concepts with greater fluidity, artistry, and perfection, but the thoughts of love are in the consciousness of most lovers. If the private correspondence of average people were as available to us as is that of the famous, this could be easily proven. Whoever knows the euphoria of love from personal experience will recognize the universal meaning of these quotations; each provides just one example among countless others that could be collected.

All lovers know, to a greater or lesser extent, that a change is taking place inside them which gives their feelings and actions a new form; because of this change, lovers perceive themselves as new people. The conception of love *as creating a new being, as becoming a new person, as a rebirth* appears in striking utterances by people of the most diverse sorts. We encounter it as far back in history as the words of that peerless genius of noble and sublime love, Dante, who dates his "New Life" as beginning the moment that he first caught sight of Beatrice.

In one of his letters to Madame von Houdetot, Rousseau portrays the effects of love thus: "This invisible flame that gave me a second life, more precious than the first, restored to my soul as well as my senses the entire power of youth."

Similarly, Lenau wrote to Sophie Löwenthal: "The circle of my life has closed.... I am as reborn. Even if I should perish as other mortals, I shall still feel reconciled with the Heavenly Powers."

Julie de l'Éspinasse wrote to Count Guibert: "My dear friend, you have divine powers. With three words you created a new soul in me."

Herder wrote to Karoline Flachsland, who later became his wife: "You ask whether I will forget you when we are apart? Does one forget a new way of existing and its cause?"

Ninon de Lenclos wrote: "Do you know what I mean by love when I sometimes speak of it? A high, powerful, active feeling that transforms the self and makes a person so different from his or her previous self that he or she becomes another person."

What connects these ideas of lovers immediately to the idea of transformation and brings in a causal factor is the idea of identification through merging two beings into an inseparable unity, the idea of undissolvable union and commonality. Alexander

Herzen wrote to his fiancée, Natalie: "You, my angel, have caused me to experience a merging of two souls into one, as noble as a reconciliation of humanity with God."

Wilhelm von Humboldt wrote to Henriette Herz: "You say that you have become happier through me? Oh, how transported I was when I read this part of your letter! It seemed to me as if our souls were not just kindred, but that they were one soul, one!"

Goethe wrote to Frau von Stein: "To me, you have become transubstantiated into all objects. I see everything quite well and yet see you everywhere. I am neither absent nor distracted and yet am always with you and always occupied with you. . . . Yes, dear Lotte, now it is at last clear to me that you are and will always continue to be my other half."

The same idea, even more unconditionally expressed, appears in the words of Robert Browning, who wrote to Elizabeth Barrett: "I wish, more earnestly than I have ever known that a person can wish, to belong to you . . and as far as is possible in this life and in this world, to be you."

And, taking to new heights the sharpest insight into the relationship of love to the consciousness of the self, Julie de l'Éspinasse wrote to Guibert: "The 'I' is an illusion. I feel so certain that I am not I, I am you, and in order to be you I need give up nothing in myself. *Your* interests, *your* inclinations, *your* happiness, *your* joys – that is the I that is dear to me, and precious and familiar."

Hebbel expressed the same idea in a letter to Elise Lensing, justifying using a dream she had shared with him in one of his books: "As a poet, I would never take or borrow the smallest thing from any other writer in the world. . . . .but you are an exception. . . . And why is that? Because you belong completely to my essential being, because between us there is no border at all."

With these words, Hebbel was perhaps also giving an explanation of how Goethe could so casually appropriate the poems of Marianne von Willemer and include them as his own in his *West-Eastern Divan*. This feeling of unity in love that erases the borders between two people was strongly emphasized by Goethe. It reached its highpoint in his relationship to Frau von

Stein, in which the idea of identification grew into the *image of metaphysical connection, the timeless unity of being*, which took on a thoroughly religious-mystical character. In one letter to Frau von Stein he added this verse:

"Tell me, what does fate have in store for us; tell me, how did it bind us so purely together? Oh, in the far distant past, you must have been my sister or my wife!"

In his passionate way, Schiller asked his beloved Laura, "Connected forever to your mouth, who will reveal to me the desire of my passion?" and he found the answer in the concept of the metaphysical unity of being: "Were our beings already interwoven? Did we already melt into one in the beams of suns, now extinguished? Yes, we did! . . . In an eternally connected existence we were once a god."

Friedrich Schlegel said in *Lucinde*: "We two will one day see in one spirit that we are blossoms of a simple plant or petals of a single flower and we will smile and know then that what we now call hope is actually memory."

A sonnet by Dante Gabriel Rossetti confesses: ". . . when first I saw you, seemed it, love, that among souls allied to mine was yet one nearer kindred than life hinted of. O born with me somewhere that men forget. . . .my soul's birth-partner . . !" And not only in poetic form, where it could be interpreted as perhaps a rhetorical exaggeration, does this concept appear; Mörike wrote to Louise Rau: "It seems to me as if we had belonged to each other for eternities, and yet – what a strange paradox – it seems to me also as if I must just today learn to experience and understand this truth."

Lenau wrote to Sophie Löwenthal: "Your birth will profoundly affect my life on earth and my eternal life. I have the strongest certainty of that. . . . Everywhere I feel God's hand, I also feel your dear hand; I often cannot distinguish between the two."

With the difference that the unity is not grounded in an ancient connection but directed toward dissolution after death, the same idea appears in the o*pus metaphysicum* of noble music and noble love, in *Tristan and Isolde*. The keen metaphysical sense of these two lovers leads to striving for unity, to the merging of subject and object, and therewith to the erasing of love itself because the consciousness of love is dependent on the nature of subject and object and receives its entire meaning from this nature. The "sweet little word *and*" prevents this separation, for with the end of the person comes the end of love. If Tristan is no longer Tristan, and Isolde is no longer Isolde, then love leads to the "love death," for which they long, "in order to be inseparable, eternally united, without end, without awakening, nameless . . . . only to live in love" – and at the same time to die for love.

Even if it is not necessarily the essence of personal bonds of love, the secret, hidden relationship between love and death runs deep. Death is the condition of the renewal of life, and conception as a means of renewal of life has death as a precondition. Herein lies the relationship of sensual love, which finds its fulfillment in sexual union, to death. For the love of the soul there is, strictly speaking, no sensual fulfillment; the marriage of souls can never realize itself as completely as the marriage of bodies. The striving for unity in the love of the soul, for which sexual union can only serve as a symbol, remains eternally unfulfilled. Therefore, in extreme cases, the idea of mutual death, of eliminating the boundaries between bodies, can exert the same seductive power as does sexual union in sensual love. Severe tension can be caused by the passion of the soul, resulting in such despair over the absence of sensual satisfaction that death is chosen as a welcome release from unsatisfiable yearning. In a certain sense, too, the condition of love, associated with the mythological archer Cupid, appears as a wound in the soul, and the self whose ego is so wounded, unlike the intact self, does not mount the slightest resistance against the temptation of non-existence – a phenomenon that emerges even at low levels of passion. Evidence of this is provided by the fact that, for various reasons, pairs of lovers frequently commit double suicide.

In the image of unending togetherness, the feeling that love is eternal reaches its highest expression although this expression is often corrupted by extreme outpourings of sentiment. However, other concepts of love give it better direction and so lead to the realm of reality. In this realm belong above all *the concepts of a secure harbor of, a home, of being safe with the beloved being.* In addition, the lover feels that the center of his or her own life is no longer the self because love has transferred the center into the beloved object instead.

Goethe wrote to Frau von Stein: "Because of your love it seems to me as if I no longer live in a tent or a cottages because I have been given a new house with a firm foundation, where I can live and die and keep all my earthly goods."

Richard Wagner wrote to Mathilde Wesendonck: "I was looking for solitude and retreat and instead I found ever more passionate yearning to find in *one* heart, in *one* certain individual the protecting, saving harbor in which I would be completely sheltered. According to the nature of the world, this could only be a loving woman."

Heloise wrote to Abelard: "As God is my witness, if you told me to do it, I would, without hesitation, follow you or go before you into Hell itself. My heart is no longer mine; I have lost it to you. If now it no longer has a place with you, it no longer has any home at all."

Lenau wrote to Sophie Löwenthal: "I cannot describe in words the feeling of security, belonging, and being cared for with which I give myself to your dear power and guardianship.... My whole life is nothing without you. You are the heart, the center of the whole world that I am."

Mörike wrote to Louise Rau, when he spoke of the zealous honesty he felt that she compelled him to express, "If I ever failed to live up to this duty, I would feel a twofold pain immediately in my own heart: I would live separated from myself and be like a man who avoided his own home out of stubbornness."

These words of Mörike's contain another idea of love – *that of truly knowing each other through zealous honesty and devotion.* Herein is mirrored love's striving toward the true understanding of a real person, surpassing every self-delusion, which is possible only through love. Mörike goes on to say, "You are the only creature who understands how to appreciate me (in the truest attainment of innermost truth); likewise, I am the only one who can lift the veil from the beautiful secret of your soul, of all your thoughts, feelings, characteristics, and expressions."

These two concepts of love and the relationship between them are brought out by Novalis, who has his Heinrich von Ofterdingen say: "Dear Mathilde, it pains me greatly that I cannot say everything to you at once, that I cannot immediately bestow on you my whole heart. . . . My entire being is destined to unite with yours. Only utter devotion can be commensurate with my love. My love is this devotion. It is a secret merging of our own most secret and most unique selves."

Robert Schumann wrote to Clara Wieck: "I want to reveal to you my innermost self, which I have never shown to anyone; you must know everything about me because you are the dearest creature to me, next to God."

Julie de l'Éspinasse wrote to Guibert: "I will never be on my guard against you, never take anything amiss. . . . I will hide from you no stirring, no movement in my heart and never blush if I seem to you weak and full of contradictions."

Fichte wrote to Johanna Maria Rahn: "I have never before experienced such an inner trust, unaccompanied by any suspicion that you could ever deceive me, nor such a desire that you could know me completely, just as I am, unaccompanied by any wish to hide myself from you."

Lenau wrote to Sophie Löwenthal: "The vanity I display to you, my desire to show you everything that I think and say and write, strictly speaking, is not vanity, but rather the expression of a great wish, dominating my whole being, to give myself completely to you. . . ." Yes, this great lover not only wants to give complete expression to his love, but also the essence of love mirrors itself in his consciousness more clearly than does anything else. Thus, he also says of the lady of his heart: "What she thinks about me is a part of my self-consciousness because, except for myself, no one knows me except for my dear Sophie." His feeling of unity was so intense that it extended into his productive activity. "Who has genius?" he wrote to his beloved. "Can a woman possess it? Foolish question! The man and the woman have it together. Before I knew love, I was working with half a soul, and I will have to do so again if I am separated from you."

In this statement is revealed at the same time the *most widespread and most fruitful concept of love – that of completion and perfection through the beloved being.* Immermann, similarly to Lenau, wrote, "The voice of my bosom was right when it told me that Marianne makes me into what I can become on earth. She is the one who really makes me into a poet."

Beethoven wrote to Bettina von Arnim: "God! If I could have such interludes with you as Goethe enjoyed, believe me, I would have produced much greater creations. . . . So much was bestowed upon me when I became acquainted with you. . . The most beautiful themes were transmitted from your eyes into my heart."

Schiller wrote to Lotte: "I no longer belong to myself. When I encounter something great in myself, I am enchanted only by the thought that I may become worthy of you, that I may come nearer to the image your love makes of me."

Similar words were written by Herder to his fiancée. He wrote that she accompanied him on his life's journey to be his muse, his companion, his invisible friend, and to lift him up to what he never could have become on his own. He concludes with the cry, "Oh God, if only I were more worthy of your love!" However, she answers with the same idea: "You, my Herder, you give me life and bliss and expand my soul – but I give you nothing but a good, faithful and complete love. . . . How often I endure pangs of suffering over my own nothingness!"

The same competition between lovers, each to place him- or herself lower than the other, is found in the letters exchanged by Barrett and Browning, whose love has the perfected quality of that between two superior individuals. Robert Browning wrote of the "strange uncertainty" regarding Elizabeth and the assessment of their love, that is, "the difficulty of identifying the giver and the receiver . . . . I cannot find a single point in which a rational person would see me as a benefactor and you as the recipient. . . . I know that you are immeasurably superior to me. . ." However, again and again, Elizabeth returned to her assertion, "You are in the position to choose, and you could have chosen better . . . It is only your love that has created a high plane for us both where we can meet each other and stand next to each other." Yet, Robert insists on his viewpoint, "Why do you belong to me if not to make me better and therefore happier? . . . Make me better – I would like to breathe and live and move according to your will and your permission – for I belong entirely, entirely to you."

That the idea of completion and perfection occurs not through the superiority of the object but through the effects on the subject of the condition of love itself is demonstrated most clearly when lovers are not equals in terms of soul and intellect, as in the case of Barrett and Browning, or for example, in that of Goethe and Charlotte von Stein. Here Goethe's own erotic genius is revealed in an inexhaustible outpouring of expression of feelings, among which the idea of completion and perfection appears most often. "If I secretly am not satisfied with myself, then you are like the ancient serpent I must encounter and get past to rectify my sins and mistakes and become healthy. . . . I would like to devote my life to you, my whole self, in order to receive myself back from *your* hands." Again and again, he asks the beloved woman to create him and reform him according to her wishes so that he can remain worthy of her, and just as often, he attests that she is his other half, that her existence is necessary for him to become a whole person.

However, perhaps most beautifully formulated, we find the idea of perfection through love in a sonnet by Michaelangelo addressed to Vittoria Colonna:

> I am only a draft of my self,
> A draft which, through you, can become
> A noble work, oh great Lady of mine.
> Put aside my excesses with patience,
> Repair the places where I am lacking, Your Grace,
> What would then be left in me to improve?

In conclusion, in order to answer the likely objection that only artists and poets indulge in such fantasies when they fall in love, let us turn to the words of a man of action, Moltke, who wrote to his bride, Marie: "I am firmly resolved to improve myself so that I can be more worthy of you. . . The long years of oppression during which I grew up did irreversible damage to my character.

Help me from now on to improve myself."

We close this sampling of quotations with evidence of how intensely the feeling of unconditional devotion in love can develop, even in a man called the "iron fist," and cite the words of Bismarck to his beloved: "My dear, dear Johanna, I must say to you again that I love you unceasingly . . . and love you as you are and not as you should be or could be. Take advantage of me, use me as you will, mistreat me inwardly and externally if you so desire: I am completely at your disposal."

What is clearly reflected in these concepts of love is above all the essence of love itself, the metamorphosis of the consciousness of the self. They reveal the nature of the changes that take place in the lovers, as well as the inner goals toward which their thoughts and actions are directed. These can emerge in either active or passive form according to whether the lover assumes the identity of giver or receiver, subject or object. In mutual love, both parties are simultaneously subject and object; the same person may take both roles. Thus, the process of transformation can take a double form; a lover may become a new person as a subject and at the same time bring about the rebirth of his or her beloved.

In its active form, the idea of transformation emerges when negative forces, distasteful prior experiences with the love object, hinder the process of merging. Then the lover imagines that the magic of his or her influence can erase all earlier impressions in order to lead the beloved creature through his or her original purity to a new, perfected existence.

The difference between illusions of love and ideas of love can be seen in the fact that in the latter lie goals of the will that may actually be realized. Accordingly, the ideas of metaphysical connection belong to the realm of illusion. However, the ideas of transformation and merging of identities also pose the question of whether they appear in the imaginations of the lovers or belong to reality. If the essence of love consists of transformation in the consciousness of the self through the incorporation of a second person, this process would have to include a temporal change of individual perception. Yet even a psychosexual merging in the sense of a lasting change of essence in both participants would not be beyond other processes of nature if one assumes that in the spiritual world the same laws prevail as in the material. There are relevant chemical and physical analogs; even the assumption that every person possesses a certain unchanging character with fundamental characteristics is hereby not contradicted. For it belongs to the nature of certain elements of personality that they can be merged, alloyed, changed by mixing.

It was such an analog that Goethe used in *Elective Affinities* to explain the attraction of love. Just as chemical materials combine with each other or remain unaffected, just as friends and good acquaintances come together without changing each other, like wine and water, so can they also in the innermost unity form a new material, as, for example, when calcium is changed into plaster by sulphuric acid. The merging into such a new unity that takes place in spite of all external hindrances is considered in *Elective Affinities* as the basic phenomenon of love. That, however, this process is opposed to the elemental moral freedom of the individual, to which it cannot be subordinated, as soon as motives from the sphere of higher ideals come into play, belongs to the second problem of *Elective Affinities,* namely the problem of marriage.

Viewed from another direction, the same phenomenon appears in Carpenter; he believes the merging of love signifies an exchange of "ethereal and vital elements" in such a way "that within each of the affected persons through the general influence that they have on each other, a process of conception occurs that is hardly less significant than that more specialized conception that results in procreation." According to the concept of high love physical union is only the immediate sensual allegory of a higher spiritual marriage. "Just as union in the physical sphere leads to physical conception," says Carpenter, "so love as union in the realm of spirit and soul leads to conception of another type."

Even when one objects to the idea that an actual merging occurs and asserts that with the cessation of erotic experience the former person remains unchanged, one must concede that during the interludes when love exerts its strongest power, there is an apparent assimilation, which the lovers perceive as transformation through the merging of their existences.

Just as affirmative ideas of love testify to the existence of love through their results, in their negation they reveal a symptom of the lack of ability to love. There is perhaps no greater proof of the significance of these ideas in the realization of love than records of the lives of the soul of those who are not able to love. An example is provided by the great poet whose love relationships have presented many riddles – Grillparzer. In his literary creations, there is so much tragic emphasis on erotic inadequacy that one must seek its basis in his lack of love and in his psychological constitution. His basic conception of the relationship between self and world, as he expresses it in the poem "Resignation," is hostile to love. Devotion seems to him to be a loss of the self; everything that causes joy or enjoyment seems to him to carry the threat of dependence, for we are bound by the things that attract us: "only when released from having them . . . do you receive that which is yours alone – your own self!"

However, in the unsettling poem "Incubus," he discusses the disturbing nature of the unreachable, closed self.: "Shuddering I saw it; I was filled with horror when my own self rose up against me" – a self in which doubt and distrust rule as evil demons. The conditions of love are irreconcilable with such a disposition of the soul, and so we find in Grillparzer a deep understanding of these conditions but no ability to bring them into being. Even during the transport of erotic experience, he never loses the feeling of strangeness regarding the creature that attracts him: "Hear this confession now, as it is torn from me: I never knew you, nor do I know you now. . . That which was opened up to me, your inner being, still remains closed to me to this very day." How disturbing is that portrait of the vain effort to come nearer to another, to merge with another, intensified into an agonizing ordeal, contained in *Memories of Green Youth*: "In burning desire, we fell together . . . but the flames found us indestructible; we smoldered, but, alas, we did not melt, for only halves can fit together: I was a whole and she was as well. She wanted to forsake her deepest essence, but it was all too firmly wound . . . she remained a woman and I remained, as always, myself."

III

It is one of the most meaningful effects of love that it removes the distinction between subject and object, man and woman. In ordinary life, the man perceives himself as subject, the woman as object; in love, however, both parties are equally subject and object, bearer of love and object of love. Also the ideas of love are in their content quite the same for both genders. Whoever studies the literature of love letters on this point will find no differences. In any case one could also argue that the idea of transformation in its active form appears mostly in women, in its passive form mostly in men – thus, quite opposite from the usual situation. The man desires to be saved by female love, the woman through her love to bring about salvation.

One need carry out no deep psychological analysis of gender differences to explain this reversal. The fact that the man usually perceives himself as a restless, changeable, confused being who must be led by the love of a noble woman to a more harmonious and purer life is less a result of his erotic nature than his way of life, which causes conflict between the demands of his sexuality and his social situation. Therefore, it happens that the man has early experiences that he does not like to remember after he has become acquainted with the higher forms of love; he wants to be "saved" from them by love. The woman, in contrast, must believe that she can bring about his salvation from the conflict and depression of such memories in order to reach the level of relationship between subject and object that higher love requires. When the circumstances are reversed, when through character and situation the man is the unified, the woman the conflicted party, the reversal is also reflected in the roles taken with regard to the idea of this salvation.

Nevertheless, there is a general view that female love is substantially different from male. We have even heard it from women: the man wants to be the master when he loves, and a woman who does not submit to this instinct is not acting like a woman. The woman can do nothing else than be subordinate when she loves. The man wants to lay his hand on the woman as on his own property and the woman rejoices in the love that has given her a master. She can rest in his power. To give herself completely and absolutely, to hold nothing back for herself, to submit to the person of the beloved, to look to him as to a higher creature: this is what a woman wants when she is in love – many people of both genders accept this view. "Let me slumber like a child in your care! To be nothing other than my own weakness in your power, to be nothing other than something of yours that belongs to you and is your property . . . I do not want you to look up to me, to admire me; I want to be less than you; I want to stand beneath you. And then – then you will lift me up to your level." (from a novella by Louis Couperus). Or, said another way: "Man and woman each understand something different by love. . . The woman gives herself away; the man takes the beloved and adds her to his own being – I think that no social contract and no intentions to pursue justice can remove this contrast in nature." However, as Nietzsche goes on, should there nevertheless exist men who love with the need for complete devotion, then they are – not really men.

Instead of explicating further discourse about love, let us compare the words of one of the most perfected men ever to appear in the human race, a master of love who knew and enjoyed the heights and depths of love more than any other mortal. "I would like to devote my life completely to you in order to receive myself back from your hands. This has already partially occurred, and that is what I like best about myself. . . It would be best if you never cease creating and forming me so that I will remain worthy of you. . . . I am always yours and with you, more a part of you than can be comprehended. I am no longer a solitary, independent creature. All my weaknesses are supported by you, my vulnerabilities protected by you, my gaps filled by you. . . Your distance from me is a true test of my self. I see how little I exist for myself and how necessary to me your existence remains, for through you my existence will become a whole."

One has reason, in matters of love, to rely more on the authority of Goethe than of Nietzsche, who never maintained a relationship of love, and never initiated a strong erotic attraction nor experienced one. Goethe, however, possessed in his erotic experience what another man adept in noble love, Friedrich Schlegel, called the "third and highest degree of the art of love," namely "the enduring feeling of harmonious warmth. A youth who achieves it loves not only like a man but at the same time like a woman. . . In him humanity is perfected; he has climbed to the summit of life."

That devotion without limits is the deepest essence of love and not only of female love is confirmed by all those who have truly understood love, as can be seen in the above quotations. Therefore, Schleiermacher places these words in the mouth of a woman: "Should love be an unchanging feeling only in us, completely developed in all its dimensions and expressions, while in you every dimension can move and change? . . . That is not the difference between the genders; the difference lies in degree, the separation of the elements. If it occurs only for a moment at a time, it still signifies a lack of development and immaturity."

Of course, this view of love comes from another time in history. Are we to believe that men at that time were so feminized in their erotic perceptions? And that the modern view of the differences between the genders in their manner of loving should be regarded as a symptom of a deeply rooted differentiation of the life of the soul? Or has the estrangement between the genders merely grown, while simultaneously the immediate as well as the theoretical knowledge of what constitutes the essence of love has been disappearing?

It is striking how often in modern literature we encounter a conception of love which assumes that sexual love involves an "egoism of two" or even a hostile battle between the sexes, as Nietzsche claimed when he wrote of the deadly hatred of the genders in love. "That sensual love inevitably moves toward hatred" is the underlying thought in Bourget's *Physiology of Modern Love* in which all the forms of sexual relationships are shown to be destroyed by the influences of civilization. In the end, Bourget portrays limitless and unchangeable devotion as a type of genuine love – not in the person of a woman but of a man. Corresponding examples of noble love can also be found frequently in Russian literature of the past century, in

Chernichevksi (*What to Do?*), Gontcharov (*The Fall*) and Dostoyevski, who created in the novel *The Idiot* one of the world's most moving portrayals of utmost devotion in love.

Even the paradoxical assertion that the difference between genders is not of great consequence in sexual love can be defended. As unacceptable as it sounds to many modern ears, the phenomenon that we know today as love between a man and a woman has often been regarded as the same as love between members of the same sex. Plato's *Symposium*, the first great work of Western culture about love, is exclusively about love between men; according to its descriptions, there is no difference between the relationships of male lovers and love between men and women. Likewise, in our day, homosexual love is the mirror image of heterosexual love – from the beautiful and noble ideas of striving for unity of the soul to all the illusions and delusions, the jealousy, the pain of love and feelings of dependence, all the way to the quarrels and petty intrigues so typical of homosexual love. The psychology of homosexual love is exactly the same as that of heterosexual love – after all, the essential aspect of the latter is not a man's dependence on a woman but the fact that two creatures, at first strange to each other, become connected by a mysterious power; this happens in both types of love.

Nowhere are the rights of individuality more unconditional than in the realm of love; at the same time, nowhere is the possibility of generalizing less. Everyone loves in his or her own way, completely according to the inner necessity of his or her being; love develops independent of all outer laws and of the lover's own plans and intentions.

In addition, there is another fact associated with love that is totally at odds with the monogamous interests of sexual relationships as arrangements to benefit procreation. We all would surely concede that whenever love has no sexual aspect, it need not be limited to a single person; the self can extend love to a multitude of people and things. It is self-evident in human love or charity in the highest sense, as exhibited in the characters of the Christian saints or in ordinary life in the love of parents or siblings that an indeterminately large number of objects can enjoy the same connection to the subject, and no one, except perhaps those motivated by feelings of jealousy and striving to be someone's exclusive object of love, would see therein a danger to or a lessening of love.

Sexual love is different. Its status in the realm of moral values is completely determined by exclusivity in the relationship between one man and one woman. Its moral value stems from other motivations, however, for as inaccurate as it is to assert that love as a non-sexual phenomenon cannot be extended to several people, it is just as inaccurate regarding sexual love, which in essence is not different from the other type of love.

In spite of all moral objections, life confirms this fact with ever renewed and multiplied examples. In particular, it cannot be denied that erotic experience produces many cases of what is called "double love," love for two objects that is perceived by the subject as completely equal. Because of the views prevailing at present, men more often confess to being in love with two women even though great efforts of family members and literary historians have been exerted to try to cover up the most noble representative of double love, Schiller's relationship to the Lengefeld sisters. That women, including wealthy, prominent women, may also succumb to double love is seen in the relationships of Marianne von Willemer with her spouse and with Goethe, as well as those between Mathilde Wesendonck and her spouse along with Richard Wagner – in both cases, relationships at the highest human level for all participants.

It is not the essence of love that requires strict exclusivity but the nature of the sexual relationship. The most painful and fateful conflicts of the life of the soul are created by this dilemma. In lower natures, such conflicts are usually resolved at the expense of sexual exclusivity, in higher by renunciation. The letters from Richard Wagner to Mathilde Wesendonck are documents for the agonized greatness of such resignation. When Goethe became conscious that his attraction to Marianne was returned, he committed himself to resignation by fleeing; in *Elective Affinities*, he showed that there could be no other solution.

IV

The most meaningful difference of level in the types of love rests on the relationship of the will to long-lasting love. The long-lasting aspect, the endurance of love, is one of its highest values. The aspects of love that reflect its essence in the souls of the lovers all have endurance as a prerequisite; the cessation of love is something that is inconceivable to the lovers, analogous to the idea of one's own death. For as soon as the beloved object is perceived as a part of one's own self, separation becomes at least a partial death of the self.

If one wants to use the emergence of the will as a criterion of love, one can differentiate three levels or types of relationships between the genders – which is not to say that this division exhausts the infinite kinds of love relationships.

At the lowest level, when a sexual adventure is just beginning to involve the soul, the lovers' own selves and their interests dominate in love. The object of love has significance in the subject's consciousness only insofar as it promises a fulfillment of desire, a contribution to a more intensified enjoyment of life.

Even if a relationship acquires the character of passionate desire that causes the utmost excitement of the soul, at this level it does not lead to the phenomenon of identification, the merging of beings. The object of love is sought as an object to be possessed, and desire is extinguished soon after possession is won, with no desire for permanent love awakened. The passion involved is simply a natural attribute of the subject and provides no evidence of a strong striving for unity. This type was labeled sensual by Stendahl because the desire for the fulfillment of desire is predominant. Because of the relationship of love to the consciousness of the self and the concentration on one's own self, it can more accurately be labeled *idiopathic*.

At this level of love, idolatry plays scarcely any role; sensual pleasure does not involve much more than the satisfaction of sexual desire without significant involvement of the imagination. Only in that type of love generally referred to as *romantic* does the power of the imagination unfold its full magical power. Subjective idolatry takes control; it is so ingrained in the consciousness of the self that the projection onto the person who awakens it is perceived as caused by that person. However the transformation of the real person into an idol requires a certain distance because the lover at this level is so caught up in subjectivity that he or she fears being disturbed by contact with reality. The need for distance lends a unique quality to this type of love; it does not cease with sexual fulfillment and in extreme cases is even accompanied by a resistance to fulfillment because of the danger that it could extinguish passionate feelings. To be sure, this type of love incorporates a desire to maintain love that does not stem from the essence of love itself and is also not directed at its realization and deepening.

In contrast, the third stage is dominated by the need for nearness, the wish to overcome all subjectivity, all self-centered constraints, through complete unity with a real person. This desire encompasses an understanding of love and desire to realize its potential in a lasting bond. In this situation, a particular intellectual function of love is helpful – the understanding that grasps the faults of the beloved as the necessary reverse side of the lover's good qualities. And so this love is, precisely through these qualities, unlike common loveless sexual intercourse whose evil consists of the fact that the double nature of the human creature is ignored. Goethe gave unique expression to such love, even making the extreme statement: "He is not really in love if he does not regard the faults of his beloved as virtues." The lover does not do so out of blindness to the beloved object but rather from intuitively gaining an understanding of the true nature of the beloved from his or her immanent form. This intuitive understanding exists only when a pre-established relationship of accord prevails between the lovers, without which the realization of love could not occur.

According to Kierkegaard, romantic love stems partly from sensual beauty, partly from the beauty of the soul, and even if "its basis is primarily in the sensual realm, it nevertheless achieves nobility in the consciousness of eternity that it acquires." Because, however, this sense of eternity has no true basis, it proves to be an illusion that one can easily regard as ridiculous. "In order to bring forth the true eternity of love, a determination of the will is necessary" – it is precisely the determination of the will that is the hallmark of *marital* love.

Our task is to create a relationship of love through the will to love. That which individuals create out of their love shows the quality of their inner nature and their ability to transform what nature has bestowed upon them into products of their own personalities. Love could not maintain the highest rank among the powers of the soul if it were not also capable of achievements of the will, if it did not carry with it the drive to overcome the inner resistance that the egoistical self mounts against assimilation as well as the external resistance that life poses to the pure feelings of love. Of course, enduring love is not absolutely guaranteed in any era of human history; it must always be won anew as unity of souls, as inner accord. Through the immanent will to love, love is realized and it gains the power to transcend idolatry, to remain attached to a real person, and to continually overcome the inevitable flaws of that person.

At this point, we see why it is only at the third level of love that the connection between love and marriage can be made within the consciousness of the person of culture. Romantic love in the age of courtly love excluded the possibility that love and marriage could merge in a unified form of life; however, true understanding of married love leads to the recognition that there is no higher content of marriage than that of love. After all, at this stage love and marriage are identical. When marriage is founded on love there is no longer any difference between the two and marriage desires what love desires.

The idiopathic type of sexual love is referred to in Nietzsche's often quoted words, stating that "its means are war, its basis the deadly hatred between the genders." In the foreground of perception, the sexual force as a drive to be satisfied is completely egocentric and so does not conflict with the struggle of the individual for maintenance of the self in the external world. This fact is seen in the whole system of erotic courtship and the arts of seduction that are employed by both men and women at this level.

If, however, Nietzsche's view of love were valid, even for love at the highest level, love would be the most purposeless of all aspects of life – for no one is less equipped for a struggle than lovers, in whose consciousness the image of the beloved being rises above all other powers and effects. A lover is distinguished by identification of his or her own self with another person; how could a lover with such a compromised being conduct a struggle for the self against the very being that he or she has incorporated into that self? According to the standards of the business of the world, the stronger lover is the weaker person; in conflicts of interest between the lover and the beloved creature, the lover is subordinate to the interests of the beloved.

The unbridled drive to conquer others belongs to the realm of common life whose law is battle: love, however, removes this law and institutes a higher standard. For lovers, the right of the mightier does not exist; because lovers are governed by voluntary devotion, they cannot place value on the very thing they oppose. The conflicts of genuine love are therefore completely different from the conflicts of common life; their nobility, their beauty, their heroism stem from the fact that they belong to a higher type of existence – this is true of both nonsexual and sexual love. With good reason, the one who strove to save humanity through the highest devotion to love said: "My kingdom is not of this world" – and that man of genuine love confirmed this claim again and again in his deeds. It is significant that in the sexual realm on occasion a man who is in love refrains from attempting to seduce his beloved when he has the opportunity because he places her interests above his own. The common, worldly person who sees a man as a mere sexual being, a conqueror of women, would regard such a man as a ridiculous figure or simply be unable to believe that such a thing could happen.

It is purely a matter of fate whether love results in personal happiness or unhappiness – it depends upon the nature of the individual and the constellation of her or her external circumstances. To be sure, love can bring the greatest happiness by elevating the individual above the limits of the self, to that realm which is free of struggles between opposite forces and is dominated by the longing for release from conflict between polarities – but all this can happen only for certain superior and select people who can achieve the higher type of love because of their nature and because of favorable circumstances. Such people possess constitutions suited to the harmony of opposites as well as to merging and salvation in love, and they are so fortunate as to find within the unsuitable and inadequate masses of people the very individuals created just for them.

When love occurs between self-sufficient natures, their subjective feelings are confirmed: when attraction leads to an episode of love between insufficient natures it ends after a shorter or longer time in disappointment and the disappearance of passion. In the first case if the real person conforms to the subjective idol created by love or even surpasses it, love brings all the happiness that it promises and the couple is able to enjoy a mutual life according to the ideas that love incorporates; in the second case when the real person does not measure up and love does not fulfill any of its promises, disappointment is attached to the person and cessation of passion to the subjective situation. There is, however, another possibility – and it belongs to the negative side of love. It happens when the real person is not like the imagined idol and the subjective feelings of love nevertheless continue due to the influence of physical attraction. Then, love transforms itself into the hellish pain as it is so often portrayed, for in this case there are unending conflicts between the expectations of the self, always looking for an idol, and the actions of the love object that again and again work to demolish the image of the idol. A torturous pendulum between attraction and repulsion becomes the dominant condition in which the lovers, in conflict within themselves, turn their destructive emotions alternately against themselves and against the objects of their love. In extreme cases, murder and suicide can result. Unhappy love in this extreme, unhealthy form is perhaps as rare as the reverse situation – perfectly happy love that stems from complete accord of the lovers in terms of physical and intellectual unity and unity of their souls. Whether such a true harmony between two persons, connected in their very beings, ever occurs naturally as a gift of fate or whether it achieves lasting unity by means of the merging process of love between nearly self-sufficient natures cannot be determined. In the great majority of couples, accord is imperfect and it expresses itself unambiguously in the lack of happiness accompanying most love relationship as soon as the initial phase of enthusiasm is over.

One wonders whether there is such a thing as a special talent for love (not to be confused with talent in erotic attraction; the great conquerors of both genders almost never enjoy love as a unity of the souls).Without a doubt frequently changing one's love object weakens the ability to transform erotic transport into genuine deep love. Where there is no basis for forging a life-changing connection, as in hearts damaged by constantly changing partners, attraction is connected to the excitement of newness, which makes it superficial and fickle.

Nevertheless, it may be that, for great, rich, and passionate hearts, changing partners or even having a simultaneous multiplicity of them does not lessen the power to love. Much less favorable to love in all circumstances is another condition of the soul. Because love is a change of the consciousness of the self through merging with another creature, this process can succeed more perfectly if the condition of the soul is more unified. The conflicted person who is essentially ununified can experience love only to a limited degree. The same is true of the asexual man whose heart is incapable of being touched by love. Such men often dedicate deep devotion to their mothers or sisters; they are sometimes devoted, self-sacrificing friends, as well as passionate animal lovers; only women as objects of erotic attraction they cannot accept as components of their own selves. When they experience attraction, revulsion is simultaneously awakened in them, revulsion toward everything sexual. This oscillation of feelings, in a modest degree a general human quality, in a greater degree neuropathological, extinguishes the striving for unity with another as soon as it is awakened; a prerequisite for unity with another is unity of the self.

If one considers all the sources of painful emotions associated with love, the incalculable types of suffering caused by the beloved objects, whether from lack or inadequacy of returned love, disappointment in the beloved, imperfection of accord, fear of loss of the beloved, or jealousy of rivals, then it seems reasonable to ask whether, also judged objectively, in light of rational consideration, suffering does not outweigh joy in love.

However, rational consideration in matters of love is an inadequate tool, for it cannot lift us to the highest levels of wisdom in life. From this height, things take on a different perspective than from the standpoint of sober insight directed toward pragmatic ends. The egocentric perspective on how to live cleverly points us only to the path of life that yields the greatest amount of pleasure and the greatest avoidance of suffering, not to the path leading to the higher plane of existence, the path of the development of the soul. For love as a problem of values, the significance of suffering as such must be recognized. Love in every form worthy of the name brings with it an increase in suffering, a heightening of the ability to suffer; and all high feelings of happiness that it creates are balanced by an equal measure of suffering. If every intensification of consciousness brings to the core nature of a creature an equivalent amount of suffering, then love, an expansion of the consciousness of the self through its extension over another person, must at the very least bring the lover the expected amount of suffering that accompanies co-existence with a second party.

The more expansive the consciousness of life, the more intense is the ability to suffer. It is inextricably connected to the ability to have great, strong experiences that transcend the vulgar.

Thus, only a very shallow conception of life can offer suffering as an objection to love. Because of the way that the human soul is constituted, it needs stimulation, the disturbance of equanimity, to maintain its necessary tension, and love as the deepest disturbance of peace of mind, as the richest stimulator of the soul, is also the most fruitful and the most full of life. After all, there is nothing except love that can intensify to the same degree all abilities of experiencing life itself and cause the individual to transcend his or her limited self while simultaneously bestowing a feeling of great happiness on that self.

The history of sexual love in the Western world has been a tumultuous process. Centuries ago, dominant attitudes, based on a worldview that condemned everything sexual in order to grant love as a societal principle the highest rank, led to an unexpected differentiation of sexual drives and a new form of the relationships between the genders. If this view has, however, by no means been generally realized as a moral norm, it nevertheless exercises incomparably more power in reality than the type of love that is supposed to be the basis of the social utopia of Christendom. Two thousand years of Christian history show that a society based on relationships of love between everyone cannot be brought about; the most that can be gained seems to be a transformation not of society but rather of the personal bond of love, especially in those relationships that are enhanced by sexuality.

That the portrayal of a human life without involvement in love leaves most of us cold and that we are intensely interested in love stories is not, as Schopenhauer would have it, to be explained by the interest of procreation alone. Rather, it is because in sexual love the two highest human interests, those of the individual and the species, are woven together. As deeply as our human interest is involved in conception as an exalted miracle of physical life, just as deeply is it involved in the realization of love as the exalted miracle of psychological life. Separated from all other creatures by the borders of the self, the human being who experiences love and thereby the transcendence of these borders receives the highest gift that his or her finite nature can offer. This person enters a world in which the most wonderful gifts of humankind are revealed – the conceptual world of love. And if there is evidence that the path of human development reflects higher planes of existence, it is found in this conceptual world.

Afterword

By Susanne Hochreiter

Viennese Modernity and the So-called *Frauenfrage*

"Female development consists of the woman transforming herself from an object into a subject, from a thing to a person." (MS, 93) For Rosa Mayreder there is no doubt that this development signified the most important change in the history of culture; it was a monumental step when women became individuals with independent personalities.

Mayreder's cultural environment was Viennese Modernity, an era of manifold, important changes in music, art, and literature, as well as in the social fabric and politics of the time. Gender was also a widely discussed topic. Male philosophers, writers, psychiatrists, and physicians created a discourse on the "true" character of women. They invented "the woman" and made up an image of femininity. Otto Weininger became famous with his notorious book *Sex and Character* (1903), in which he made various claims, including the assertion that the "female" is simply incapable of contributing to culture. In this study, he reproduced and even reinforced the misogynistic views that so many men (and women) at this time shared.

As a leading feminist of the fin de siècle, Rosa Mayreder sought to lay bare and defy the predominantly misogynistic world she lived in. She traced the importance of gender in culture and its history and investigated the complex development of culture, focusing on gender as well as exploring how a culture shaped by male hegemony generated certain concepts of masculinity and femininity.

Gender and Culture (*Geschlecht und Kultur*) is Mayreder's second volume of essays. Her first book, *A Survey of the Woman Problem* (*Zur Kritik der Weiblichkeit*, 1905) was very successful and was translated into several languages. She had already planned the second volume when political and personal events made it impossible for her to continue working as she had before. Only in

1923, eighteen years later, did *Gender and Culture* come out. Even though interest in Mayreder has increased since the growth of the feminist movement in the 1980s, these essays still have not received the attention they deserve. In the past, readers were often interested in her pacifist engagement and her philosophy of love, and they hardly noticed her social criticism and political demands. Today's readers recognize her political views, but they tend to focus on *Kritik der Weiblichkeit*, often ignoring *Geschlecht und Kultur*.

Today in many respects, we have gone far beyond the restrictions women in the early twentieth century experienced. In our current state of intellectual and cultural development, we can understand Rosa Mayreder's groundbreaking work better than ever before. We know Simone de Beauvoir's *Le Deuxième Sexe* (1949). We should also get to know Rosa Mayreder's essays in *A Survey of the Woman Problem* and *Gender and Culture*.

Rosa Mayreder

Rosa Mayreder was born in 1858 as the eighth child of Franz Obermayer, a well-to-do innkeeper and owner of a popular restaurant in Vienna. Her mother was quite well read, a fact Rosa learned only later in life. Unfortunately, her mother had kept her books secret and never offered any critique of existing gender roles. Rosa suffered early on from restricted access to education despite the fact that her father, a politically liberal and self-made man, was very anxious to give his sons and daughters the best education. However, for the girls, he supported only lessons in painting and piano. Later, Rosa joined her younger brother in his Latin and Greek lessons. In addition, she attended a young lady's college in the city, which provided little intellectual stimulation. Almost everything else she learned was self-taught. At sixteen, she was interested in the works of Schopenhauer and Nietzsche, and later she was also fascinated by Richard Wagner's music. By this time, she had already gotten to know the works of Goethe and Schiller. With her multiple talents, Rosa Mayreder soon realized that she wanted to write. Music and painting would have been acceptable for a lady of her class (*"höhere Tochter"*), but writing definitely would not. She was accused of being a bluestocking, a way of discouraging female misbehavior. Not to be a "real" woman meant that she would risk losing the only possibility for a good life prescribed for a woman of her class: to marry a suitable man.

Indeed, she did marry. After four years of engagement, she celebrated her wedding to the architect Karl Mayreder in 1881. This marriage was quite happy, despite Rosa's extramarital affairs, until 1912, when Karl was diagnosed with a mental disease. For a long time, she had idealized her relationship with him as a perfect harmony of two free and equal spirits, though she fell in love with two other men. But when Karl's depression became worse, she felt her world break down and wrote in her diary that she felt that their life was "destroyed."[2] Her disappointment was, of course, very personal and excruciatingly hard for her to bear because of her intense struggle for the possibility of a partnership between woman and man based on freedom, respect, and equal rights. To live that possibility was important to her as an intellectual woman, as a feminist, and as the daughter of a patriarch who did not care at all about women's rights, aside from providing a good education for his daughters as defined by his society.

Reading Mayreder's diaries makes it clear how difficult her lifelong conflict was with the social norms that she encountered as a young girl and as a grown woman. As an adolescent, she wrote: "I suffer awfully. First they tell me the world of antique poetry is paradise ... and then they answer: 'You? You are a girl, you don't need Greek.'"[3] Mayreder's biographer, Hilde Schmölzer, explains: "The theories being constructed to keep women away from higher education were ridiculous and absurd and show once again that no argument is too silly when it is necessary to maintain the status quo in power relations."[4] Rosa Mayreder fought against specters of

---

[2] Hilde Schmölzer, Rosa Mayreder: *Ein Leben zwischen Utopie und Wirklichkeit* (Wien: Promedia, 2002), 188.
[3] Schmölzer, 37.
[4] Schmölzer, 37.

self-doubt her whole life, but she resolutely followed her beliefs, shedding her corset – in the literal and metaphorical sense. She continued the acceptable "feminine" art of painting but also started to write novels, plays, and poems as well as scholarly literature.

At the beginning of the 1890s, Mayreder became strongly involved with the women's movement. Together with Auguste Fickert and Marie Lang, she founded the General Austrian Women's Association (Allgemeiner österreichischer Frauenverein), and from 1893 until 1903, she held the office of vice-president. Her first public speech, in 1894, was about prostitution. In the city hall of Vienna, she argued against conventional concepts of decency and against state control. A few years later, in 1897, she founded an art school for women and girls, together with Marianne Hainisch and Olga Prager. She also started one of the most important feminist publications of that time, the magazine *Women's Documents* (*Dokumente der Frauen*), together with Auguste Fickert and Marie Lang; its first issue appeared in 1899. Although she quit her official activities for the Austrian Women's Association in 1903 in order to concentrate more on her writing, she continued to concern herself with its work.

Mayreder kept on writing and was productive despite the worsening illness of her husband. While those years at the beginning of the new century were disturbing to her, the most horrifying event was the outbreak of the World War I. She was shaken to the core, not only because of personal losses but also because she was witnessing the collapse of a culture that seemed to be facing its ultimate end. However, because of the acceleration of decline she had experienced since the turn of the century, she was not particularly surprised by the war. Rosa Mayreder did not understand the euphoria so many people shared about war and felt devastated by the inhumane brutality of modern weapons that reduced human beings to objects.

In the foreword to *Gender and Culture*, Mayreder delineates what tremendous changes had occurred during her life:

> Death and illness have taken a cruel toll on the
> small circle of people nearest to me, and just as

> cruelly war and disaster have taken control over the German-speaking world to which I belong. In the midst of such devastation, for a long time it seemed impossible to maintain the world of intellect. (MS, 1)

In continuing her work and publishing these essays, however, Mayreder proved to herself that she would not give in and would not allow destructive thoughts and powers to conquer her. Even though she had fundamental doubts about humankind's capability for creating an advanced and humane culture, she obviously still believed in reading, writing, thinking, intellectual discourse, and political commitment.

When Rosa Mayreder died in Vienna on January 19, 1938, the National Socialists were soon to take over Austria. The catalog that was published for the auction of her furniture and other belongings a few months later had a swastika on its cover. It was clear by then that her hopes for a better future would not come true for a long time. The barbaric Nazi dictatorship destroyed all that was left of culture, as she had understood the term.

Rosa Mayreder was a highly respected person and a well-known writer, whose work has gained considerable national and international recognition.[5] Despite this fact, her work was almost forgotten until it was rediscovered in the 1980s in the context of the new women's movement in Austria.[6] Important research on Mayreder has been contributed by Hanna Schnedl-Bubeniček, Harriet Anderson, Eva Geber, Ursula Kubes-Hofmann, Hilde Schmölzer, and the American scholars Jane Sokolosky and Kate Mittnik, all of whom understand the importance of Mayreder's

---

[5] A Czech translation of *Kritik der Weiblichkeit* was published in 1911, a Swedish translation of *Geschlecht und Kultur* in 1921, and a collection with the title *Kvinnlighet, manlighet och mänsklighet* in 1910; an English translation of *Kritik der Weiblichkeit* with the title *A Survey of the Woman Problem* was published in 1913.

[6] Except for an unpublished diploma thesis by Herta Dworschak, *Rosa Obermayer-Mayreder: Leben und Werk*, (Universität Wien, 1949).

work and have provided invaluable insights into her thinking. Despite their groundbreaking studies, additional research is needed before Mayreder's significance is fully recognized.

Rosa Mayreder's Concept of Gender

The major topic of these essays is stated plainly in the title: *Gender and Culture*. More precisely, Mayreder deals with the social and cultural values that underlie the patterns of life of each gender. She clearly designed this volume of essays as a continuation of *A Survey of the Woman Problem*. The first volume explored the question of what women *are*, according to the nature of their gender. In the second part, Mayreder discusses the question of what women are *supposed to be*, according to their basic nature. There was an intense debate about gender at the beginning of the 20th century, but it was predominantly misogynistic despite some works that tried to achieve a more differentiated perspective on the issue. Feminists, a feminist movement, and feminist theory existed and had had predecessors since the Enlightenment in the 18th century but were in Mayreder's day simultaneously confronted with a rigorous anti-feminism and a radically changing social and political situation that made it even more difficult to fight for women's rights. Conditions were indeed challenging for the field of feminist theory and terminology. The term "gender," for instance, has a long history of complex and diverse discussion in many fields of study, but it was a relatively new word in scholarly debate at the turn of the 20th century.

Mayreder's use of the term "nature" referring to "gender" might irritate today's readers, but it is crucial for the understanding of these texts to consider their contemporary context. "Nature" was a pivotal term at that time and the "nature of woman" one of the most intensely discussed issues. Because of the assumed "natural" disposition of the female body and psyche, women were said to be weak, susceptible to illness, and morally and intellectually inferior. The book *The Woman as Criminal and Prostitute* (1894), by Cesare Lombroso and Gugliemo Ferrero, is a typical example of publications on the "woman question" at the end of the 19th

century. The authors stated that "the female [is] a half criminaloid being of mental inferiority."[7] Statements of this sort mirror political and legal conditions; for example, electoral law and university admissions were especially misogynistic. Women were not allowed to study at Austrian universities before 1897 because of "intellectual inferiority," as scientists and philosophers insisted.

Rosa Mayreder could not argue beyond the discourse of her time. The art of her writing is to summarize (often with irony) various theories and perspectives that represented the actual scholarly status quo in order to discuss and evaluate them before she presented and substantiated her own positions. Thus, she used terminology such as the "nature of gender," now considered outdated. Her concept of gender can be seen as an attempt to accept certain biological facts *and* to reject any generalization about gender characteristics as a consequence of biological disposition. In reproduction she sees the cause of gender inequality:

> Let us once again consider the following: nature placed the heavy burden of the reproductive task entirely upon the female gender and let the man be free of it. ... In addition, it should be noted that culture as one of the human species' distinctive attributes has strengthened this naturally bestowed inequality. (MS, 73)

It is obvious that Mayreder had to deal with what science was just beginning to explore: the human body and the degree to which it determines the individual. We cannot compare today's knowledge with yesterday's scientific knowledge. Hormones, for instance, were not discovered until the beginning of the 20th century. Even though many facts about "human nature" had not yet been proven, sciences in those days had become so important that a philosophical argument about gender alone could hardly be taken

---

[7] Nike Wagner, *Geist und Geschlecht: Karl Kraus und die Erotik der Wiener Moderne* (Frankfurt am Main: Suhrkamp, 1982), 76.

seriously. References to philosophical, psychological, anthropological, and medical writings are therefore components of Mayreder's method of argumentation in her essays, and she certainly believed that it was not possible to omit consideration of the body. However, despite all the new research and data of the time that tried to verify "female inferiority" as biological fact, she clearly was also convinced that there is no evidence for a certain and unchangeable character of each gender (*Geschlechtscharakter*).

This point is something we have to keep in mind when we read Mayreder's reflections on the "nature of gender of women and men, on motherhood, and on the important role women have in changing culture. Today, we would question whether a person's physical ability to bear a child defines this person as a "woman". We would also deny any notion that reproductive possibilities could be a sufficient or even a necessary reason to constitute a binary opposition of genders. Today's state of gender studies concerns the analysis of the construction of gender concepts and finding ways to deconstruct them. Rosa Mayreder's approach is much closer to modern thinking than is seen at first glance.

Mayreder postulates a "teleological nature of gender" that would explain certain tendencies in the behavior of men and women. At the same time, she insists on an indeterminable variety of individual characteristics which do not allow general assumptions about masculinity or femininity. The question of "what women are supposed to be" includes several aspects. It refers to the contemporary normative discourse of Mayreder's day but also to her ideas about how women could contribute to a positive development of culture. It is, of course, also related to the question of "what women are" and to all the contradictory answers that were given at that time.

Mayreder's experience with war convinced her of the utmost urgency in finding an answer to this question. She thought that war "represent[ed] the most extreme manifestation of male being, the last and most terrible consequence of absolutely male activity." (MS, 82) On the other hand, she sees a primary antagonism between women and war. Mayreder argues here in a twofold way:

"the law of the essentially female, according to its most original and most general function, is the *maintenance of life*" (MS, 83). She sees two principles represented by the two genders – two opposing principles that are based on the differing responsibilities of men and women concerning reproduction. However, there is more importantly a social argument supporting women's special responsibility for peace. Women are supposed to fight against war because of their position in society. To defend social achievements in a law-governed state based on individual freedom, women have to oppose any challenge to these rights. It is war that suspends the law-governed state and thus "the woman loses equality or declines in status" (MS, 83). Mayreder wants women to realize that their mission in life has to be completely different from that of men. In this assertion, she makes a fundamental critique of patriarchal society and its values. Mayreder makes it clear that the whole gender debate is not only about equality based on male values but rather about a change in the existing society and culture.

Still, Rosa Mayreder takes a different line in her argumentation in Gender and Culture compared to that in her first volume of essays. Even though there is a decidedly more biologically oriented approach in the later volume, I do not agree with Eva Geber, who thinks that Mayreder gave up her anti-biologistic position. I also cannot see that Mayreder would adjure a "world-healing motherhood."[8] Motherhood itself is not at all a major issue in these essays and definitely not an ideal to which one needs to aspire. Motherhood *and* fatherhood instead are seen as pivotal for the history of culture in terms of gender relations. Mayreder argues that the existing hostile civilization needs to become more balanced. Because modern civilization has indeed been constructed by men and dominated by male values, it will take feminine values to overcome the disparity between civilization and culture. Mayreder quite obviously deduces an abstract masculinity and femininity from the teleological gender character she described earlier. Her argument is not so much about biology as about

---

[8] Eva Geber, "Der Verlust der Hoffnung" Afterword to *Gender and Culture*, by Rosa Mayreder (Wien: Mandelbaum, 1998), 325.

cultural values traditionally linked to women and men. Although she sees a biological disposition that might influence behavior and values, she clearly transforms this idea into a more abstract concept of gender.

Hanna Bubeníček explains Mayreder's way of representing femininity as a combination of observed and ideal types based on a general typology of persons.[9] Her idea of a "progressive ideal type" was influenced by Friedrich Schlegel and Friedrich Schleiermacher, both important German philosophers and theorists of Romanticism. Their influence helps explain why the idea of love is so very important for Mayreder, who was committed to the value of marriage and the concept of destiny. Unlike the male Romanticists, however, she overcame re-idealizations and restrictions on women. Consequently, she develops a new type of differentiated and progressive masculinity as well.[10] However, Mayreder goes beyond these ideas to offer radically innovative thoughts that anticipated some of today's debates and theories, for instance, in her discussion of the connection between sexual morals and social repression. It will take more academic effort to explore her complex thinking, elucidate the seemingly paradoxical reasoning we find in some of her essays, and ultimately understand and appreciate the richness of her work.

Composition of *Gender and Culture*

The book is composed as an exploration of Mayreder's topic, beginning with a definition of the terms "culture" and "civilization," followed by a reflection on the current status of culture, and leading to a historical analysis of important cultural topics concerning gender such as parenthood, sexuality, eroticism, marriage, and love.

---

[9] Hanna Schnedl-Bubeníček, "Grenzgängerin der Moderne: Studien zur Emanzipation in Texten von Rosa Mayreder," in *Das ewige Klischee: Zum Rollenbild und Selbstverständnis bei Männern und Frauen*, ed. Autorinnengruppe Uni Wien (Wien: Böhlau, 1981), 183.
[10] Schnedl-Bubeníček, 186.

In "On Culture in General," Rosa Mayreder identifies a conflicting relationship between culture and contemporary civilization that does not allow a higher refinement of life. She thinks that the existing civilization in her time might develop according to rules that do not correspond with the aims of culture and clearly sees the negative effects of rampant industrialization and growing capitalism. A technically perfected civilization would effect a mechanization of life and would destroy culture. Mayreder arrived at this conclusion many years before Günter Anders wrote *The Outdatedness of Human Beings*,[11] in which he describes the relation of civilization and culture in a similar way. Her study was not mentioned by Anders.

The second essay, "Civilization and Gender," claims that an imbalance in how much the two genders contribute to life is one reason for the hostile character of modern civilization and its hubris. For the first time in this volume, Mayreder stresses the unequal responsibilities of men and women concerning reproduction. "Male" productivity ignores the importance of "female" reproductivity. For Mayreder, the solution lies in a fundamental change in society, such that "the woman becomes the measure of all things" (MS, 28).

"The Crisis of Fatherhood" is an in-depth examination of the development of fatherhood, which highlights a crucial step in history, namely the appearance of the idea of property on which the patriarchal order is founded. In patriarchal societies men had almost unlimited power over their wives and families. But Mayreder observes a change that challenges this anachronistic concept of masculinity and fatherhood. With the new social position of the female gender and the emancipatory youth movement at that time, the absolute power of the father seems to have been overcome. She pleads for a fatherhood that disengages from the concept of property and finds in free affection a new and appropriate social form beyond the principle of authority.

---

[11] Günter Anders, *Die Antiquiertheit des Menschen* (München: Beck, 1956).

After a short comment, "Double Standards of Morality," the next essay is called "Gender and Social Politics." Mayreder asks what the aim of women's newly gained freedom could be: "Freedom – to what end?" (MS, 64) Discussing the difference between male and female personality, she concludes that women have to find their own task and mission in society and life, a mission that will necessarily be different from that based on "male" values and ways of behaving, as terrifyingly manifested in war.

The center of this volume, in which many topics culminate, is the essay called "Sexual Ideologies." In more than sixty pages, Rosa Mayreder explores a fundamental discrepancy about sexuality that runs throughout the history of Western philosophy. The dominance of a dualistic worldview caused a fundamental struggle between body and soul. Mayreder shows how thinking of body and soul as being in irreconcilable opposition negatively affects the attempt to achieve gender equality. She argues that sexuality is not only a tool to maintain the species; it is also a means of developing the species.

"Culture up to now has never done justice to human nature by incorporating sexual drives" (MS, 119), Mayreder states. The consequences of this lack have been hypocrisy and indecency, resulting in double moral standards and prostitution. Realizing that reproduction is *not* the motive for the sex drive challenges many existing norms about sexual behavior. Homosexuality, for instance, is then as normal as other "aberrations" that are, in fact, just variations. Although Mayreder personally did not support homosexuality, she clearly concluded that there was no reason to pathologize or to punish it. Prostitution, on the other hand, had to be fought. According to Mayreder, a higher sexual culture depends on the concept of personality. Throughout cultural history, prostitution had sunk in prestige because of an increasing level of development of the *female* personality. She condemns prostitution as a degradation of personality because it lacks the presence of the higher human soul and therefore represents an absolute negation of the female personality.

Based on the cultural history of sexuality outlined in this essay, Rosa Mayreder explores female eroticism and the problems of marriage and love in the following essays. In "The Evolution of Female Eroticism," she discusses problems of personality, marriage, and prostitution that are causally linked to the stages of development of female eroticism. All these stages are still represented by individual women and lead to fundamental differences between them. Mayreder explains that unity solely based on gender is therefore absolutely impossible. Women involved in the later women's movement realized the same fact that Mayreder explicates in this essay. To deal with these differences and to find political strategies that still allow people to fight together against oppression was, and still is, one of the most difficult problems for all emancipatory movements.

The theoretical significance of marriage and its essence are the topic of "The Evolution of Marriage." Mayreder defines marriage as the will to achieve permanence in love. In addition to the historical and philosophical explanations, she poses concrete political demands – some having provocative power even today. For instance, she thinks that lifelong monogamous marriage should not be the only form of gender relation that is granted social acceptance. She also believes that the state should legalize a form of a temporary marriage and support marriages financially.

In opposition to many contemporary thinkers like Nietzsche who describe love as an illusion or a mere egoistic drive, Mayreder identifies in her essay "On the Essence of Love" the unique quality of love as the only means of transcending the limits of the consciousness of self. Mayreder refers to Plato's *Symposion* when she explains that love induces a growth of the self and creates fundamental joy beyond any selfish motivation.

The volume ends with "An Excursus on the Imaginary Self." The last essay in this ambitious cultural study is an examination of a topic that is one of the most important for Mayreder: love. Her idea of love is not only romantic: she is interested in the character of the phenomenon, in its cultural importance, and its powerful influence on the individual. Love allows the individual to overcome the limitations of the ego. But one must be aware of illusions arising from an imaginary self. It takes self-reflection to be capable of real love. This is true for its various forms but especially for sexual love. For Rosa Mayreder, love means equality between partners, which she therefore acclaims as an opportunity for the realization of true gender equality.

Perspectives

Rosa Mayreder dealt with many questions that are still relevant. We must ask ourselves why it is that, even though gender equality is widely discussed today and many valuable measures have been taken towards achieving it, we still see women in many areas of life in inferior social positions. Why is it that men on average earn more money, own much more land, and still hold the highest positions in politics and in the economy all over the world?

Why is it that one in every five women becomes a victim of physical or sexual violence?

In spite of all academic efforts to break open the binary gender structure that keeps many women in an inferior position, not much seems to have changed in everyday life and in the basic structure of gender relations in many countries. Despite the fact that women's education and access to the job market in many Western countries have clearly improved, there are no data to show that men engage significantly more in domestic and family work than they did a few decades ago. Today, we definitely see more women than men carrying the double and triple burden of household duties, family care, and employment.

Mayreder's demands made eighty years ago obviously concern us still: Women must realize that they will not succeed if they do not stand up for different values. Of course, Mayreder did not claim a general female identity, but she was well aware of the fact that it does not make much sense to achieve equality in a civilization lacking an orientation toward the values of a higher culture. Mayreder's analysis helps us to understand her times as well as our own, offering essays that are of historical interest and that also present interesting ideas and perspectives on solving today's problems.

BOOKS AND PAMPHLETS BY ROSA MAYREDER:

Der Corregidor: Oper in vier Akten. Mannheim: Heckel, 1896.
Aus meiner Jugend: drei Novellen. Dresden: E. Pierson, 1896.
Die Abolitionisten-Föderation. Vienna: s.l., 1898.
Die ersten fünf Jahre des allgemeinen österreichischen Frauenvereins. Berlin: s.l., 1898.
Idole: Geschichte einer Liebe. Berlin: S. Fischer 1899.
Die Frau und der Internationalismus. Vienna: Frisch, 1900.
Pipin: Ein Sommererlebins. Leipzig: H. Seemann, 1903.
Zur Kritik der Weiblichkeit: Essays. Jena: E. Diederichs, 1905. [ed. Eva Geber. Wien: Mandelbaum Verlag, 1998.]
Übergänge: Novellen. Vienna: Hugo Heller, 1908.
Zwischen Himmel und Erde: Sonette. Jena: Eugen Diederichs, 1908.
A Survey of the Woman Problem. Translation by Herman Scheffauer. New York: G.H. Doran, 1913.
Der typische Verlauf sozialer Bewegungen. Vienna: Anzengruber, 1917.
Anda Renata: Ein Mysterium in zwei Teilen und zwölf Bildern. Vienna: Österreichisches Journal, 1920.
Fabeleien über göttliche und menschliche Dinge. Leipzig: Anzengruber Verlag, 1921.
Sonderlinge: Novelle. Berlin: Hermann Hillger, 1921.
Geschlecht und Kultur: Essays. Jena: E. Diederichs, 1923. [ed. Eva Geber. Wien: Mandelbaum Verlag, 1998.]
Askese und Erotik. Jena: E. Diederichs, 1926. [ed. Tatjana Popovic. Dornach: Geering, 2001.]
Ideen der Liebe. Jena: E. Diederichs, 1927.
Mensch und Menschlichkeit. Vienna: W. Braumüller, 1928.
Die Krise der Ehe. Jena: E. Diederichs, 1929.
Der letzte Gott. Stuttgart: J. G. Cotta, 1933.
Gaben des Erlebens: Sprüche und Betrachtungen. Darmstadt: Darmstädter Verlag, 1935.
Aschmedais Sonette an den Menschen. Privately published, 1937.

Diana und Herodias: Ein mythisches Spiel. Privately published, 1937.
Krise der Väterlichkeit, ed. by Käthe Braun-Prager. Graz: Stiasny Verlag, 1963.
Zur Kritik der Weiblichkeit: Essays, ed. Hanna Schnedl. Munich: Frauenoffensive, 1982. (selected texts)
Rosa Mayreder oder Wider die Tyrannei der Norm, ed. Hanna Bubeniček. Vienna: Böhlau, 1986.
Mein Pantheon: Lebenserinnerungen. Dornach: Geering, 1988.
Tagebücher, 1873–1937, ed. Harriet Anderson. Frankfurt am Main: Insel, 1988.
Das Haus in der Landskrongasse: Jugenderinnerungen, ed. Eva Geber and Käthe Braun-Prager. Vienna: Mandelbaum, 1998.
Meine theuren, fernen Freundinnen: Rosa Mayreder schreibt an Ellen Kleman und Klara Johanson. Copenhagen: W. Fink, 2004.

LETTERS

Wolf, Hugo. *Briefe an Rosa Mayreder. Mit einem Nachwort der Dichterin des Corregidor,* ed. Heinrich Werner. Vienna: Nikolo, 1921.
All the other letters she wrote and received are still unpublished. There is a collection of 1204 manuscripts in the City Library of Vienna. (www.wienbibliothek.at)

SECONDARY LITERATURE:

Anderson, Harriet Jane. "Beyond a Critique of Femininity. The Thought of Rosa Mayreder (1858–1938)." (PhD diss., University of London, 1985)

―――― "Der Feminismus des Sich-Erinnerns: Zum Verhältnis zwischen dem Persönlichen und dem Politischen in Autobiographien der österreichischen Frauenbewegung um 1900," in *Autobiographien in der österreichischen Literatur,* ed. Klaus Amann and Karl Wagner, 61–73. Innsbruck, Vienna: Studienverlag, 1998.

———— "Rosa Mayreder," in *Major Figures of Turn-of-the-Century Austrian Literature*, ed. and with an Introduction by Donald G. Daviau, 259-290. Riverside: Ariadne Press, 1991.

Bachler, Sigrid Ingeborg. "Rosa Mayreder: eine exemplarische Antizipation." (PhD diss., Universität Frankfurt am Main, 1994)

Braun-Prager, Käthe. "Rosa Mayreder," in *Frauenbilder aus Österreich. Eine Sammlung von zwölf Essays*, 35–63. Vienna: Obelisk Verlag, 1955.

Brehmer, Ilse: "'Kraft meiner Wesensart dem alten Ideal der Weiblichkeit entgegengesetzt ...' (Mayreder). Bildungswege bedeutender Frauen am Übergang vom 19. ins 20. Jahrhundert," in *Geschichte der Frauenbildung und Mädchenerziehung in Österreich*, ed. Ilse Brehmer, 55–71. Graz: Leykam, 1997.

Der Aufstieg der Frau: zu Rosa Mayreders 70. Geburtstag am 30. November 1928. Als Ehrengabe dargebracht vom Verlag Eugen Diederichs in Jena. Jena: E. Diederichs, 1928.

Dworschak, Herta. "Rosa Obermayer-Mayreder. Leben und Werk." (PhD diss., University of Vienna, 1949)

Freund, René. *Land der Träumer: zwischen Größe und Größenwahn, verkannte Österreicher und ihre Utopien. Mit Porträts von Jakob Lorber, Leopold von Sacher-Masoch, Rosa Mayreder und Marie Lang u. a.* Vienna: Picus, 1996.

Gläser, Bärbl. "Rosa Mayreder und ihre Ideen," *Welt der Frau* 1 (1990): 4–5.

Herminghouse, Patricia, and Magda Mueller (Ed.). *German Feminist Writings*. New York: Continuum, 2001.

Hildebrandt, Irma. "Der weibliche Kulturanspruch. Die Philosophin und Frauenrechtlerin Rosa Mayreder, 1858–1938," in Hildebrandt, Irma. *Hab' meine Rolle nie gelernt. 15 Wiener Frauenporträts*, 105–119. Munich: Diederichs, 1996.

Johnston, William M. "Rosa Mayreder: Connoisseur of Woman's Role," in *The Austrian Mind*, 156–158. Berkeley: University of California Press, 1972.

Klugsberger, Theresia. "Die Modellierung der Norm im Text. Zur Analyse eines Konzeptes in zwei Texten von Rosa Mayreder u. Irma von Troll-Borostyáni," in *Schwierige Verhältnisse. Liebe und Sexualität in der Frauenliteratur um 1900*, ed. Theresia Klugsberger und Christa Gürtler, 133–149. Stuttgart: Heinz, 1992.

Kubes-Hofmann, Ursula. "'Etwas an der Männlichkeit ist nicht in Ordnung.' Intellektuelle Frauen am Beispiel Rosa Mayreder und Helene von Druskowitz," in *Die Frauen der Wiener Moderne*, ed. Lisa Fischer and Emil Brix, 124–136. Wien: Oldenbourg, 1997.

_____ "Berichte über zwei 'Entartete.' Rosa Mayreder und Helene von Druskowitz," in *Die Frauen Wiens: Ein Stadtbuch für Fanny, Frances und Francesca*, ed. Eva Geber, 126–140. Vienna: Der Apfel, 1992.

_____ "Die Kunst des Gedankens ist Erinnerung: Das Rosa-Mayreder-College in Wien." *[sic!] Forum für feministische Gangarten* 59/60 (2007): 40–43.

Mittnik, Kay L. "Rosa Mayreder and a Case of 'Austrian Fate': The Effects of Repressed Humanism and Delayed Enlightenment on Women's Writing and Feminist Thought in Fin-de-Siècle Vienna." (PhD diss., Rice University, 1990)

Prost, Edith. "Weiblichkeit und bürgerliche Kultur, am Beispiel: Rosa Mayreder-Obermayer." (PhD diss., University of Vienna, 1983)

Reiss, Mary-Ann. "Rosa Mayreder. Pioneer of Austrian Feminism." *International Journal of Women's Studies* 3 (1984): 207–216.

Rosa Mayreder 1858–1938. Vienna: Mitteilungen des Instituts für Wissenschaft und Kunst 44, 1. 1989. (special edition)

Schmölzer, Hilde. *Rosa Mayreder: ein Leben zwischen Utopie und Wirklichkeit*. Vienna: Promedia, 2002.

(Schnedl-)Bubeníček, Hanna. "Rosa Mayreders Essays und die Erkundung eines komplementären Erfahrungsraumes als Ort des Denkens," in *Frauenbilder, feministische Praxis und nationales Bewusstsein in Österreich-Ungarn 1867–1914*, ed. Waltraud Heindl, 61–70. Tübingen: Franke, 2006.

―― "Ein Resümee zu theoretischen Ausführungen und literarischen Darstellungen Bertha von Suttners und Rosa Mayreders." *Wiener Beiträge zur Geschichte der Neuzeit* 11 (1984): 96–113.

―― "Grenzgängerin der Moderne. Studien zur Emanzipation in Texten von Rosa Mayreder," in *Das ewige Klischee. Zum Rollenbild und Selbstverständnis von Männern und Frauen*, ed. Autorinnengruppe Uni Wien, 179-205. Vienna: Böhlau, 1981.

Sokolosky, Jane Elizabeth. "Rosa Mayreder: The Theory in Her Fiction." (PhD diss., Washington University, 1997)

―― "Primitive or Differentiated? Constructions of Femininity in Rosa Mayreder's Theoretical and Fictional Texts." *Modern Austrian Literature* 30/2 (1997): 65–83.

Spreitzer, Brigitte: *Texturen: Die österreichische Moderne der Frauen*. Wien: Passagen 1999.

Tanzer, Ulrike. "'Ob ich klar bin über mich?' Selbstbeobachtung und Selbsterziehung bei Rosa Mayreder und Alfred Freiherr von Berger," in *Literatur als Geschichte des Ich*, ed. Eduard Beutner, 139–153. Würzburg: Königshausen & Neumann, 2000.

Witzmann, Reingard. *Aufbruch in das Jahrhundert der Frau? Rosa Mayreder und der Feminismus in Wien um 1900*. Vienna: Eigenverlag der Museen der Stadt Wien, 1989.

Wobbe, Theresa. "Politik, Macht und soziale Bewegung. Rosa Mayreder (1858–1938)," in: Dölle, Gilla (Red.): *"... das verheißene Land der Freiheit und Gleichheit"? Der radikale Flügel der bürgerlichen Frauenbewegung*. Kassel: Archiv der deutschen Frauenbewegung, 1995.

Wucherpfennig, Wolf. "Kulturideal und weibliche Identitätsarbeit. Rosa Mayreder und ihr Briefwechsel mit Ellen Kleman und Klara Johanson," in *Österreich und Skandinavien. Kulturelle Beziehungen zwischen Wiener Kongreß und Erstem Weltkrieg*, ed. Wolf Wucherpfennig, 135–156. Copenhagen: Fink, 2004.